THE KITCAR BUILDER'S MANUAL

BUYING □ BUILDING □ TRIMMING

Peter Coxhead
and
Martin Foster

Foulis

Haynes
®

A **Foulis** Motoring Book

First published 1990

Published by:
Haynes Publishing Group
Sparkford, Nr Yeovil
Somerset BA22 7JJ, England

Haynes Publications Inc
861 Lawrence Drive, Newbury Park,
California 91320, USA

**British Library Cataloguing in
Publication Data**

Coxhead, Peter
    The Kitcar builder's manual,
    1. Cars, Design & construction
    I. Title II. Foster, Martin
    629.23
    ISBN 0 85429-801-0

Library of Congress Catalog Card Number
90-84257

Editor: Robin Read
Design: Tim Rose and Peter Kay
Typeset in 10/11pt Frontiera med roman and
printed in England by J.H. Haynes & Co. Ltd.

Contents

Introduction   4

Chapter 1   The first steps   7

       2   Doing your homework   19

       3   Visiting the Maker   27

       4   Counting the cost in time and money   57

       5   Preparing for the build   65

       6   Basic techniques   75

       7   The process of building   91

       8   Rebuilding donor car components   106

       9   Collecting or receiving the kit   128

      10   Preparing and fitting out the chassis   130

      11   Fitting the body   138

      12   Taking on the electrics   143

      13   Interior trim and fitting out   153

      14   The final touches   161

      15   Getting on the road   170

Introduction

Cars have long represented a great deal more than a mere mode of transport. Like fashions in clothing and interior design, the car has become for many people a pronouncement of personality, a statement of style: the ecologically aware drive Morris Minors, Citroën 2CVs or Fiat Pandas (although in reality they may be less environment-friendly than many more practical models); the country casuals drive anything with four-wheel-drive, or something cheap and cheerful to cope with muddy kids and dogs; the upwardly striving are made mobile by power-packaged boxes, with their turbocharged or fuel-injected name tags.

So however much we may try to resist automotive pigeon-holing, the modern car says a great deal about the people we are.

But like all fashions, as trends gain popularity so it becomes more difficult for the individual to make his mark: if you drive a 2CV you will automatically be classified among the stripped pine and yoghurt

Below and right: These two very different cars typify the wide variety of kits available. The lightweight GP Porsche Spyder replica is based on VW mechanics; the mighty Atlantis, seen here thundering around the track at Castle Combe, is Jaguar XJ6-based.

fraternity; a Range Rover will ensure you receive at least one pair of green wellies for Christmas. How then to be different?

It is largely because of this desire for something different that the specialist car sector of the market has evolved. Tired of the homogeneous, computer-outlined, ever-so-efficient, but oh-so-boring mainstream production cars, an increasing number of modern motorists are looking towards the only real alternative: the kitcar.

Combining the virtues of practical mechanical components with original styling, the kitcar can also bring otherwise unobtainable designs within reach of the mere mortal, and allow the owner actually to play a part in the manufacturing process. Buying the car in component form also means still more opportunity to tailor the car

to the builder's personal requirements. No two kitcars are exactly the same: so an original automotive statement can be made.

What might appear to be advantages, however, can turn against the unsuspecting newcomer: too much choice can result in the wrong decision; over-optimistic calculating of the time and money required can result in abandoned projects; a careless or hurried build can produce a car that is unreliable, unattractive – and possibly even dangerous.

The Kitcar Builder's Manual sets out to guide the kitcar enthusiast through the entire process of planning, choosing, buying and building a kitcar. It is written by two kitcar journalists who have a wealth of experience to draw on, and advice to give, for they have edited *Kitcars and Spe-*

cials and *Classic Replicas* magazines, and have actually built kitcars.

Building and owning a kitcar can be a rewarding experience, in more ways than one, but before you start, read through *The Kitcar Builder's Manual*. You'll need to come back to it again during the buying and building of your car. But one complete reading of this book is the next best thing to building a kitcar. Nothing, however, beats experience!

Authors' Note

The authors would like to express their thanks to Link House Magazines for allowing the use of many photographs from the archives there.

6

CHAPTER 1:
THE FIRST STEPS

What is a kitcar?

Given modern man's desire to present an individual image to the world, and the important part played by the car in many people's projection of that image, the innocent car has been quite dreadfully hacked about over the years.

At first, the search for automotive individuality was a preserve of the rich – as indeed was any form of motoring. But with the arrival of the affordable popular saloon, and particularly with the availability of even cheaper secondhand examples, a whole new concept was born even before anyone had begun to use the word 'concept' in this connection. Like most new areas of motoring, it grew out of racing, where heavy production saloon bodies were discarded in favour of lightweight aluminium sports shells; entrepreneurs saw their opportunity and the 'specials' industry was open for business.

The 1950s supplied just the right environment for growth: plenty of cheap but boring secondhand production cars; a growing expertise in a relatively new material called glassfibre; and an increasingly rebellious youth, with a decent pay packet in the back pockets of their jeans, just looking for a new way

to leave their mark on society. That's not to say that only the young wanted cheap sports cars: older generations, too, were becoming tired of driving sensible Morris Oxfords and were dreaming of Healeys, and the low-cost special meant they could afford to run a second car.

The favourite basis for the specials were Austin and Ford saloons, from the Austin Seven to the Ford Popular, produced well into the 1950s. Ripping away the saloon bodies left a simple ladderframe chassis on to which racily styled, two-seater bodies – with names like the Caribbean and the Falcon – could be bolted. The running gear could be left virtually unchanged, although engine 'tuning' equipment had become widely available from specialist companies, and wind-in-the-hair motoring was just around the corner – even if negotiating the corners did sometimes prove something of a challenge for the crude running gear.

This highlights one of the problems of the early specials, and kitcars as they were to become known: the cars were only ever as good as the components on which they were based. This is still true today, of course, but the standard

of design and production is much improved, and the arrival of the monocoque chassis has meant that kit manufacturers have to design new chassis specifically for the purpose – usually, but not always, to better effect.

One revolutionary monocoque design that had as great an effect on the kitcar industry as it did on the mainstream market was the Mini, designed by Alec Issigonis. The self-contained front and rear units, with all the mechanical components bolted into simple, compact subframes, was the perfect basis for a sports car; and if BMC had no interest in exploiting its potential (the company was content to develop faster versions of the saloon, thus improving sales of the basic model), then several small companies were happy to oblige.

The two best-known early examples were the Mini Marcos and the Mini Jem, which housed Mini subframes in very suspect beetle-shaped bodies to provide cheap sports cars in the mid-1960s. In later years the design was much modified and improved to become the Midas.

At a time when mid-mounted engines were relatively new even in racing cars and 'exotics', the compact Mini front subframe assembly

The Mini-Marcos used subframes from the Mini to provide competent, inexpensive alternative transport in the mid-1960s.

kits, and one that is suffered even now by Metro-based cars, is that the height of the transverse engine/gearbox assembly results in a relatively tall front bulkhead and waistline. It doesn't appear tall on the Mini or Metro, but build it into a sports car and it takes a good stylist (like Richard Oakes, who has done such a clever job on the Midas Gold) to keep things in proportion. The diminutive Mini components also restricted the overall size of the finished car, and the market was hungry for alternatives.

The alternative mechanical components came in the distinctive,

used at the rear, with the steering blanked off, was also found to be a good basis for a budget mid-engined sports car. Again the idea lives on, and GTM still produce a Mini-based, mid-engined coupé.

The problem with the more common front-engined Mini-based

Right: Years of development have resulted in this Midas – a compact car with superb performance.

love-it-or-hate-it shape of that other great landmark in mass-market automotive history: the Volkswagen Beetle. Among its many engineering innovations, the Beetle uses a flat floorpan on to which the bodyshell is mounted; its design dates back to the 1930s, when all cars were built on the separate chassis and body principle.

The Beetle's rugged simplicity has been exploited in many ways over the years. The most famous – or notorious – design is the beach buggy, which itself was a development from sand dune racers built in America. Its arrival in Britain coincided with the frivolous 1960s

The GTM is another Mini-based car which, thanks to its neat styling, continues to be very popular.

Fatal attraction. One of the earlier kitcars, which still enjoys healthy sales, is the VW-based Madison. Designed by Neville Tricket, the Madison was the car that was responsible for the authors' first involvement in kitcars.

Using the full-length VW floorpan, more sensible tyres, and often heavily modified engines, these 'budget exotics' proved far more effective than the buggies, and some live on today. But while they offer the advantage of a relatively easy and cheap build, it must be remembered that under the skin there is still a humble saloon car, the original design of which dates back some 50 years; and it will never produce the sort of mid-engined spaceframe handling and performance suggested by the styling.

Volkswagen's close relationship with Porsche is well-known, of course, and the former's compo-

when function gave way to fun – the 'fun car' had arrived.

Back in the United States, the buggies cruised the streets of the West Coast, carrying bronzed teenagers to beach parties and surfing competitions. On the wet streets of, say, Hartlepool, the appeal wasn't so immediately apparent. But these were fun cars: who needed practicalities? Needed or not, the buggy offered (or offers – they are still manufactured, and sold, in the United Kingdom and abroad) little or no weather protection; their short, chromed exhaust systems had all the discreet unobtrusiveness of a chainsaw. The questionable handling of the original VW was further worsened by the .fact that several inches had been cut out of the wheelbase, and tyres (in the early days, illegal racing tyres) like rubber road rollers were stretched across banded steel wheels. Bump steer is an undesirable handling characteristic that will be explained later, but for a perfect demonstration, try driving a buggy on anything but perfectly smooth road surfaces and at any speed more than about 30 mph. Credit where credit's due – but the buggy deserves none at all for improving

Beach buggies helped to introduce low cost, fun car motoring to the youth of the Swinging Sixties and at the same time they paved the way for the more sophisticated designs that followed.

the reputation of kitcars.

However, it didn't stop there. Beetle floorpans soon found their way under all manner of body shapes. The low and (at least apparently) streamlined, closed-top, two-seater sports car will always have its fans, and in the 1970s came the introduction of numerous VW-based versions. The most famous of these was probably the Nova – another Richard Oakes design.

nents are certainly more at home as the basis of replicas of the latter. There are currently manufactured replicas of the Porsche RSK and 550 Spyders, 356 Speedster and the classic 911. All of these are available in VW-based form, although the trend is definitely towards purpose-designed chassis and Porsche engines and gearboxes, or even water-cooled Ford and Alfa Romeo power units linked to the trusty VW transaxle by adaptor plates.

Despite its part in the plague of buggies, the VW Beetle has made an important contribution to the development of the market as it is today. However, with the wider availability of more sophisticated components, and the higher expec-

Despite its space-age styling, the exotic Nova sits on a Beetle floorpan.

tations of today's car builders, it would seem its days are numbered: much to the relief of those who still enthusiastically restore and modify the original cars.

While most of the kitcar industry experimented with Beetles, Minis and other production car chassis-based models (the Triumph Herald also proved popular for a while), one company came up with an original design that was to change the future of the industry. The company was Lotus, the designer Colin Chapman, and the car the Lotus Seven.

Sold in kit form, the Lotus Seven was a development of the similarly styled Lotus Mk6, and owed a great deal to Chapman's revolutionary racing car designs. The principle was brilliant but, like the all the best ideas, simple. The Seven differed from the rest of the small volume cars produced at that time in that it used a purpose-designed, lightweight multi-tube chassis, with the emphasis on design. In the best traditions of kitcars it used components from mainstream production models. They were, however, taken not from one car to keep things simple; rather they were chosen from a number of cars to keep things efficient. The Triumph Herald was perhaps best known for having the turning circle of a supermarket trolley, but it took Chapman to make the most of the potential of its front suspension uprights and hubs. The Seven subsequently

inspired the often-misused expression 'four-wheeled motorcycle'.

Form followed function in that given the location of the running gear, and the race-inspired position of the driver, the bodywork just covered things over, with a nose cone between the front wheels and a crude, wrap-around rear end with an externally mounted spare. The bonnet, side panels and cockpit tub were aluminium (often polished rather than painted), the nose cone and wings were glassfibre, and the result was truly classic.

This deceptively simple car and its Mk6 ancestor (performance and perfectly balanced proportions of this order are no accident) inspired a whole sports car movement. The styling has influenced numerous designs (and led to a few downright rip-offs), and the engineering principles involved have shown that

The Lotus Seven lives on. The Caterham Cars company has carefully developed the Series Three Caterham Seven so that it retains its original qualities, but gives even better performance.

it is possible to produce an affordable sports car that is easy to drive fast and safely. A true fun car.

Lotus ceased production of the Lotus Seven and moved on to different, arguably better, things. The design and rights of manufacture were, however, taken up by Lotus dealers Caterham Cars, who still produce an only slightly more sophisticated version today.

So what of the rest of today's market? Having briefly examined its history, it is necessary first to determine what is meant today by 'kitcar', and also to look at some of the other terms used in the marketplace.

A kitcar, then, can now be crudely defined as a specialist car using an original body and chassis (except where the latter is from the donor vehicle) in conjunction with production car running gear. The body is usually glassfibre, although it is sometimes aluminium, or a combination of the two. The chassis is usually a ladderframe or multi-tubular design, although a few kitcars use a combined body/chassis monocoque shell. We will be looking in more detail at the pros and cons of these various designs later.

Most build-ups involve buying a 'donor' vehicle from which the mechanical components are taken, or the sourcing of new or second-hand parts, or both, from appropriate suppliers; the fitting of the reconditioned or new running gear on or into the new chassis; the fitting and fitting out of the bodyshell, wiring, painting, detailing and registration. And if a kitcar manufacturer ever makes it sound that easy, bid that company a hasty farewell.

The design of the body, the most

important single factor in most people's choice of kitcar, will certainly be distinctive and individual in comparison with the wind-tunnel-tested boxes of the big motor manufacturers. However, even a brief examination of the vast range of designs available shows that they've come a long way since the early days of crudely rebodied saloons. Such diversity defies precise definition, but we can indicate the broad categories now before examining them in more detail in subsequent chapters to help you decide what best suits your individual requirements.

The largest single category, and the one that is growing most rapidly, is in fact the least original. Replicas attempt to recreate, with varying degrees of accuracy, the overall lines and detail features of classic sports cars, so as to give enthusiasts a taste of classic car motoring, but without all the inconvenience and expense of the originals, thanks to modern mechanical components.

It is the expense that is really the key. Everyone knows that there is nothing like a genuine Ferrari, for example; but most people also know they will never be able to afford one. Indeed, as classic cars become more desirable as investments, more and more are disappearing into private collections, inflating prices still further. Inadvertently or otherwise the classic car press has played a part in this process by concentrating on car

LR Roadsters' Jaguar D-Type replica is quick, reliable and great fun all at a fraction of the cost of the real thing.

prices and auction trends. It has left these magazines with an increasing readership – reflecting the ever-growing interest in classic cars – a dwindling number of whom can actually afford to buy the cars. The magazines' solution seems to be to bestow 'classic' status on newer, humbler cars, and owners of Mk 1 Cortinas are surprised to find they now have an appreciating classic in the garage.

For fans of the true classics, the Ferraris, Jaguars, Porsches, ACs and so on, buying one is simply not feasible. They are therefore turning to the replica manufacturers for cars that closely resemble the originals, and provide real sports car handling and performance. These are often up to, and sometimes better than, the standard of the cars from which they take their inspiration. Providing the budget is big enough, replicas can often match the original, litre for litre, cylinder for cylinder. Quite acceptable performance, however, can often be obtained from a smaller engine, particularly since the replicas are often lighter. The 2-litre Lancia engine, available in three states of tune, used in the JH Classics Ferrari Dino replica is a good example of this. Infinitely cheaper than the original to buy, run, service and insure, it is still powerful and flexible enough to make the car a delight to drive.

John Tojeiro, the designer of the original AC Ace, forerunner of the Cobra, says that Cobra replicas such as this V12-powered Dax handle far better than the original.

Despite an initial resistance, many owners of original classics are now accepting that it is impractical to use a car worth hundreds of thousands, or even millions, of pounds on any sort of regular basis. They are buying themselves replicas to drive – in much the same way as an art collector might display good copies of paintings and keep the originals safely locked away.

As the more mundane sports cars grow in value, so it becomes economically viable to reproduce them in replica form. Probably the cheapest to put on the road is the Mk 1 Sprite replica produced by the Frogeye Car Company – the firm has received the official stamp of approval from the Healey family, along with the right to use the Healey name.

Generally, however, rarity value and some indefinable element of attraction are the necessary requirements for a suitable subject for 'replication'. Competition cars are generally produced in smaller numbers than other types and make up the majority of the popular replicas: Jaguar C and D Types, Ford GT40, Lola T70, Lancia Stratos, Ferrari P4 (an original of which changed hands in 1989 for £6,000,000 – a clear statement of value) and, of course, the AC Cobra.

The most-copied car of all time, the AC Cobra would not be nearly so well known in Britain had it not been for the first replica bodyshell which made its way from the United States in the early 1980s. Since then replicas have appeared on ladderframe and multi-tubular chassis, with engines from Ford Cortina to Jaguar V12 (and includ-

This Austin Healey Sprite replica by the Frogeye Car Company is almost indistinguishable from the real thing and carries the approval of the Healey family.

The Cobra must be the most copied car ever.

ing more authentic American Ford V8s). They have given the kitcar industry, and the replica sector in particular, a very healthy shot in the arm. Manufacturers have come and gone, but the top six or so have been around for some years now and have all diversified into other models, funded by their Cobra replicas.

For the beginner, some replicas could prove an over-ambitious first build. In a later chapter we will look in more detail at the time and money involved, but the standard of finish set by the originals usually demands considerable helpings of both, plus just the right detailing to make the replica really accurate. Virtually complete versions can be bought (more on that later, too), but this puts up the initial purchase price, so doing this is seldom any cheaper.

'Component car' is a term originally adopted by some companies in the kitcar industry in an effort to distance themselves from the 'kitcar' label, which they felt still had something of a stigma attached to it from the early, less professional days. In fact 'kitcar' proved a tough name to shake off – as generic terms often are – but some companies do advertise their cars as being available in 'component form' (a phrase coined by Lotus in the 1950s), which might prove less confusing to those who still think a kitcar comes in 1/32 scale with a tube of polystyrene cement.

Another term often used in the context of kitcars is 'specialist cars'.

This has been given official recognition by the formation of the Specialist Car Manufacturers' Group (SCMG), a section within the Society of Motor Manufacturers and Traders (SMMT). The SMMT is a huge trade organization representing all the mainstream car manufacturers and it has given its full support to the SCMG, which was formed by the specialist manufacturers themselves to promote higher standards – ostensibly within the kitcar market as a whole but, as it has turned out, more particularly among a small, select group of companies.

Membership of the SCMG has been severely restricted by strict requirements such as a minimum turnover, minimum term of trading, and a no-replica rule unless permission has been given by the original designer. As a result, at the time of writing the SCMG consists of relatively large, long-established companies producing original and successful designs, with only one replica manufacturer on their books.

Apart from obviously wanting to distance themselves from manufacturers who have not put their cars through the extensive and expensive SCMG testing programme, the reason for adopting the 'specialist car' tag is that most of the member companies admit that they produce cars in component form for con-

venience only. The only thing that prevents them from selling complete, new cars is a law stating that in order to do so, manufacturers must first get what is known as Type Approval.

This is an official test procedure whereby every component used in a car is submitted for testing. Assuming the parts meet the required standard, that 'type' is then approved, and providing the manufacturer does not change the car's specification, every complete car produced is also approved and can be sold in complete 'turnkey' form alongside the Fords and BLs. Unfortunately, the Type Approval test programme, which includes the infamous 'crash test' when a complete car is crashed into a very large and very stationary block of concrete to test its behaviour in this dire circumstance (and if it fails, another car must be submitted), is prohibitively expensive for most companies. The law states, however, that cars sold in component or kit form for assembly by the customer are exempt from Type Approval. The specialist manufacturers exploit this by selling complete cars, including all the running gear, with one or two components to be fitted by the customer. It has been known for some companies simply to leave off the steering wheel, but this is generally held to be pushing a point. The Ministry's requirement of 'one major mechanical component' is more usually interpreted as the engine or complete front suspension assembly.

Some of these specialist companies – they include Midas, whose Mini-based car we have already mentioned, and Caterham Cars, continuing with the former Lotus Seven project – do offer genuine kit form options, which involve a little more work and actually save the builder some money. The SCMG is, however, lobbying hard for a limited form of Type Approval – often referred to as 'junior' or 'small volume' Type Approval – that would allow these companies to build and sell complete cars. If, as seems likely, such a scheme is introduced, perhaps in the early 1990s, it wouldn't be surprising to find that the frustrated car manufacturers among the SCMG membership will stop selling the kit versions and concentrate on complete vehicles.

If that does happen, it will still take only half a dozen or so companies out of the kitcar market. It is the others, and the kits they sell, that we are concerned with here. In fact these companies, too, recognize that some customers lack the time, inclination or ability to build the car themselves. Not wanting to turn customers away, some of them therefore offer a similar 'virtually complete' sales service. Naturally the much higher labour and material costs are reflected in the price and a near-finished car will cost many thousands of pounds more than a basic kit of parts. However, there are usually a number of options between the two, so it would be appropriate now to examine 'the typical kit' (and thus prove there is no such thing), the various options, and what you can expect for your money.

The naming of parts

Manufacturers' price lists usually start with 'body/chassis', or a similar heading, so we must first determine just what they mean by this, beginning with the three basic chassis designs used in kitcars: the ladderframe, the multi-tube (sometime referred to as a 'spaceframe') and the monocoque.

The ladderframe is the most common and the most traditional; it formed the basis of most production cars until the 1950s (including all the traditional sports cars of the 1930s), and of some until the present day. In its crudest form it consists of two heavy parallel members running the length of the car,

The Lightspeed Tarrogon chassis is a basic ladderframe. It has a minimum of cross-bracing and relies on the bodyshell to stiffen it.

with crossmembers between the two at right angles to give extra strength and provide mounting points for mechanical components. Such a construction will, of course, be very susceptible to twist, so extra rigidity is often provided by additional members running diagonally across the rectangle, or by vertical tubes joined again across the chassis, or by both. These literally take the chassis into an extra dimension, and are sometimes linked up again along the length of the chassis to form the beginnings of a box structure, which has far greater strength and resistance to twist, plus extra side-impact protection. This additional tubing is also used for mounting components such as seat belts and door hinges, which require more secure mountings than the glassfibre bodyshell can offer.

Taking this box theory still further, with extra vertical, horizontal and diagonal tubing, we move into

The ASD Hobo chassis takes things a step or two forward, for it has extra vertical tubing carrying a perimeter frame on a second level. This creates a boxlike structure, which is more resistant to twist and provides side-impact protection. At the front are mounting points for the windscreen, pedalbox and Mini front subframe. This is a typical example of a kitcar chassis – inexpensive to make, strong and twist-free but not very sophisticated, and a little overweight.

the multi-tubular chassis. This is sometimes called a spaceframe – although strictly speaking this term applies to a complete, multi-stressed construction. And this is not practical because of the apertures required on a car frame, for doors, bonnet, boot, etc. The far greater strength and rigidity offered by the multi-tubular design also means that smaller, lighter gauge tube can be used, resulting in a reduced overall weight with all the inherent benefits of improved performance, handling, fuel economy, and so on.

The disadvantage of this design is inevitably one of cost. More individual pieces of tubing mean more measuring, cutting and welding, and all that extra time puts money on the final price. However, there is nothing to beat the multi-

The Hobo's chassis forms part of the bodywork of the completed car, so neat welds are of the greatest importance.

Above and below: The multi-tubular design used on this CCC Challenger offers the greatest strength and rigidity of all the methods of chassis design and construction. The extra work involved in the manufacture inevitably results in higher cost.

There are other chassis designs which will not fit neatly into either of these categories. The centre backbone chassis concentrates the tubular structure in the centre of the car, forming a boxed tunnel. This is often then literally boxed in with steel sheet for still more torsional strength. Outriggers support the car body and provide side-impact protection. This panelling-in principle can also be applied to the more elaborate ladderframe designs, providing box structures in areas of greater stress.

Monocoque construction, used by most mainstream car manufacturers, where whole body, floorpan

tubular design for any form of competition work – and many would say for any fast road car as well.

The design of the Evante Cars backbone chassis is based on that of Colin Chapman's Lotus Elan.

and inner panels form a rigid box, is rare in the kitcar industry. It is popular among the big manufacturers because mass-produced pressed steel panels can be easily assembled, often now by robot, on production lines and in huge numbers. The numbers involved in the kitcar industry preclude such methods; but one company, Midas Cars pioneered the glassfibre monocoque with great success. (Midas Cars went into liquidation in early 1990 but Pastiche Cars have purchased the project and production is continuing).

Sceptics' doubts of the strength

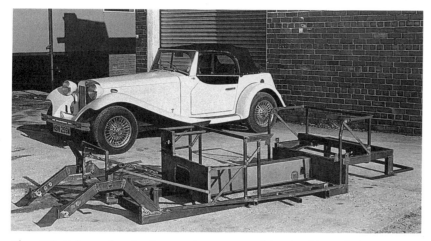

The JBA Falcon chassis does not fit into any of the main chassis design categories, but incorporates a boxed-in backbone with ladderframe outriggers and additional vertical structures on to which major components can be mounted.

Some kitcars consist of a simple glassfibre body mounted on a production car chassis. However, the monocoque construction of most modern production cars means that kitcar manufacturers are limited to older designs such as the VW Beetle and the Triumph Herald. The VW floorpan pictured here has formed the basis of a variety of kitcars over the years, but is proving less popular now.

The Midas Gold, a glassfibre monocoque design, undergoing the destructive crash test. It passed with flying colours, allaying some people's fears regarding the strength of glassfibre.

of a glassfibre monocoque construction were answered when Midas put one of its cars through the gruelling crash test that all production models must pass as part of the Type Approval procedure. Careful computerized measurements were taken and the Midas Gold passed with flying colours. However, the monocoque principle remains a more complex method of construction than separate body and chassis units, and its popularity seems unlikely to

spread in the kitcar industry.

There are also those kitcars, already mentioned, that are really rebodying exercises in which the manufacturer supplies a glassfibre body to fit on a production car chassis. The monocoque construction of most mass-market cars limits

the choice of base vehicle to VW Beetles, Triumph Heralds, etc., so generally this method is dying out. The only exceptions are where a kitcar body is bonded on to *part* of a monocoque production car, i.e. the floor section; or where kitcar body panels actually replace some of the panels on the production car. The former is a tricky exercise because the production car becomes 'floppy' immediately the top section is removed, and although the strength can be replaced by the new bodyshell, the actual conversion is best undertaken by the kit manufacturer. The second exception, the replacement panel conversion, is ideal for the beginner in that it doesn't require any mechanical work, and all the running gear and the interior

remain untouched.

Having established what constitutes the two basic units of most kitcars – the body and chassis, usually sold as one package – the would-be purchaser can then select additional packages, or options. A more detailed examination of the parts necessary for each stage of the build will be provided in Chapter 4, where calculating the total cost of a project is dealt with, but it is important to have at least a basic understanding before the

Triumph Herald chassis have been used under a number of kitcar designs in the past, but they are simply too old now. However the efficient front suspension components are still being used on some cars.

Above and right: This early version of Robin Hood Engineering's Ferrari Daytona replica involved the bonding of the new glassfibre body on to the 'floorpan' of a cut-down Rover SD1 monocoque. This skilled operation was carried out at the factory, and was superseded by a more conventional separate body/chassis design.

sight of a completed kitcar turns your head. Normally level-headed people have been known to cast aside all considerations of practicalities after falling head-over-wallet in love with the car of their dreams.

The next important factor in the build will be the mechanical components, and these can come from a number of different sources.

Some kitcars require components that are unique to that model – suspension parts, perhaps, or a shortened steering column or prop-shaft – and these will often be included in the basic body/chassis package. They are sometimes listed on an options list, however, and this then becomes something of a misnomer since they are not optional at all but vital to the build. Again this will be examined in more detail elsewhere, but the reminder cannot be given too often: check and double-check what the kit includes, and make sure your budget allows for additional parts.

In most cases, the majority of the mechanical components will be from a production car, and again there is a whole range of alternative sources open to the builder. At the top of the pile, for convenience, quality and cost, are brand-new parts. The use of all new parts, whether bought from the kit manufacturer – many of whom can supply at competitive prices – or

The breaker's yard is one source of mechanical parts, but you need to know what you are looking for. See Chapter 7 for advice on buying the donor vehicle.

from conventional suppliers, will obviously result in a completely new car (which will then be liable to car tax).

Many kitcars are designed around one 'donor vehicle': that is, a production car from which components can be taken. The proportion of usable parts from the donor will vary, from engine/gearbox or suspension to a complete package of components down to wiper blades and door catches. Most builders will want to recondition, repair or

replace at least some of the major parts, and an all-new brake system must be considered a minimum requirement. Advice on buying the donor vehicle, and reconditioning and replacing parts, is given in Chapter 7.

Continuing with our definition of that mythical 'typical kitcar', and a basic introduction to the build process, the sequence moves on with the assembly of components, incorporating donor, original and other production car parts into the basic body/chassis unit according to the instructions. The more ambitious builder can usually opt to take on the plumbing, wiring, painting, trimming and final detailing: the companies usually supply the necessary parts, materials and instructions in additional packages, which has the added bonus of spreading the cost of the build. It also gives the builder the option of sourcing, or even making, his own parts for some jobs. The scope for individualism knows few limits in the kitcar industry, but it leaves the would-be purchaser with more choices than he would face in most consumer markets: hence the need for careful research and decision making. Those with a larger budget may choose to let the kit manufacturer, or other specialist companies, carry out some of the more difficult jobs; but for those with enough ability and time, enormous financial savings can be made. Then at the end of the project you will be able to say, in all honesty, 'I built it myself'.

Have you got what it takes?

Having some grasp of the basics, it's now time to ask yourself whether you've got what it takes to build a kitcar. That includes practical ability, equipment, time and, of course, money. We will be looking at all of these aspects in greater detail, but if you have difficulty changing a wheel, live in a flat without a garage, have no spare time and had problems raising the money to buy this book, then perhaps you should be thinking of taking up a different pastime.

The kitcar builder does not in fact have to be a technical genius, but he does need to be familiar with how a car works and have the basic skills necessary to strip one down to its basic components, refurbish them, and build them into the kitcar. It's worth bearing in mind, too, that not everything will fit perfectly (ignore what the manufacturers might say) and a little problem solving, modification, or even fabrication, might be required. Some manufacturers also provide poorly written and ambiguous instruction manuals, so it would help if you can scratch your head over a problem and come up with something useful. Patience and perseverance can mean the difference between an abandoned, incomplete project and a successfully finished car.

The builder should only need a basic toolkit (again, we'll be covering this in more detail later), but a roomy, warm, dry and well-appointed garage or workshop is going to make life a lot easier (although necessity is the mother of invention, and we have known a kitcar to be built in a tent on the front lawn). If you are trying to do things with the minimum of equipment, it would be useful if you had even occasional access to more sophisticated gear, and maybe the odd word of advice. A problem shared is often a problem halved; and it may take a fresh pair of eyes to spot a solution that has been staring you in the face.

Many builders get involved in projects with friends, and this can have huge benefits both in terms of

A roomy, warm, dry and well-appointed workshop such as this is going to make life easier, but kitcar builders have been known to improvise.

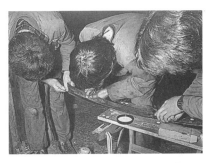

Many hands don't always make light work! But it does often help to have the assistance, advice and encouragement of a friend.

problem solving, and as a source of encouragement and extra momentum when things are getting sticky, as they inevitably will at some point. Problems and laborious jobs are never quite so daunting when shared. On the other hand, there is a saying in the service industries that two men working together will always take twice as long to finish a job! That's not strictly true when it comes to building kitcars, but it is a dangerous assumption that two people working on a project will halve the estimated time that one would take. More realistic would be a reduction of about one third.

Estimating the time and money required is a complex affair, which is why we have devoted an entire chapter to it; but again we can cover a few basics here by way of

preparation. Both cost and time will depend on the options chosen: obviously, the nearer to completion the selected kitcar, the less time it will take to finish, but the price will be correspondingly higher. As a rough guide, a complete build-up, from basic body and chassis kit, through removing, reconditioning and refitting donor parts, to fitting the body and finishing off, is likely to take in the region of 300–400 hours. Clearly it will take longer if very time-consuming jobs, such as interior trimming and painting, are undertaken, although this will save you money.

Cost is the most variable factor of all, and is determined by the type of car chosen, how complete the kit is when supplied, the desired quality, and the intended final specification. At current prices it is possible to put a basic, two-seater sports car on the road for under £4000, and a better-appointed, high performance model for around £8000. High standard AC Cobra and Ford GT40 replicas are more likely to cost upwards of £12,000. However, the more expensive examples are generally more desirable to other enthusiasts, and it is possible to see a handsome profit when the time comes to sell.

It must be said that this is not the case with some of the less popular kitcars. It stands to reason that if there is little demand for a particular car in kit form, there will be an equally limited demand for the completed vehicle, resulting in low resale prices. An ugly or poorly finished kitcar often costs just as much to build as a good one, so if

The final cost of building the car will obviously depend on the kit and specification chosen, but it is still possible to put a cheap and cheerful sports car, such as this Pilgrim Bulldog, on the road for less than £4000.

your own taste dictates that you build a three-wheeler Reliant Robin-based Cobra replica, with a textured Ripolin finish, you can expect to lose out when you try to sell it! Remember, too, that taste in styling is a very personal, subjective matter, and your meat could be another man's botulism. The important thing here is that it might just be worth judging other people's honest reactions to a particular car before you commit yourself.

There now follows a golden rule regarding a subject that prompts more reader queries in kitcar magazines than any other.

Do not choose a kitcar on the basis of utilizing an available donor vehicle. If you have run a good reliable car for some time, it is understandable that you would want to use its running gear in a kitcar, to prolong its active life. The cost of the donor vehicle, however, will actually represent only a small proportion of the total cost of the completed kitcar. It is far better therefore to consider carefully which kitcar best matches your requirements, then buy the appropriate donor vehicle. If it so happens that the kitcar can be based on the car you brought back from the garage with an MOT failure certificate, all well and good. But building a kitcar requires con-

siderable commitment and it would be soul-destroying to invest time and money only to find that the finished article was unsuitable. Better to sell your car for spares to help finance the right project.

If you lack the inclination or ability to build your own car, but still desire the sort of original designs found only in the kitcar market, it is possible to have the vehicle built for you by one of the many profes-

Something like this Marcos Spyder would cost upwards of £10,000 to build, but many of the trickier jobs will have been done before the kit leaves the factory. Completed cars also hold their value.

sional companies around the country.

First a word of warning: the law that makes it possible for small specialist companies to produce cars in kit form without the need for expensive test procedures and the like, also prohibits the assembly of those cars by the manufacturer or any other company. If professional build-ups were permitted, a manufacturer would only have to set up a separate company to look after manufacture and

assembly. He could then operate as a conventional car manufacturer, but without having to bother with any of the restrictions that currently apply to mainstream manufacturers.

Thus the build-up companies operate in what they like to call 'a grey area'. Yet if complete build-ups were offered, this would clearly be illegal. A way around this problem has of course been found: they offer to build cars to a near-complete state, as do some kitcar manufacturers themselves, but leave the customer to bolt in a main component. This is often the engine/gearbox, and is frequently done on the build-up company's own premises. Thus the customers complete the build themselves and the law is kept.

The quality of work carried out by these companies varies enormously, and the most frequently experienced problem is one that often afflicts the private, individual builder: estimating the time needed to do the work.

Given the widely varying quality and 'buildability' of kitcars, it makes sense to find a build-up company that already has experience of the car you have in mind, and also to examine as much of its work as possible. Manufacturers are constantly being requested for complete, or near-complete, cars and those not offering their own build-up service will almost certainly be able to suggest or recommend a company familiar with their cars, as will an owners' club. A reputable, established build-up company will be happy to pass on the names and phone numbers of previous customers, whose views are invaluable.

The kitcar market, however, has more variable factors than a British weather forecast, and a multiplicity of models. First you need to do a little groundwork.

CHAPTER 2:
DOING YOUR
HOMEWORK

Basic groundwork

Before attempting to choose the right kitcar, the complete beginner will first have to do some very basic groundwork to familiarize himself with the market. Even for the more experienced enthusiast, a detailed knowledge of what is available from the kitcar industry is vital.

Before the current explosion of coverage in the specialist and mainstream motoring press, it was all too easy to see an isolated kitcar advertisement, or a particular kitcar, and to become obsessed with that one model without realizing that there were many alternatives. Today, would-be kitcar owners have a wealth of information available to them. There are now around 250 different kitcars on the market,

This shot, taken at Castle Combe racing circuit, shows just a sample of the variety of machinery available from the kitcar industry. It could be all too easy to fall in love with the shape of one car, or the performance of another, and make a hasty decision. Choosing the right kitcar is probably the most important stage in the whole process.

manufactured by some 120 different companies. At least basic information on them is best found in specialist magazines and at kitcar shows.

As authors we should declare an interest here because both of us have been involved in *Kitcars and Specials* and *Classic Replicas* magazines. The other three magazines (at the time of writing) are *Kit Car*, *Which Kit* and *Kit Car International*. Since, despite our declared interest, neither of us has any axe to grind, we feel we are able to comment on the three of them. First impressions are certainly favourable. All of them offer plenty of good quality colour photographs and apparently informative text, not to mention the occasional 'exclusive' tag. To evaluate the magazines' own assessments of the kitcars, however, it is necessary first to know something of the nature of the publications and the market they cover.

The kitcar industry, as you will discover, is made up of small companies operating, like all such bodies, on tight budgets, and they need all the free and low-cost exposure they can get. The magazines are very specialized in nature and in turn cannot afford to upset too many companies with heavily critical reports, for fear of losing advertising revenue. That is not to say that payola and bribery are rife in the industry, but most journalists would agree that reporting in the kitcar press is not as objective as the readers would like.

The other problem facing the kitcar press concerns the subject matter itself. Most of the cars tested are professionally built by the manufacturers, and if they can't put together a good example the kit is really in trouble. So the cars tested are not necessarily representative of the marque or model; any suspect areas on the finished car could have been concealed by modifications or a little cosmetic surgery; and the manufacturers are hardly likely to admit to any problems during building.

The magazine tests can – and sometimes do – give a good idea of what the car is like to drive, the look of the finished vehicle and of

The specialist magazines often take kitcars to circuits in order to test their handling on the limit. The note-taking process is vital – for professional and amateur alike.

the standard of the workmanship in construction. A company is unlikely to use, for example, a poorly welded chassis on its demo car, so a good magazine report will also comment on the quality of bodies and chassis in construction or in stock.

Unfortunately, the hand-built car is by definition an individual animal, and no single example can really be said to be representative of the model as a whole. This is a problem that the prospective purchaser must also overcome when visiting the factory, but it would be fair to say that his motivation will be different from that of the kitcar journalist.

Ironically, there is another problem that besets the better magazine (and this caused us numerous headaches on *Classic Replicas*, and its predecessor *Kitcars and Specials*). Despite all the above comments about companies being able to present the perfect demonstrator, this is often far from the case. Manufacturers have been known to apologize for everything from faulty instruments ('we haven't had the speedo recalibrated yet') to suspect brakes ('they haven't really been bedded in yet').

All these faults are 'going to be sorted out soon', of course, but the fact that the company has not bothered to do it for the press, who could do the firm a great deal of good or harm, does not bode well.

We know that some companies count on the magazines either not recognizing the faults, or if they do, not mentioning them. (We're happy to say that the industry knows that neither was true of the magazines with which we were involved). Kitcar magazines have a role to play in providing information that will help you choose a kitcar, and it might seem that we are being rather critical here. We simply feel that it is important that readers are aware of the magazines' limitations, and should be prepared to do additional research of their own. We will be looking at ways of getting the best from factory visits and road tests later.

Both *Kit Car* and *Which Kit* produce annual guides to the kitcar market, and with their photographs and basic specifications these can prove very useful as references. Again we must issue a brief word of warning. Most of the companies featured in the guides have paid for the privilege of appearing there and some of them write the words themselves. They are therefore really little more than a collection of advertisements. Again there is nothing really wrong with that, just so long as everyone knows.

Kitcar shows play an invaluable part in the process of choosing the right kitcar. They bring together all the main manufacturers under one roof, where cars can be compared – and awkward questions asked!

A fragmented industry leaves the kitcar shopper with the options of a great deal of legwork, or visiting a place where manufacturers congregate. Although a certain amount of the former is necessary, the early

and at the biggest events most, of the companies under one roof, so questions can be asked, cars compared and armfuls of literature gathered.

Whether you just wander around in an attempt to see it all, or spend time examining specific cars and asking their manufacturers difficult questions, will depend on your familiarity with the market. If it is specific cars you are after, it is worth a telephone call to the company a few days before the show.

having to filter the genuine enquiries out from the time-wasters. To that end it is also worth making a mental note of what you want to ask them on the stand. Most companies will be helpful – they want to sell cars after all – but public shows can drain exhibitors' reserves of patience and considered questions are more likely to get an informative response than the more vacuous variety. On the other hand, don't be intimidated: you might be interested in a particular car, but you're certainly not going to part with any money until you know just what you'll be getting. It's the company's job to allay your doubts and convince you that its car meets your requirements.

Collecting company literature, either from shows, or by post through magazine advertisements, is another useful method of accumulating information. The huge demand, and the cost of producing the literature, means that most companies make a charge. At shows you will obviously have the opportunity to assess the worth of these brochures, but you might want to check by phone what you'll be getting before sending any money. Other companies supply less glossy literature free of charge, but they do often require a stamped and addressed envelope. If you are contacting a company that has been mentioned in a magazine feature, again it's worth a telephone call first.

The standard of company literature varies enormously, from a simple photocopied A4 sheet to a full-colour, glossy brochure. Romantic, creative copywriting aside, it's the facts you want. Pretty pictures may give you a clear impression of what the car actually looks like, but a full-colour catalogue isn't necessarily an indication of a good product. As we have seen, many of these kitcar companies are small, and if the people involved are primarily engineers, they may lack marketing skills. That they haven't used a marketing or advertising agency might say something abo'' them; but do wait until you h at least seen a car before r a judgement.

Action Days are really outdoor kitcar shows held at racing circuits. They are usually organized by the kitcar magazines – and give the would-be buyer the opportunity to drive (or at least ride in) cars in a controlled environment.

stages of market research are best supplemented by visiting kitcar shows. These bring together many,

Even when booked, companies do sometimes have to cancel, or a last-minute hitch sometimes means they arrive but without the new model you have driven two hundred miles to see.

A phone call can also register you in the mind of the proprietor or salesman (try to speak to someone who will be at the show), and some recognition can make a difference on the day when companies are

A surprising amount of basic research can be undertaken at shows – just sitting in the car and asking yourself whether you would like it on a regular basis is a good place to start.

Factors to consider

When you have gathered together a wealth of literature and magazines, and visited as many kitcar shows and events as possible, it is time to think about your own requirements and compile a short list of cars that meet them. Start by considering the following factors:

Cost

For most people the cost will be the biggest single factor in choosing a kitcar and for this reason, and because calculating the complete cost of a build is a very complex business, this is looked at in more detail in Chapter 3. When comparing cars, you might like to cross-refer between the factors listed here, and the advice given in that chapter. However, for the newcomer to the market, who first of all wants to thin out the huge number of models available, it will probably be enough (allowing for a little 'maker's optimism') to work on the manufacturer's own estimate of what it would cost a customer to build one of them. It might be useful to relate the price specific car, one shown in the

company literature, perhaps, or on a show stand. Cars that are out of reach will soon become obvious and, unless funds are limited, those at the bottom of the price range may already have been rejected for reasons of quality or lack of certain features.

When you know which cars are within your price range, you can start to look at different options, or consider whether compromises necessary to keep a certain car within the limit are actually acceptable. It might, for example, be possible to afford a Cobra replica if it is one of the versions based on Ford Cortina or Granada running gear, but not if it uses Jaguar suspension, and a Rover or American V8 engine and gearbox.

Number of seats

By far the greater part of the market is made up of two-seater sports cars, so if you need four seats, your decision will be made much easier. There are a number of 'two plus two' models on the market, but be warned: the 'plus two' passengers often seem to be expected to be minus legs.

Hardtop or convertible?

Convertibles account for a large slice of the market, and again most of them are two-seaters. The appeal

Although this Buckland (AYX 428) is great fun to drive, the tiny aeroscreen is the only weather protection. The Gentry (VNX 889H) does at least have a full screen and hood to cope with showers.

of the open-topped car is timeless, but it might not be the most practical choice if it has to be used in all weathers. It takes an exceptional hood to provide the sort of protection you can expect from a hardtop, and the best hoods will only

Hardtops are available for some open cars, and this DJ Sportscars Dax Tojeiro would be practical transport all the year round.

be found on the more upmarket (i.e. expensive) models. The section in Chapter 3 giving advice on road testing includes the suggestion that you should conduct it in the worst possible weather. For the convertible this is particularly important because it's the only way really to test the quality and fit of the weather equipment. Then when you're sitting there with draughts blowing about your ears, and water trickling on to your trouser leg, ask yourself if you are going to be able to stand it. Many do, of course, and if the car is to be used as a second or third vehicle, the worst of the weather can be avoided.

The open-top supplied with an optional hardtop offers the best of both worlds, although the hardtop obviously can't be taken along 'just in case' and British weather is notoriously unpredictable. Much of the sensation of open-top driving can be created by removing the roof panels in a 'targa-top' design. Some of these have the added advantage of providing space for the panels to be stored in the car, so the roof can be replaced in a sudden downpour.

The styling
In addition to the basic choices of seating capacity and hard or soft

Styling is very much a personal thing, but these two – a Jago Samuri (Q529 NTB) and a Teal Type 35 Bugatti replica – show the extremes of what is available.

tops, there is a whole range of different body styles, original designs and replicas of classic sports cars. These extend from the traditional 1930s-style sports car to a

replica Group C racing car; and then there are offroad models (a good percentage of which are more accurately described as 'offroad-style'), modern sports cars, saloons and estates – in fact, something for everyone. The sheer diversity of the market makes it impossible to encompass them in words. They really have to be seen, in some cases, to be believed!

The sports car trap
One final word on sports cars. In the enthusiasm to own one, it would be easy to convince yourself that a two-door, soft-top with room in the back for the kids is a practical replacement for your current family saloon. It simply isn't. Apart from problems with weather pro-

Beware the sports car trap! If you think a two-plus-two soft-top could take the place of the family bus, think again! The kitcar market is diverse enough to meet every need, however, and something like this Rickman Ranger is ideal for the family man kitcar enthusiast.

tection, access is poor, luggage and storage space is very limited, and even with a good hood the wind noise can be wearing. Yet nothing is as much fun to drive; and if your kitcar is to be a second or even third car, as many of them are, who needs to consider practicalities?

The choice of engine
The type and size of engine used, and its state of tune, will have a bearing on a number of other considerations. A big or highly tuned engine might provide superlative performance, but it will also be more expensive to run. Kitcar insurance is looked at in more detail later, but the basic rules are the same as for conventional production cars: sports cars are more expensive, and high-performance sports cars are the most expensive of all.

It's worth remembering, too, that a smaller Ford, Fiat or even BL Ital engine will provide much better performance in a small, lightweight, glassfibre sports car than it ever did in its original saloon car body. Then,

too, straight-line acceleration isn't everything: the quickest car getting from A to B on typical British roads will generally be the one with the best roadholding and most effective brakes.

Again, if the kitcar is to be a second car these considerations might not be so important, and several insurance companies now operate limited mileage schemes which work out much cheaper than the more comprehensive policies.

The ease of construction
This can only be accurately assessed by someone who has built the car you are interested in. The responsible manufacturer should give you a

There is no point in paying for more power than you will need, but if you are planning to build a replica, like this LR Roadsters D Type, the engine too has to look right.

good indication, but it is better to have it backed up by a less biased view from existing owners. The manufacturer will normally be happy to pass on a few names, and the owners' club will prove invaluable because members will have discovered any common problems and devised ways of overcoming them. It is really only possible to get a broad indication at this stage, but a close examination of the build manual will prove more revealing later. Again it's impossible to look at this category in isolation because a bigger budget will allow you to buy a more complete kit, where more of the awkward jobs will have been carried out by the manufacturer.

External dimensions
Will it fit in your garage? Some models are considerably longer than the average production car; others (like the utility-style estates) are taller. Bear in mind, too, that the car will probably be on axle stands during building and you will need room to move around it.

Legroom and cockpit-width
These will become evident when you test drive the car. Some models, particularly the traditional roadsters, are very narrow, and

some of the closed sports cars have restricted headroom. It's worth trying the car for size at one of the shows, or even making an initial enquiry by telephone to save a wasted journey.

Panel damage and replacement
A one-piece front-end can be expensive to replace in the event of damage. Check, too, that replacement panels are available.

This Durow might fit the bill – but would it fit the garage? Remember, too, that you will need extra room during the build-up.

Access can be tricky when the hood is up – try getting in with an armful of groceries – and women soon discover that traditionally styled roadsters and skirts don't go well together.

Availability of demonstrator
Another golden rule: never buy a kitcar without having driven a completed version. If it means waiting for the company to complete its demonstrator, then wait. It is sometimes possible for companies to bring in a customer's car for you to drive. There is more on test drive procedures in Chapter 3.

Self-colour GRP or paint finish
GRP is glass reinforced plastic, an alternative name for glassfibre. Some companies use a process by which colour is impregnated in the bodyshell at the moulding stage. This gives a high-gloss finish that does not require painting, which saves time and money. The standard of finish achieved by this means is acceptable to many people, but some prefer to go for a more traditional, high quality sprayed paint finish.

Number of kits produced

Everyone has to start somewhere, and someone has to buy the first kit: but unless you are satisfied that it is a genuine production version, and that any teething problems have been sorted out, it is better not to be that pioneering someone.

SCMG and STATUS membership

As we have seen, the Specialist Car Manufacturers' Group is a section of the Society of Motor Manufacturers and Traders set up to improve the standards of the kitcar and 'specialist car' industry. SCMG's conditions of entry have restricted membership to a small section of the industry, but have ensured that it includes the largest, more established manufacturers.

Even before companies are considered suitable to embark on the rigorous SCMG test procedures, they must have been in business for at least three years, and have a minimum turnover of £100,000 (although this figure is defined as 'automotive business turnover', so companies run in conjunction with a garage or some similar business could include those trading figures). For replica manufacturers there is also the requirement that they should have written permission from the original designer. This explains why there is only one replica manufacturer (Autotune, which produces a not very accurate replica of the Jaguar XK120) among the membership.

The cost to a company of bringing its car up to standard for the SCMG Certificate of Conformity will vary, but the high standards mean it will never be cheap. There is also the seat-belt anchorage test, and this can cost around £2000.

Besides the size of the company, and its willingness to make a substantial financial commitment, what else does SCMG membership tell the prospective customer about a company? The standards of the test are based on the Construction and Use regulations, which all road-registered vehicles should conform with, plus the seat-belt tests and

Autotune, which produces this Aristocat, is a member of the SCMG, which means the car will have undergone extensive testing. Knowledge that the car meets SCMG requirements can dramatically cut the amount of research necessary.

track testing of the completed vehicle. The inspection and testing is undertaken by the West German technical inspection organization, Technischer Überwachungs-Verein (TÜV), through its British operation, TÜV UK Ltd. In Germany, TÜV runs a similar Government-recognized scheme for small-volume car manufacturers who cannot afford the Allgemeine Betriebserlaubnisse (ABE), the German equivalent of our Type Approval.

After the seat-belt test comes a three-part engineering assessment. First is the examination of company documents, including a set of diagrams (showing the chassis, general body shape, position of lights, steering columns, seats, etc.), an assembly manual, parts list, complete kit description and seat-belt anchorage certificate. The importance of a good assembly manual cannot be over-emphasized and the SCMG standards are very high.

The second part involves a factory visit by the TÜV vehicle inspection engineer, who examines a full set of components and a completed vehicle. The standards are again very demanding, covering everything from lights to switches and

controls, and companies often have to carry out comprehensive, and expensive, redesigns or modifications in order to conform.

For the third part, a car is taken to a private test track (often the Millbrook Proving Ground in Bedfordshire), where 12 performance tests are conducted, covering braking performance and stability, handling, full-lock steering behaviour, response to load transfer, and wet road performance.

If the car passes all three parts, and the 92 checks and tests of the assessment, it then receives the Certificate of Conformity.

The other two sections of the SCMG Code of Practice cover business integrity and customer care. Included here are the preclusion of any replica for which the originator's permission has not been obtained, and a recall clause ensuring that if a fault comes to light, all customers will be told about it and necessary action taken. Manufacturers must also provide an adequate level of supporting information (in addition to the assembly manual), and a 12-month warranty with the car or kit.

All in all, SCMG membership – not granted without receipt of the Certificate of Conformity – is a unique assurance of quality and safety standards that takes a good deal of the work and worry out of selecting a kitcar.

Membership of the other industry organization, the Specialist Transport Advisory Testing and Utility Society (STATUS), requires no such testing at the time of writing, although a Code of Practice along the lines of the SCMG's is in the pipeline. Ideally, the industry needs a Ministry-recognized standard, similar to the TÜV scheme operated in West Germany. This is certain to come before long, particularly in view of the 1992 'single market' agreement.

Unlike the production car market, where one three-door saloon really isn't that much different from another, there are a great many factors to consider when assessing a kitcar; there may be others that the individual will want to add to the list we have given. The hours spent poring over the literature and considering the above factors may have been enough to confirm an earlier favourite. However, if your shortlist still isn't short enough, a useful additional exercise is to note down those features your final choice must have. Keep it fairly short and definitive, for example:

Total project cost of £5000
Two-seater, open-top sportscar

Full weather equipment (hood, tonneau cover)
Two litre engine
Traditional styling
Self-colour GRP finish

Now look through all the kitcar guides, brochures, and any notes made at shows, and discard any that do not include all your 'musts'. If you don't have the relevant information, call the manufacturer and find out. Now apply a second list of 'would likes' to the remaining cars, for example:

Black as a colour choice
Luggage space for at least one suitcase
Roll-over bar
Optional hardtop

If one or more of your shortlisted cars meets all these requirements, you've struck gold. If not, pursue the car or cars that meet most of them.

Of course, choosing a kitcar is not quite as clinical and soulless as this, and you should never spurn gut reaction, self-expression and maybe even a little risk-taking.

Nevertheless it is a big commitment, and the huge number of choices available make it all the more important to get it right. For the newcomer, the process we have suggested is a useful guide through a very complex market.

You may by now have made what you feel is a final decision, or at least arrived at a shortlist of kit-cars that seem to meet your requirements. But in order to ensure that you spend your leisure time happily building the car rather than repenting, having acted in haste, there is a great deal more research to be done.

The next stage is the factory visit. If the company or companies under consideration are members of the Specialist Car Manufacturers' Group or STATUS, at least some of the work has been done for you (see the 'SCMG membership' section earlier in this chapter). Even so, the importance of a factory visit should not be underestimated, and driving the kitcar you are considering is possibly the most important stage of all.

CHAPTER 3: VISITING THE MAKER

Taking a look at the company

This is a vital part of the decision-making process for a number of reasons.

Firstly, it gives you the opportunity to find out something about the company itself. The production processes of the big manufacturers like Ford and BL are taken for granted and seldom given a second thought. The kitcar industry, however, consists of many small specialist companies, and unless you already have experience of the firm in question you have no way of knowing whether it operates out of a couple of lock-ups or an efficiently run factory unit.

Secondly, you will either be able to see bodies, chassis and other components in the production stages or, if these are not manufactured on the premises, at least be able examine the car in its unassembled state. Buy a kit on the strength of having seen just the completed demonstrator and you might well be horrified when the kit arrives in all its nakedness.

Thirdly, you will have the chance to test drive the company demonstrator and assess objectively whether you could live with the vehicle in the long term.

Finally, it is the perfect opportunity to ask all those awkward questions while the company representative has the time, and a workshop full of examples, to answer them.

There are companies in virtually every corner of the country and, life being what it is, those on your shortlist are likely to be hundreds of miles apart, but a visit really is worth the trouble and expense. Even if travelling and staying over costs you a few hundreds of pounds now, it will still represent a small part of the overall cost of the purchase and build, and could save a very expensive mistake.

First make the appointment. Most companies only have one demonstrator and a small staff, so that the boss may be involved in production, sales – and making the coffee. Some of the very small operations are run on a part-time basis, so if you call in on the off-chance, you could find they are without a demonstrator, the person you need to speak to is picking up parts, or even that the place is locked up and deserted.

The factory visit is so important, and includes so many different areas and items of information, that it is easy to forget something. Even journalists sometimes have to call a company after a visit 'just to check'. So, like journalists, it is best to arm yourself with a note pad; and if you can take along a small tape recorder to get down everything you are told, so much the better. The note pad is a vital *aide-mémoire*, and you should in no way feel foolish about taking it along. It will show the company that you know what you are doing, and save those unsatisfactory after-thought phone calls.

It is simplest if the notes you make in advance are chronological, running through in the order you would like things to happen. If circumstances dictate changes of plan, so be it, but at least there will less chance of your missing something.

Top of your list, should be the premises. You need to assess the sort of people and company you are dealing with, and this is best done by looking at the way they run their business.

As has been mentioned, parts of the kitcar industry are far from affluent. This is due partly to the fact that some companies have been under-capitalized from the beginning. Often their biggest failing is, however, a simple lack of confidence: a few are virtually apologetic for the 'kitcar' label, and

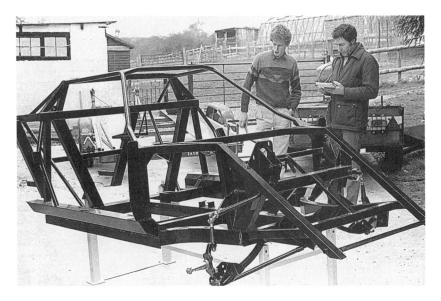

Follow Mike Taylor's example and make notes during your factory visit. Here Mike is inspecting a Transformer Cars HF 2000 (Lancia Stratos Replica) chassis.

seem to price their kits accordingly. The result is that the company operates on tiny margins and never really becomes established. There are many exceptions to this, of course, and the new breed of small volume manufacturers are pricing their kits far more realistically. With this more progressive attitude

Southern Roadcraft's premises occupy what used to be a car showroom and are fairly typical of the kitcar industry. However, don't be surprised to find the company you choose operating from a Nissen hut.

comes better premises, and although Nissen huts and converted farm buildings are still common among the smaller companies,

more and more are moving into efficient – if less characterful! – industrial units. Whatever the design and scale of the premises, however, there is never any excuse for things being scruffy and badly run. Even the poorest workshop area can be kept tidy and work-manlike.

The provision of a plush, carpeted reception area, with potted plants in profusion, is an indication of the company's awareness of image. Many companies are, however, run by engineers, as has been pointed out, with little feel for marketing;

Working with glassfibre is a messy business. At Pilgrim GRP the floor of the laminating shop is covered with sheets of hardboard, which are replaced regularly for safety and cleanliness.

and some have actually told us they deliberately keep away from 'all that sort of thing', channelling all their efforts and resources into producing cars. The best and most immediate way to judge a company's efficiency is still by its workshop, its 'business end'.

If the company makes its own glassfibre panels, there is certain to be a good deal of mess about – laminating is a mucky job – but it is still possible to have a degree of order and maintain a certain standard of cleanliness. The better run, more caring company will have its materials stacked and tools on racks. The floor need not be

covered in a sticky carpet of glass-fibre mat and resin – and for safety reasons should not be – and too much dust can be damaging as well as unsightly. First impressions do count, so make this your first observation and note it on your pad.

Kitcar companies operate, characteristically, in a number of different ways, depending on how much of the actual manufacturing process is conducted on the premises. At one extreme are those firms that produce virtually everything themselves – moulding the bodies, welding the chassis, and casting or machining the smaller components. At the other are those who subcontract the whole process and simply act as a gathering point, bringing together all the various parts, and sending out the complete packages.

Marlin's factory has an efficient workflow system. Each chassis is assigned to a customer and carries his name with it as it travels through the system.

If you visit Jago's Chichester factory you can see chassis being fabricated and examine the jigs used in the manufacturing process.

If the chassis are welded on the premises, this too provides an indication of the company's working practices and it is reasonable to expect a certain level of tidiness and cleanliness. The standard of equipment, and the jigs used to hold the chassis components during fabrication, can also be examined.

The general level of activity in the factory is another good indicator: a stack of bodies and chassis will prove useful when it comes to examining them, but if they are sitting under a pile of dust and cobwebs, or are being used as shelving units, be warned. Look for a healthy 'movement' in the production and sales process. Some smaller companies produce kits to order, so there is unlikely to be a stock of bodies or chassis. In most cases, however, to enable orders to be processed within a reasonable period of time, some level of stock is necessary, particularly in the smaller items such as trim kits, windscreens, chrome trim, etc.

If no stock is held, be prepared for a lengthy wait, which can be very frustrating if the car is finished but for the odd small part that prevents it from being driven.

As you are shown around, be aware of the logic, or otherwise, of the production process, and the general system organization. Some companies assign a kit to a customer almost before production begins, so it immediately acquires an identity from his name tag.

If you are compiling a detailed breakdown of cost (see Chapter 4), the factory visit is the ideal opportunity to fill in the gaps, but again it is important to make notes in advance. Many brochures and price lists are impressively comprehensive, but there will always be questions like 'Are the doors already hung on the basic kit?', or 'How much extra is the tonneau cover?' Jot them down before you leave home.

More general questions to be asked should include how many kits are sold. Just how accurate the answer is, and how much 'optimism factor' has entered the calculation, is for you to decide, but it should be obvious if a wild claim is not supported by the activity going on in the factory. As a very general rule, one kit a week is considered fairly good, and one a month would be acceptable providing it was a more upmarket model with

A completed Marlin Roadster.

a decent profit margin. Less than that and the company must be involved in some other business – general glassfibre fabrication, light engineering, or a conventional garage, perhaps. This is by no means a bad thing, but do try to judge the company's degree of commitment to the kitcar side of its operation.

All these, and the more obvious questions about the time the firm has been trading, the number of people involved, etc., are all intended to give some indication of the company's integrity.

The last thing you want is for your company to disappear after you've bought the basic chassis kit and before the bodyshell has been supplied. Even if you are buying the complete package at one go, you will inevitably need to get back to the supplier – hopefully not too often – during the build. And whether you build a kit or buy a virtually complete car, there is every likelihood that you will need spares in the future.

Ask, too, for the names and addresses of a couple of previous customers, preferably in your home area. If the firm can't easily come up with two satisfied customers, be suspicious; but the more practical purpose of this exercise is to provide you with a possibly more independent source of opinions. Ask also about an owners' club.

'Possibly more independent' is deliberate because owners are often very protective of their cars, and not always as objective as you would like them to be: more on that later.

The next stage is to inspect the chassis. It is worthwhile leaving the inspection of the finished car, and the test drive, until last because it is all too easy to be swayed by an impressively prepared demo car. That might sound patronizing, but in fact most journalists use the same approach in order to keep their objectivity.

The chassis

The basic types of chassis are covered in Chapter 10. If you are a novice, it is as well to get some basic idea of their design in your mind in case the makers try to baffle you with science. Only a real expert can begin to know how a chassis will perform, or whether it will be strong enough, so unless you have an engineering background it is best to restrict design-orientated questions to the more

Below: Steer clear of a chassis that looks like this. With no crossbracing the centre section is weak and liable to twist – the company that made it, Daytona Classics, went out of business.

Below: This Standard Ten chassis is a simple – some would say crude – ladderframe, but it is still going strong today after covering thousands upon thousands of miles with no sign of fatigue.

Although it may be a little over the top, and perhaps overweight, this JPR Wildcat chassis is strong and twist-free, and the twin perimeter rails give side protection.

practical aspects.

Top of many people's list will be safety and a general enquiry as to the protection offered in the event of an accident should indicate immediately how much priority has been given to this aspect of the design. Don't expect anything up to Volvo standard, but it is reasonable to expect consideration to have been given to some form of crumple zone – to absorb at least some frontal or rear impact – and side impact protection. Some body styles preclude consideration of such factors. They weren't in the original 1930s. '40s or '50s designs, so they cannot be incorporated in similarly styled, or identically replicated, cars today. The same absence of safety factors would, of course, apply if you bought and drove one of the original classics.

Seat belt mounting is one aspect of kitcar safety that has received a great deal of publicity in recent years, and rightly so. The importance of seat belts has been taken for granted since they became com-

pulsory in the United Kingdom, and the same laws apply to kitcars. However, they are only as effective as their mountings. The tremendous forces acting on the mountings in the event of a collision rule out simply bolting them to convenient glassfibre panels, and the manufacturer often has to fabricate a suitable framework specifically for the purpose (although the same framework can also be used for

mounting other components requiring strength and rigidity, such as door catches).

As the law stands, seat belts must be fitted to kitcars, but the anchorage points do not have to be tested. However, some manufacturers, and particularly those within the two industry organizations, the SCMG and STATUS, voluntarily put their cars through a thorough test procedure in order to conform with the EEC standard 14.02. If the company you're visiting has successfully put its car through this test, you need have no more fears concerning seat belt mountings.

Matters such as chassis tube size and wall thickness, positioning of suspension mounting points, and the effectiveness of crossbracing must be left to the integrity of the designer. There are, however, a number of other aspects of construction that can be examined.

It is important that all the necessary mountings and pick-up points are provided, and that no fabrication is required. Most manufacturers will clearly state in their literature that 'no welding is required', but do always check. It has been known for companies to sell a budget version of their chas-

A Jaguar E–Type lookalike, the JPR Wildcat is a competent performer.

One of the earlier Westfield chassis undergoing seat belt anchorage testing at Manchester Polytechnic, the home of STATUS. (Picture courtesy Arnold Wilson)

sis unit requiring the welding and drilling of all the mounting points, which is not something to be undertaken by anyone without considerable engineering skills – and a good deal of time and patience. Check also to see if holes drilled in chassis tubes are bushed with tubular spacers to prevent crushing when bolts are tightened.

The strength of welds obviously cannot be detected by simply looking at them. However, a good weld will be of even quality and neat appearance and, if you look carefully, you will be able to see where the weld has penetrated the steel. Most manufacturers use a method called MIG welding, and this gives consistently good results in the hands of an experienced operator; so if the welds look like bits of bubblegum stuck to the chassis, be suspicious. Like every other profession, welding has recognized standards and enquiring after the qualifications held by the employees can also give an indication of company standards.

Another useful and easily conducted visual check is to make sure that the ends of the steel sections are sealed. If they are left open,

water and salts can get inside and cause rapid corrosion – undetectable until serious damage has been done. They should be closed by welding a plate over the end, or by capping with plastic.

It is important that the insides of the chassis members are protected from rust in some way, and this is sometimes carried out by the manufacturer. Probably the best method is Waxoyl, or a similar preparation, which is applied under pressure and dries to form a waxy protective coating that will not

Look for neat welds and capped ends to the chassis tubes and check that mounting points are provided.

vibrate loose and is self-sealing in the event of a scratch – when bolting on mechanical components, for example. It is possible to carry out the treatment during the build-up, but this is a fiddly and often less thorough method – particularly if the chassis tubes are sealed.

Chassis are supplied in a variety of external finishes. Aware of the rustproof qualities of the glassfibre body, a few manufacturers attempt to offer extra protection on their chassis by offering an optional galvanized finish. This will obviously cost more, but the protection it offers makes it worthwhile.

Other offerings from the industry include primer, a protective paint finish like Hammerite, and plastic coating. This last option is superb, providing a smooth, protective surface, although it is necessary to make sure that no moisture is allowed to get inside the coating at bolt holes, etc.

What finish you choose, providing you have a choice, will again depend on how much time and money you wish to spend. Careful chassis preparation can add years to the working life of the car, so if you intend to run it for some years, a more thorough preparation might be worth while. Even if you don't plan to hold on to the car that long, the sense of protection it offers is reassuring and future buyers will surely be impressed.

Working on the principle of 'If you want a job done properly . . .', you might choose to have the chas-

sis supplied untreated and undertake the work yourself. It is unusual for companies to offer this as an option, however, and they might require a special order – and the extra time for delivery that this entails. Treating the chassis yourself does have the added bonus of allowing you to see the welds before they are covered up by paint.

The body panels

Continuing the note-making process, it is now time to cover the main points to examine on the body.

This shows the bare bones of the Triton and the extensive use made of aluminium panelling. Note that the chassis is resting on a jig, so don't mistake the open-ended tubes beneath it for chassis members.

top end of the market, hand-beaten into beautiful compound curves by highly skilled craftsmen. Needless to say, such craftsmanship does not come cheap. In most instances, the aluminium body is used only as a skin over the multi-tube frame from which the car takes most of its strength.

In kitcar construction, GRP (glass-reinforced plastic – or plain 'glass-fibre') is widely used for body

The Foers Triton is one of the few aluminium-bodied kitcars available.

This section will concentrate on glassfibre panels, which constitute the vast majority of bodyshells used.

Aluminium does feature on some of the cheaper designs, and a few more expensive but simple body designs like the Caterham Super 7. It is used on this model for flat or simple single-curve panels. Aluminium also appears right at the

A typical set of kitcar body panels. These are from the GP Vehicles Porsche Spyder replica.

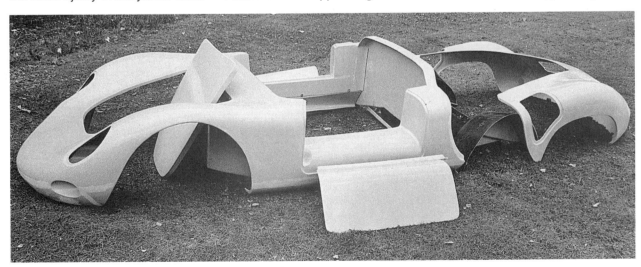

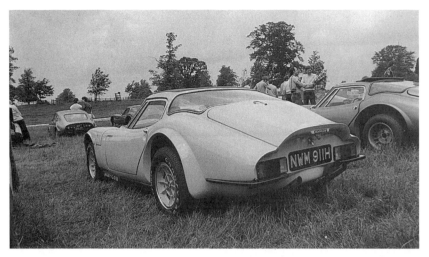

Above: The flowing lines of the Marcos not only give the car its beautiful appearance, but the compound curves of the body panels add stiffness. Also, the generous returns on the wheel arches impart rigidity and give a nice tidy finish.

panels in place of steel. In comparison to the complex procedure of making compound curves in sheet steel or aluminium, glassfibre production requires no big outlay in machine tooling, and a fabrication shop can be set up in most reasonably sized establishments. The technique of making moulds and laying up the glassfibre is easy to learn and the material lends itself to one-off moulding or short production runs. In short, GRP is

the answer to a kitcar designer's prayer.

The material does, however, have its limitations. The tensile strength/weight ratio of GRP is high, but the stiffness is low compared to steel. It is therefore important that the designer specifies a

Below: In contrast, this budget-priced Dutton does not have returns on the wheel arches or bonnet and an edging strip, such as Titanfast, is usually used to give an acceptable finish. This, however, does not contribute to panel stiffness.

material thickness sufficient to prevent panel shake. Alternatively, he can employ various devices, such as moulded-in ribs or channels, or introduce lips and curves, to stiffen panels.

Sandwich construction can also be employed. This is where a core material, such as plywood, balsa wood or a paper honeycomb, is sandwiched between two layers of GRP. It is possible to increase the tensile strength of glassfibre by including carbon fibres or woven glass strands in the lay-up.

GRP is not as ductile as steel or

Left: The Triple C Challenger E-Type Jaguar replica has a double-skinned and ribbed bootlid for rigidity and an authentic appearance.

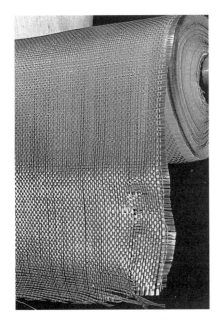

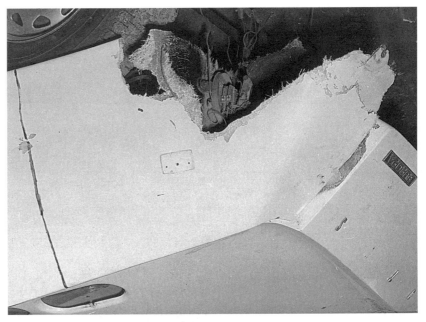

Above and below: Glassfibre reinforcement can be in the form of chopped strand mat or woven cloth. Other materials, such as carbon fibre, can be used where a really lightweight, strong laminate is required. **(Pictures courtesy Arnold Wilson)**

Above and below: Glassfibre is not so ductile as steel or aluminium and the material will break under heavy impact. However, unlike metal panels, any damage is usually localized and is easy to repair using replacement panels if necessary. **(Pictures courtesy Arnold Wilson)**

of GRP compare favourably with steel and aluminium. All things taken into consideration, a properly designed GRP-bodied car is just as strong as its steel counterpart and much more weather-resistant.

So much so that with the passage of time, as a steel car starts to rapidly rust and weaken, the scales tip heavily in favour of GRP.

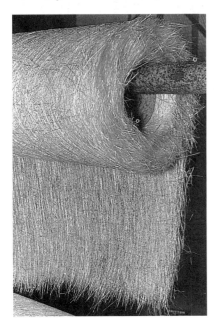

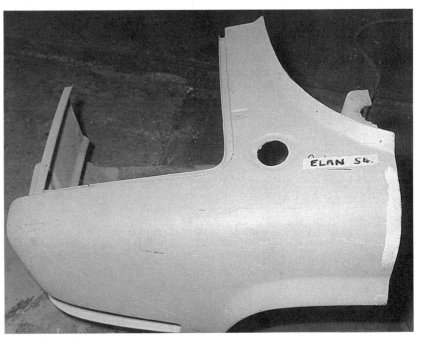

aluminium: it doesn't dent, but when it is hit sufficiently hard it will break. In other words a typical car parking mishap that would normally put a dent the size, say, of a dinner plate in a steel car would only scratch a GRP- bodied model. However, an accident that was a little more severe, enough to dent the wing of a steel car extensively,

would crack through and break the wing of a GRP body.

Of course, glassfibre doesn't rust and it is very weather resistant. It is also a good electrical and heat insulator, and the fatigue properties

In reality, the only thing preventing the big car manufacturers from making more and more panels from glassfibre is the fact that it does not lend itself so easily to mass production, and the cost of

Above: This steel bodyshell has been severely weakened by rust after a few years' use. This will never happen with GRP panels.

Production cars, such as the Renault Espace, are beginning to use GRP bodypanels.

the raw materials is higher. Nevertheless, its use is on the increase.

GRP: the process

To produce a car bodyshell, a female mould is made to the exact design and shape of the car. The mould itself is usually made of glassfibre and it has a perfectly smooth and blemish-free finish on the inside. It is against this that the mat and resin mix is laid up.

First the mould is washed and any minor imperfections filled. It is then rubbed smooth with wet and dry paper. If the mould is multi-sectional it is bolted together and any joint cracks are filled and covered with Sellotape (this is why you sometimes see the impressions of the tape in the gelcoat). Then the whole mould is polished and sprayed with a release agent.

The gelcoat is then applied and it is this that becomes the outside surface of the car. Some manufacturers offer a self-coloured finish. In this case a pigment is mixed with the gelcoat, which results in a very high-gloss, coloured surface. Other

companies specify a semi-gloss finish, which is suitable for spraying.

This is followed by a layer of surfacing tissue which gives the gelcoat a good base and helps to prevent air bubbles forming. Then come the layers of glass mat, or woven glass cloth and resin – the layers are added until the desired thickness is achieved. In most cases this process is carried out by hand,

Left: Here a layer of mat and resin is being applied to a mould. Most kitcar companies carry out the laminating procedure by hand, but specialist GRP fabricators sometimes spray a mixture of chopped strand mat and resin onto the mould.

but some glassfibre fabrication shops use a gun to apply a mix of resin and glassfibre.

Some manufacturers finish off with a layer of fine tissue or a coat of thick pigmented resin. This gives a smooth finish to the inside of the moulding, which is easy to clean and ensures that there are no splinters or rough areas.

A badly made laminate may display some of the following faults:

1   Areas of dry mat are exposed on the inside of the laminate. This indicates that insufficient resin has been used and the glass fibres are not saturated. This could mean that the whole moulding is starved of resin; or it might be a localized fault. It would pay to examine the whole of the moulding carefully. If there are extensive areas of dry mat, reject the bodyshell.

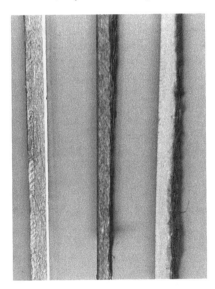

These are sections through three different laminates. The laminate on the left is of even thickness and is a dense, solid lay-up. The example in the centre shows an uneven lay-up with air holes and voids. On the right is a laminate that is resin-starved on the inside face, which presents a rough surface with dangerous splinters of glassfibre.

2   Tiny broken blisters in the gelcoat, which give the surface a rough, broken appearance, are usually caused by applying the first layer of resin before the gelcoat has cured. There is no real remedy for this and if the visible parts of the bodyshell are affected badly, the whole moulding should be rejected.

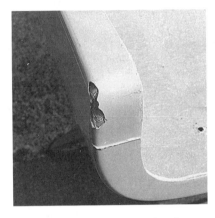

Careless application of the first layer of glass mat can cause voids like these behind the gelcoat. The exposed glass fibres will draw water into the laminate if this is not attended to.

3   Hollows behind the gelcoat can cause pits in the surface and, more often, in the edges and corners of mouldings. These are usually caused by air bubbles behind the gelcoat and the first layer of mat; they can be gouged out, filled and painted, so they are not usually a serious problem.

4   Ridges and bumps (detected by drawing your finger tips over the surface, or looking along the surface against the light) can be caused by poor quality moulds or by the laminate being removed from the moulds before a complete cure has taken place. Most car bodyshells have some imperfections of this sort and if the shell is to be painted, the pre-paint preparation will get rid of them. On a gelcoat finish there isn't too much you can do about it, and it is up to you to decide if you can accept it or not.

5   Varying thickness of the laminate can be caused by careless laying-up. Some variation in thickness can be allowed, but thin, waferlike laminate at the edges of running boards and wings is not acceptable. It should be appreciated that the laminate will also vary in thickness depending on the stresses in certain areas.

Star cracking can occur when the laminate has a gel-coat that is too thick, or when an impact on the reverse side has occurred. **(Picture courtesy Arnold Wilson)**

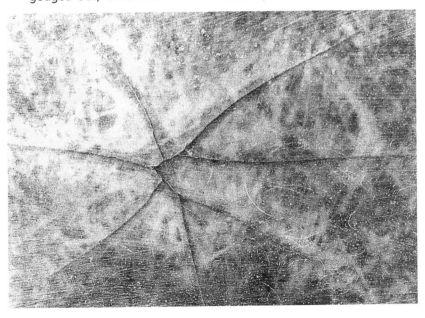

Some panels are stiffened by sandwiching plywood, foam and various other materials between two layers of glassfibre. The example on the left shows a plywood sandwich. On the right is a section through a laminate of uneven thickness, which could make for a weak panel.

These panels will be trimmed when they have cured. Careless trimming could result in an undersized panel. **(Picture courtesy Arnold Wilson)**

6   Careless trimming of the bodyshell can leave very little tolerance for final fitting. Also, the panels can become chipped and scratched at the factory and this happens surprisingly often.

Having noted all the disasters that can occur, we should point out that most kitcar bodyshells are made to high standards and they are getting better all the time. So don't expect to find too many problems. It is surprising, too, what can be done to repair damaged GRP: chips and scratches are easy to deal with, so don't go rejecting mouldings on these grounds alone.

Don't be alarmed if the glassfibre appears to be translucent, especially in strong sunlight. This is quite normal: it does not indicate a weakness, although it can be somewhat disconcerting. However, there is something you can do about it and we'll be talking about that later. Anticipating the problem, some manufacturers pigment their laminate right through its thickness with the same colour as the

Panels for the Riley MPH-inspired Brooklands by Swindon Sportscars are supplied in a non-pigmented finish which has to be painted. Many people prefer this for the control they have over the quality of the final finish.

gelcoat. This makes the moulding opaque and it has the added benefit that if the gelcoat becomes chipped, the damage is not so noticeable.

One other important factor concerning GRP is whether it is structural or non-structural. A bodyshell designed to be used in conjunction with a simple ladderframe, for example, will need to contribute a good deal of the combined structure's strength: the chassis is prone to twist and the bodyshell stiffens it. In that case the main bodyshell panels would be expected to be about $\frac{1}{4}$ in thick. A bodyshell intended for use on a multi-tubular chassis does not need such strength because the chassis is inherently far stiffer. The body is little more than a skin, to keep the occupants and mechanical components covered, and to appeal aesthetically; a thickness of around $\frac{1}{8} - \frac{3}{16}$ in would be acceptable.

The above remarks do not constitute a hard and fast rule, because of the many variable factors involved, some of which have been mentioned. However, it is important that you are convinced the thickness has been carefully considered, that strength is imparted by other means if not by panel thickness, and that corners have not been cut for reasons of cost. Such an exercise would be the falsest of false economies.

It is not always possible to see the panel thickness, of course, and you will often have to take the manufacturer's word for it. Make a note to look around for any glassfibre offcuts that might be lying around the workshop (or does the company score so highly on the cleanliness front that there are none to be seen?). If available – and you could always ask – they will give you an accurate idea of what is going on under the surface, both in terms of lamination methods and thickness of the moulding.

Returned edges are another feature found on good quality moulding. Instead of wheel arches, doors and other panels ending in a trimmed glassfibre edge, the panels should be turned over to give a smooth, neat finish. It also adds considerable stiffness in areas that might otherwise flex and prove prone to damage.

Just what you consider to be an acceptable standard of glassfibre moulding is ultimately up to you. But don't listen to excuses like, 'It's a difficult panel to mould', because the industry is full of top quality glassfibre fabrication companies who simply do not make mistakes in this area. You might be prepared to accept the odd flaw in order to get the type of car you want, but do at least be aware of any compromises.

Many manufacturers refuse even to supply bodies in self-coloured gelcoat because they believe the standard of finish is unacceptable. It's true that a well-applied professional paint job cannot be beaten, and for the more expensive builds, like the upmarket replicas, there is really no other finish worth considering. At the cheaper end of the market, however, there is a lot to be said for self-coloured body panels, which are certainly better than an amateurish home spray finish. You could opt for the best of both worlds: self-coloured GRP, sprayed with the same colour. This allows a high quality paint finish,

Supplied with self-coloured GRP panels with a high-gloss finish, the Lomax is an inexpensive three-wheeler using Citroën 2CV mechanical components.

and provides instant colour in the event of chips or small scratches in the paint.

The subject of glassfibre safety is a contentious one. Everyone has a horror story concerning a glassfibre car – usually a three-wheeler – seen 'shattered' after an accident. We have seen several glassfibre-bodied kitcars after accidents – some of them high-speed shunts on the racing circuit – and this simply wasn't the case. The Midas Gold was tested officially and survived the immovable wall of concrete test impressively. That says a great deal about the Midas design, of course, but it also speaks highly of glassfibre.

It is true that badly damaged glassfibre requires a different repair technique from steel. However, providing you check that the company can replace panels – and that a damaged front wing doesn't necessitate replacing the entire bodyshell – you shouldn't have any real problems. Remember, too, that some ocean-going boats are made of GRP, and they withstand the severest of punishments in rough seas.

With the factory and kit inspection out of the way, and questions concerning company history, kit prices and ease of build all asked and answers carefully noted, it is time for the road test.

The road test

Curb your enthusiasm a little longer. Driving the car is only part of the story and, unsurprisingly, a kitcar road test is like no other you've ever conducted. A few notes of explanation.

For a start, the kitcar you drive will not be the kitcar you buy – unless you make an offer for the company demonstrator. What is more, kitcars possessing the infinitely variable specification we know them to have, it might not even be much like the kitcar you intend to build. You could copy the company demonstrator, but the chances are you'll want a different engine, or at least a different state of tune; or maybe a different interior, and different wheels and tyres; and the paint might not be quite what you have in mind. So if the car available is so different from the one you hope to build, what's the point of even testing it?

In fact, we would go so far as to say that you should never buy a kitcar without having first driven an example. That doesn't mean being driven in one, or a spin to the end of the industrial estate cul-de-sac. It means a genuine test in which you are able to drive the car, ideally in a variety of different traffic and road conditions, so that you can assess whether you could use the vehicle on a regular basis.

Test driving a kitcar means testing the car's total design, not checking on the position of the ashtray, or the colour of the 'turbo' badges. If you are going for an Escort, Maestro, Astra, or some similar car, the final choice will be down to styling and detail touches. Choose a kitcar and two apparently similar models could be completely different to drive; two identical models could be built and finished so differently that choice simply doesn't come into it.

When you go to see a kitcar, then, you will be looking for general quality of design and production in the workshop inspection already described, but also for quality of design and production on the completed car. You can take nothing for granted. Is the front suspension geometry correct? Are

Escort door catches really suitable? Are the door hinges mounted securely enough? Do the window winders work? Is the boot sealed? Assuming that everything is fine on the demo car, will it be so on yours? Is it just an assembled kit, or have modifications been made? Will it be possible to get the demo car's quality of finish on your own car, on your own?

Yet when you think about it, could it be any other way? You are considering buying a car, featuring an original design of chassis, and original or replica body style, in kit form. You intend to build a complete vehicle from these parts, to register it, and to use it as you would any other car. Surely it's not unreasonable that you should undertake a few hours of careful research and consideration.

The kitcar requires thorough examination if you are to be 100 per cent sure of your decision. It is important, however, that you don't make excuses for it. You may have adjusted your standards somewhat, accepting that the company won't have spent millions of pounds on a safety design development programme, and not expecting an ergonomically perfect interior design. However, when you examine and drive a kitcar, it is a mistake to think that you can tolerate shortfalls because it looks like a famous Italian sports car, or even because it looks like nothing else on

earth. A knee constantly knocked against the dashboard of a car is just as painful if you have built the car yourself: and your pride, too, can take a bit of a bashing.

We have established the importance of first test driving a kitcar. It is important now for you to establish the status of that kitcar. That is, was it built from a production kit? Could you build a similar car?

What can happen is that a company develops a prototype of a new car, then discovers and – it is to be hoped – corrects any inherent faults, and puts the car into production. Unfortunately, limited resources (time and money again) push the original prototype into service as the company demonstrator, even though it is not representative of the improved kits actually being sold by the company. The result is that the test drive is littered with phrases like 'of course that's been changed on production versions', and the prospective customer has an even more difficult evaluation to make.

Ideally, then, the demonstrator should reflect the company's product, and should be finished to a standard that is both reasonably attained and of acceptable quality.

Dutton demonstration cars were built to a standard that the average home builder working to a budget could achieve.

Featuring a tuned Jaguar V12 engine, this Dax demonstrator was certainly not built down to a price.

There are, inevitably, companies who offer opposite extremes in this respect. On one hand there are companies who produce cheap and cheerful cars and build their demonstrators as cheaply as possible to show what can be done on a small budget, arguing that those wanting to spend more money can obviously do so to achieve a higher standard. Then there are companies who adopt the opposite philosophy and build their demonstration cars to an impossibly high standard which the amateur builder would find difficult and very expensive to emulate.

Most companies will fit demonstrators with sensible engines and complete them to a reasonable standard to show the customer what can be done; it takes little imagination on the part of the would-be builder, and little effort from the company representative, to say what could be achieved should the customer decide to invest more or less in the project.

The timing of your road test may be out of your control; but just as it is a mistake to view houses on glorious, sunny days, so it can be misleading to test kitcars in good weather. Driving along with the

The Mini Minus shrugs off the worst of the British weather.

wind in your hair is one very enjoyable aspect of open sports car ownership, but it is only one aspect. Try it again when the rain is pouring and the wind is howling, and you might look at things in a very different light. It might be less convenient, and less comfortable, but the worse the weather at the time of your company visit, the better. There's nothing like a heavy shower to wash the colour off rose-tinted glasses.

The exception, of course, is if you are considering buying something like the Britton Hazelgrove, which has nothing but a small screen to

protect you from the elements. Then again, in the British climate it's really not practical to restrict use to warm sunny days, so take along your flying jacket, sensible hat and scarf, and get a real taste of adventure motoring.

So there you are, face to radiator grille with the car of your dreams, with the sound of jingling ignition keys in your ears. But first comes the examination.

The first part of the examination is first impressions. It might seem like an old wife's tale, but first impressions really do count. So stand back from the car and take it in: does it sit well? Does the ride height look right? If it's the first

You'll need your long johns and woolly hat when testing the Britton Hazelgrove in the winter.

time you've seen the car in the flesh, does it look as good as in the photographs? Is the styling less effective when viewed from different angles? You will be examining things in more detail later, but having quickly taken it in, does it impress? Remember it will cost you anything between £4000 and £24,000 to get this show on the road – you deserve to be impressed. If you are considering a replica, check the overall lines and detail items for accuracy. Take along reference books or magazines, because it's easy to forget original detailing when the replica in front of you looks so right.

You next need to turn your attention to the bodywork. Assuming that it is glassfibre, you might have spotted flaws on the bodyshells inside the workshop. Are they still there in the finished car? If not, ask what work was involved to get rid of them. If they are still there, are they acceptable? If you are not sure, ask whether it is a gelcoat or paint finish and, if paint, how the finish was achieved. If the work was carried out by an outside company, you could pay a call to seek an opinion; expect the people there to be a little biased, but every clue helps.

Are the chrome items unique to this kitcar or lifted from a donor car? If the former, check them for quality – look for cast pitting, patchy areas, flaking, etc. – and if they are not part of the basic kit specification, make sure you know how much extra they are going to cost you. Stainless steel detailing won't suffer plating problems, but isn't easy to work with and usually costs more.

Next you should pay attention to the quality of the moulding. We've already talked about surface quality, and the accuracy of replicas, but do the panels fit properly? Hanging doors is probably the worst job of a build – it's well worth having them hung by the factory if this service is offered – and is aggravated by irregular mouldings. Check

LR Roadsters' Ram has the doors fitted at the factory, thus saving the builder a tricky job.

mously from company to company; in content, as you would expect, but also in standards of finish. Neat wiring and a clean and tidy engine doesn't make the kit any better, but it does make its examination a lot more pleasurable. Equally, it doesn't help if thousands of pounds have been lavished on non-standard equipment like dry-sump kits and turbo-chargers and any modifications to the standard kit which that

Photographs below: In an ideal world all cars would have removable panels to allow access to the mechanical components, as in this Ginetta G27.

Mini components are very much at home on the Pimlico, but not all kits make such a sensible choice of donor car ancillary items.

for signs of 'doctoring' – edges of panels that have been cut or ground off – and the all-important equal gap around the doors, bonnet and boot, which is the mark of an accurate bodyshell. If you can see a pre-paint bodyshell with opening panels showing equal gaps, give it not another thought.

Most kitcars use components from production cars, but on some the integration is more successful than on others. If donor car parts are used on a replica, they will sometimes stick out like sore thumbs; but on original designs, too, it can be obvious where parts like windscreens have been utilized because they were available on a donor car, rather than because they suited the design. We have seen many an impressive designer's drawing suffer all sort of compromises in the 'productionizing' because the manufacturer wanted to use as many donor car parts as possible. Pay particular attention to windows and even complete panels, which can't be changed; to catches, handles, lights, and so on, which could perhaps be substituted after some avid breaker's yard searching; and wheels, mirrors, etc, which can be more easily tailored to your own taste during the build-up.

Engine compartments vary enor-

effort went. Traditionally styled sports cars, just like those of the 1930s and '40s they took their inspiration from, offer little such capacity, although this is sometimes supplemented by an authentic luggage rack. More modern sports car models are usually small and luggage space seems to come low on the designer's list of priorities. Mid-engined cars are notorious, although some do manage a narrow but deeper boot behind the power unit, and more conventional styles offer at least 'weekend luggage' space. If you're hoping to carry big dogs and golf clubs about, look towards the big utility-style estate vehicles: but that decision will have been made before you start visiting factories.

One final note on luggage capacity: do ensure you have at least one

might involve. Look for the provision of appropriate mounting points for components and a general businesslike appearance. Consider also accessibility, not just for maintenance and repair, but also for the build. Exotic mid-engine designs look very impressive, but you could find yourself on your back with a multi-extended, ratcheted socket just to get to that last plug.

If the demo car uses an engine much smaller than the unit you

Photographs above: A forward-hinging bonnet gives reasonable engine access on the Griffon.

plan to use, make every effort to see another car. The manufacturer might be able to suggest a previous customer close to home, or the owners' club might be able to help.

Production car designers pay a great deal of attention to providing storage space, and after looking at some kitcars you can see where the

lockable area, particularly if choosing a sports car, because it will prove useful for protecting your valuables.

The boot area should be neatly finished and trimmed and this can be a fiddly job if a suitable trim kit is not supplied. If it is neatly trimmed, lift the carpet to see if any uglies lie beneath: look for signs of waterproofing problems and poor quality glassfibre work. Check, too, that the catches and hinges are

Above: Both the Rickman Ranger and the NCF Diamond have room for your dogs and golf clubs.

Space is at a premium in most of the sports cars on the market, so it's perhaps too much to expect for the spare to be mounted as conveniently as on most production cars. If the demonstrator hasn't got one on board, bear in mind that it will take up a good deal of the

Room for two and a weekend suitcase only in this NGTD.

well-mounted and operate correctly. This is a good example of a small detail that is taken for granted on a production car, but can sometimes be lacking on a kitcar – and very irritating on the completed vehicle.

This is an appropriate point at which to mention spare wheels.

The Mini Cub has a lockable underfloor compartment to keep valuable items safe from casual thieves.

This Merlin Monro (Paris Cars) has a neat solution to the problem of where to stow the spare wheel.

available boot space – if it fits in there. Externally mounted spares certainly look the part on traditional sports cars, but some form of security device will be necessary. A stud-mounted wheel can be protected by a locking nut, but a wire wheel might need a crude but effective padlock.

If the car has different-sized wheels front and rear, (it is quite common for narrower wheels to be used on the front), the law says that both sizes should be carried as spares to avoid the temptation to use different sized wheels on the same axle. The only alternative is to carry no spare at all.

Door catches and handles will almost certainly have come from a production car and, providing they are installed correctly, shouldn't present any problems. It is worth examining the catchplate mounted on the rear pillar, however, because it will take a lot of strain. Ideally, the catchplate should be mounted directly on to the chassis, or on to a framework attached to the chassis, as should the hinges. Holding the open door and attempting to rock the car is a simple test that will say a good deal about its structural rigidity. There should, of course, be no give in the hinges or their mountings.

With the external checks complete – they actually take longer to read than to carry out – it is time to get into the driver's seat and close the door. On some traditional designs, doors are considered an

The well-engineered Marlin Roadster has strong doors with similarly well-engineered locks and hinges. However, getting in and out of the car with the hood up in the pouring rain, and with an armful of groceries, would not be easy.

unnecessary luxury, which simplifies things, but do have a few attempts at getting into the car with the hood and sidescreen in place. Then consider the same operation in the rain with your arms full of shopping, and with you or your partner wearing a skirt. We're not trying to be killjoys, but it is easy to overlook such practicalities.

'The doors shut with a satisfying clunk' is one of the great motoring journalist clichés, but if you have to lift the door, or really slam it, before it will close, it could indicate misalignment, or at least inadequate hinges. It would be unreasonable to expect to experience that much satisfaction from the clunk of a lightweight sports car door, but neither should there be flexing or rattling.

It is advisable to spend a while settling into the interior, and it is to be hoped that you will be able to conduct this part of the examination at your leisure, perhaps in the workshop, showroom, or even at a show. Ideally, we would suggest the following examination, followed by the first part of the road test with the company's representative behind the wheel, and then driving the car yourself. Things are seldom ideal, however, so work out the best practical compromise. Be sure to make notes of your findings either during the check, or immediately afterwards in the case of the road test. This is the way we have conducted magazine road tests, and it works.

Don't rely on your memory make notes during the test.

Photographs right: The dashboard of the Adams Roadster with its engine-turned dashboard is suitably period.

As you look around the interior, first impressions are again important. Is it the company's basic trim package, a more expensive one-off job, or something between the two? Are the seats as supplied, or a more upmarket alternative? If it's the company's own trim, does it fit and is it well finished off? Likewise, are the carpets as supplied, and do they fit? If production car parts are used – instruments, controls, seats, etc. – do they integrate well into the interior design? If it is a replica, is it accurate (again you will need some kind of reference material to check details)?

Next, consider the driver's seat. Its importance will depend on its interchangeability: most sports cars use closely fitting seats that wrap around to prevent sideways movement, as well as to support your back. Since bodies vary enormously (and enormous bodies vary most of all!) it might not be just right for you, but this will not be a problem

Below and right: The William Towns-designed Hustler Highlander has a dashboard that wouldn't be out of place on Starship Enterprise.

if it can be changed. If, however, a narrow cockpit dictates that the fitted seat is the only choice, you

might find yourself lumping it more than liking it.

Thousands of words have been

written on the theory and practice of selecting the right car seat, and much of it has been totally ignored by even the big manufacturers. Basically, you should look and feel for good support of the back, particularly the lower back, sideways support from the side panels, and enough cushion length to support your thighs. It might help to consider your own shape and then whether the seat is a 'negative' image of it. The human body is very adaptable, but it will not adapt to a badly shaped seat. Trying to drive in one, and particularly attempting to drive fast, will be like running in ill-fitting shoes. Give it some thought.

If you intend to fit an 'after-market' seat, take measurements now, and pay particular attention to headroom, allowing space for a subframe if appropriate.

Another time-worn journalistic cliché is: 'The gear lever and controls fell easily to hand . . .'. Such expressions only become over-used because the subject they refer to is important, and the importance of being able to feel easy and 'at home' in a car cannot be overstated. The seating position and the location of controls and switches

Check that the controls are right for you.

are obviously interrelated, and there is often some room for tailoring to personal requirements. Some aspects can't be changed, however, and it must all be considered within the confines of the car's interior dimensions.

The chances are that the steering column will have come from a production car, probably with its switchgear, but its mounting probably can't be changed and should be considered a fixed feature. The pedal boxes on sports cars are often rather cramped affairs, with the result that operation of the pedals themselves is restricted, or at least very different to other cars you have driven. If you can't move your foot easily from one pedal to another, and there is no room for improvement in the limited space available, the car must be rejected (brake pedals much higher than the accelerator are positively dangerous and alarmingly common). Having somewhere to rest your left foot, rather than floating it above the clutch pedal, is less vital, but a real boon. If you go in for fast, or even competition driving, check whether you can heel-and-toe without dislocating your ankle.

Some manufacturers seem to design their cars with orang-utangs in mind, so make sure you can reach the important switches.

Although the layout of the dashboard may be variable, make sure that there is at least space for the speedometer and rev counter to be mounted directly in front of the driver, and the more important small gauges within easy sight. There is a temptation to use all that open space in front of the passenger to mount the radio, and maybe even a few less vital controls or instruments. This is great for giving the passenger a sense of involvement but a real pain, and potentially dangerous, when you're on your own.

As with the exterior examination, if production car parts are used inside, ask yourself if they are well integrated or very obvious add-ons; and ask the manufacturer if the dashboard is supplied, and if so in what form. Dashboards are focal points of the interior, but often the builder is supplied with a blank piece of plywood or GRP, so find out what work was involved in producing the final version seen in the demonstrator.

Next, consider all-round visibility. Low, fixed-top sports cars are generally the worst, and more radical examples, like the Lamborghini Countach replicas, the worst of all. Check side vision for dissecting door pillars, and rearwards for small, steeply angled rear windows and wide, sweeping rear-three-quarter body panels (particularly on mid-engined cars), which make reversing, and sometimes overtaking, a real gamble. The rear view mirror is little help, although thoughtfully positioned door mirrors can fill in some of the blind spots. Rear wings and spoilers are equally effective at creating them.

Steeply raked windscreens can also suffer from odd reflections, and light-coloured material on the top of the dashboard can cause a virtual 'white-out'. The 'exotics' can also become fashion victims, courtesy of a drop-away 'bonnet' line. Again the Countach replica perfectly exemplifies the worst case: seeing anything of the coachwork forward of the screen base is impossible. Again it makes parking something of a challenge. Large areas of glass can also distort, so examine the view through the

Above: Most Lamborghini Countach replica drivers are too busy trying to see out to appreciate the attention the car receives from other road users.

screen carefully.

Traditional roadsters are at the other end of the visibility scale. Not only can you usually see all corners of the car, but also the front wheels

Below: No visibility problems with the JBA Falcon, with or without the hood up. Some hoods do present a real safety problem – so check this out.

turning and the front suspension hard at work (not always a very reassuring sight). Don't forget to compare things when the hood is erect and the sidescreen fitted. Visibility obviously won't be as good, but modern hoods are much better than those of old, and with side, or scuttle-mounted, mirrors they needn't be too bad.

Following our hypothetical ideal order of things, the next stage should be a drive in the car with a company representative at the wheel. This gives you the opportunity to make various checks and notes without your being distracted from your driving.

On a general level, does the driver look comfortable, and does the car appear easy to drive? The company will obviously be familiar with the car and its idiosyncrasies, but if using controls looks awkward, or if allowances appear to be made for worn or faulty components, you will need to check them for yourself when you drive, and any advance information will help.

Pay particular attention to noise levels, from the engine, exhaust and wind. The annoyance factors of high noise levels should not be underestimated. On a short journey it's easy to make allowances for a noisy, draughty hood, or to accept (and even enjoy) a loud exhaust, but on a long trip it is likely to

become very wearing. A lot of owners (private customers and manufacturers themselves) of cars with loud, side-mounted exhausts have admitted that they would choose a quieter, full-length system next time. Can you hold a conversation without shouting, and could you hear an in-car hi-fi system? Not unreasonable requirements, but both impossible in some cars.

Whereas engines and exhausts can be silenced, wind noise is often a difficult problem to solve, as the owners of some production cars will confirm. Mainstream manufacturers spend millions on computer-aided wind-tunnel development to come up with today's slippery shapes, and kitcar manufacturers can't be expected to compete. A traditionally styled sports car with a near vertical screen, projecting period mirrors and accessories and a simple hood will never be silent. In fixed-top models, however, it is worth paying attention to the noise around windows and doors, which could indicate ill-fitting panels.

Other noises to listen out for are rattles and squeaks from the body of the car itself. Flexing in the body or chassis can cause friction between the two with noisy results, and rattles from the doors, windows, dashboard, etc. would indicate poor design or poor construction. Being driven for the first part of the road test gives you

the opportunity at least to attempt to trace them and question the company representative. If an acceptable explanation is offered, and a likely solution suggested, ask for a more detailed explanation when you get back to the factory, perhaps with an examination of the offending part or parts on an unbuilt kit. If you are told that it, or any other feature, has been changed on later production kits, again ask to see proof on an unbuilt kit.

If the car to be tested is a convertible, ask if you can conduct part of the test drive with the hood up or down (the opposite to what the prevailing weather suggests) so that you can assess all options. It will also give you the opportunity to see how easy or difficult the hood is to erect and dismantle.

Some companies offer two or more different quality versions of weather equipment. In our experience it is generally better to go for the more expensive: there is little point in an ineffective hood, for example, and the fact that it saved you a few pounds is little compensation when you are wringing out your trouser legs. The material used will vary enormously, but the superior quality variety is known as 'double duck' and is superb.

As has already been pointed out, you should ideally road test a kitcar in the worst of weathers to see all its weaknesses. If you decide that any shortfalls in weather protection are acceptable, that's your decision, but don't let it come as a surprise when you get caught in the first shower. An automatic carwash is a brilliant test of a kitcar's weather equipment and seals, but whether you can convince the company it's in its interests depends on your powers of persuasion. Ultimately, we suspect that what the company will be prepared to do for you will depend on how close you are to deciding upon its car, and how much the order will be worth!

So, finally, we come to driving

Ideally you should test the car in all weathers, but at least you know what to expect with the UVA Fugitive.

the car. You will have to remember these findings and make notes afterwards. You should be sure to make these notes because the memory can play some strange tricks and the chances are you will recall perfectly the sound of the exhaust, and the admiring looks the car received in the High Street, but not what it was like to park.

We have already said that we would never buy a kitcar without having driven a finished car. However, we know of companies, some selling cars that cost well over £10,000 to complete, which do not allow test drives, yet this seems to have little adverse affect on sales. The companies' reasons for not allowing prospective customers to drive are largely economic: the demonstrators are too valuable to let sometimes inexperienced visitors drive; and in any case, they say, getting insurance to cover them is too expensive.

If therefore the 'no drive, no buy' rule is applied, it will immediately put some models out of the running. If it includes your favourites, that might be unacceptable. We would again say that if a company doesn't trust you to drive its cars, or can't afford to insure them so that you can, you shouldn't be trading with it; but if you just have to have that particular car, you will have a pretty good idea of its merits and otherwise if you have followed the factory visit procedure this far.

For those who are able to drive the car, the road test will provide the best possible indication as to its everyday performance. It is not possible to test speed, acceleration, roadholding and handling to the limits – journalists have to use private roads or, ideally, racing circuits – and it would be most unwise to attempt any high-speed driving in a car with which you are unfamiliar.

On the subject of performance and roadholding, it is worth stating the obvious here and saying that you shouldn't look for qualities you simply don't need. If your preferred driving style is fairly sedate, it doesn't have to change – and probably won't – if you purchase a sports car, so only buy the power you need. The attainment of power

The Mini Cub is undoubtedly strong, but you don't have to take testing to extremes!

and better roadholding and handling is subject to the law of diminishing returns. As the standards improve, it costs more to get less improvement; and the last few bhp and extra mph on cornering speed will cost far more than earlier increases. Having 350 bhp under the bonnet of a Cobra replica

sounds impressive through the side-pipes, and through your own trumpet in the saloon bar. It will, however, hit a discordant note with bank managers, and insurance brokers will rejoice.

The most important factor on the

Don't look for performance and handling qualities you don't need – not everyone will want to go flying, like this Kingfisher Kustoms Chenowth driver.

road test is an abstract, hard-to-define quality probably best called 'feel'. Assuming you're quite familiar with the controls by now, start by simply driving the car. Don't attempt to assess or check anything – the most obvious points will become immediately apparent – and just drive as you would any other car. If you feel at home behind the wheel, or think you soon would, the signs are good. If, as was the case on one car we tested for a magazine, the pedals are several inches higher than the level of the seat cushion, the most comfortable seating position involves canting your head at 45 degrees, and your knee collides with the bottom edge of the dashboard every time you change gear, you could start planning a visit to company number two on your shortlist.

Try to drive in as many different traffic conditions as you can, but at least include the two extremes of heavy traffic and fast open road if at all possible.

Having become accustomed to the car's layout, driving position and size, confirm your earlier conclusions on all-round visibility before giving some thought to the mechanicals. The condition of the engine, gearbox and clutch is not

too important in terms of the kit quality, although faulty components are very annoying and distracting, and perhaps say something about the company's priorities. More important is how effectively donor car components have been put into service on the new kitcar. The effective and efficient operation of the steering, for example, depends on

Try to drive in a variety of traffic conditions. Sometimes the magazines organize a drivers' day at one of the circuits but a good test in traffic and on a fast, open road will tell you what you need to know – this Spyder Sport Spyder driver is no doubt discovering why the car has been called 'the definitive sports car'.

the kitcar designer's ability to reproduce the delicately balanced geometry of the original donor car. When this is not achieved, or when a redesigned system is not successful, the most frequently experienced problem is lack of self-centring, so that the steering has to be deliberately straightened after a corner with all the loss of speed and potentially dangerous problems that can cause.

Excessively stiff or heavy steering will also be obvious, but it must be remembered that very wide wheels and tyres will create heavy steering, particularly at low speeds, and this shows up most noticeably in town driving.

Most donated suspension components come from saloon cars – Ford Escorts and Cortinas, Jaguar XJ6s, BL Itals, etc. – so modifications are usually necessary before fitting them to much lighter sports cars. Generally this involves the fitting of different rate springs and often adjustable dampers, but it can't be taken for granted that all manufacturers will have got the new settings right. If adjustable dampers are fitted, the final ride can to some extent be 'dialled in', but an excessively hard ride can generally be attributed to incorrectly rated springs. Remember, however, that the improved roadholding and handling associated with sports-cars doesn't come without some cost. It

is personal comfort that suffers, so expect the ride to be considerably harder than in a saloon car.

An excessively 'wallowy' ride, and 'bottoming' on bumpy roads with a great deal of body roll on corners, would indicate unnecessarily soft springs or dampers, and you would need a fairly convincing argument from the manufacturer before your doubts were answered.

Although the absolute limits of adhesion cannot be safely tested on public roads, and it really wouldn't be reasonable to expect the company representative's nerves to be up to it in any case, it is possible to make some generalizations. A front-engined, front-wheel-drive

A car set up to give flat cornering will have a firm, not to say very hard, ride.

model (more than likely Mini- or Metro-based) can be expected to show signs of understeer: that is, trying to go straight on when the driver is steering to the left or right. A front-engined, rear-wheel-drive car is more likely to display signs of oversteer: trying to turn a tighter corner than the steering would indicate, with the result that the rear end breaks away. A mid-engined

A mid-engined car like the Reflex is likely to display neutral handling characteristics.

car will be far more neutral, with no signs of break-away from the front or rear end up to impressively high speeds. But when it does go, it is less easy to correct it and the consequences are often more serious, so for on-the-limit driving and motorsport, the mid-engined car needs an experienced driver.

Now these are, as we said, generalizations and innumerable factors will play a part in determining a car's behaviour (a heavier Jaguar engine in the front of a rear-wheel-drive car can create understeer, for example). At the speeds you are likely to experience on a road test they are unlikely to be very obvious. However, we did once experience very obvious, and potentially dangerous, oversteer in a new kitcar we had on test, and only after careful experimentation with spring and damper rates did the company bring things down to an acceptable level. The better companies will talk quite honestly about the handling characteristics of their cars, so it does help to have some knowledge of terms used.

One thing that sets the specialist kitcar press apart from the mainstream motoring journals is that the former will generally look at kitcars in context. While the label 'kitcars' should never be used as an excuse, it is not reasonable to expect them to compare directly with production cars. Where they do score over their mass-produced cousins, however, is in their individuality, and this again is something with which many journalists have problems. Specialist vehicles are by definition produced for a specialist market, and the wide variety of models available cannot all be expected to appeal to everyone. Journalists, then, can talk about the pros and cons of, say, a Lotus Seven-style sports car, but ultimately they should evaluate the model as an example of that genre. The prospective customer should also look at the car in the same light.

On completing your road test, ask yourself therefore if the car has lived up to your expectations. You will consider your notes later and, if you have other cars and visits to weigh up, you will have comparisons to make.

The voice of experience

There is another source of information, which can prove invaluable: word of mouth. Personal recommendation is said to be the best form of advertising simply because it is the most reliable kind of information, coming as it does from those who have personal experience and less bias. As we have mentioned before, however,

do beware, because having spent several hundred hours building a kitcar, the owner is sometimes reluctant to admit, or even remember, that he has had problems along the way. Asked specifically about various stages of the build, however, most owners will be honest. Getting them to speak

Owners' and kitcar clubs are a good source of information.

about their cars will certainly not be a problem!

There are two different methods of contacting existing owner-builders, and both are worth trying. The first is to ask the manufacturer for names and addresses of previous customers, which has the added advantage of giving you some idea of how worried the manufacturer might be about passing on such information. Ideally you should talk to someone who has already built a kit, and to someone who is in the process of putting one together – preferably a car with a similar specification to the one you have in mind. The second approach can be made through the owners' clubs. These are usually set up by an owner or owners for practical as well as social reasons. Their regular meetings in pubs, at kitcar shows and on club-organized activities, always include the discussion

and, they hope, the solution of problems.

Attending a meeting or at least talking to one of the club officers – some clubs have members who specialize in the practical and technical aspects of kitcar building and ownership – can provide a tap into an invaluable source of information: what the problems are; how they can be solved; how money can be saved, what modifications are worthwhile; and, more fundamentally, what it's like to own and run the car in question.

At the risk of labouring a point, although the process of planning, examination and consideration described here might seem long-winded and deliberate, the complexity of the kitcar market, with all its available models, options, and choices, is such that it is necessary to make a great many decisions to ensure you have got what is the

right kitcar for you. Only by following some form of detailed, step-by-step process can you take a large part of the uncertainty out of those decisions. If you fall in love at first sight with a particular kitcar, following this process will at least give your head the opportunity to question your heart. If you choose to cast aside all considerations of practicalities, at least you have considered the alternatives.

It is important that you should try to form a more accurate picture of what the build will cost, and how long it will take, before making the final decision. Or maybe you have already bought the kitcar and – better late than never – are looking for a breakdown of where your money and time will go, or are already going. It is time to talk figures.

CHAPTER 4: COUNTING THE COST IN TIME AND MONEY

Money matters

To anyone in the fortunate position of having unlimited financial resources, this chapter may be of little interest. For the rest of us, however, cost is an important consideration and to underestimate the final figure could result in a poor-quality project, or even an incomplete one.

Building your own car suggests a DIY, low-cost alternative to conventional motoring. In truth, although building a kitcar can save money, it is important to keep things in perspective. Cost should be looked at in relation to mainstream motoring. Better still, the kitcar should be looked on as providing something that can be found nowhere else: what single production car could meet your needs in the way that a carefully chosen and built kitcar could?

In Chapter 2 the section 'Factors to consider' includes a checklist of required features. To appreciate the value of a kitcar fully, try finding a production car that will meet the same requirements, and for the same money. If you find such a car, ask yourself whether it can match those other features that are found in the well-built kitcar: fully reconditioned (or even new) running

You can't put a price on the satisfaction of building your own car.

gear; new and fully rustproofed chassis; interior and exterior colour and trim to your own requirements. In short, the builder decides upon his own priorities and then spends the money accordingly. All the limited edition, luxury-economy, performance options in the world couldn't match that.

There remains one factor on which it is impossible to pin a price tag: satisfaction. The sheer enjoyment value of building a kitcar, like that of playing a round of golf or a game of squash, is incalculable, and will be different for everyone. Then, too, the simple knowledge that you've built it yourself can make all the difference to owning and driving the finished car.

Having said all that, however, only millionaires and the downright foolish would start a project without calculating a more or less accurate figure: '£4000 upwards' is too vague for even the most sympathetic of bank managers, and garages up and down the country hold the evidence of deserted projects that have simply run out of cash.

Given the importance of cost as a factor in deciding which kitcar to buy, it is almost impossible to separate the two ('almost' because for the purpose of logical presentation we have done just that), so ideally this section and 'Factors to consider' should be used together. The serious purchaser will be referring back for help in selecting cars within the appropriate price range.

It would obviously be impractical to attempt detailed price analysis for the entire kitcar market, so it is assumed that the following exercise would be applied to a shortlist of perhaps two or three different models. The final decision may even have been made, but still the importance of a detailed budgeting of the proposed build cannot be over emphasized: like some of the other exercises suggested for this preliminary stage, it is time well spent.

The cost of building a kitcar and the time it takes are of course linked: pay out for a nearly built car, and quite obviously it will take less time to complete; build one from the ground up and you will save money. Between these two extremes are an infinite number of alternatives. Once you start to know your way around the market, it will become easier to estimate at least roughly the work involved in a build, and to approximate the cost. When you've got that far, you can start a more detailed analysis.

Inevitably, it all starts with more list-making. In order to come anywhere near an accurate costing, you first have to establish exactly what it is you'll need. That might seem obvious, but it's not so easy to achieve.

It will help the budgeting if you list materials roughly in the order in which you will need the parts (having a detailed list of all the parts required might also help when it comes to negotiating a discount from a motor factor; but more of that later).

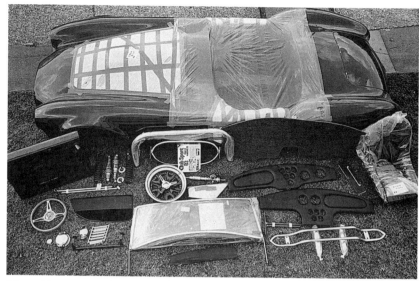

Most kitcar manufacturers are able to supply every part needed to complete their cars, but you will often be able to buy the parts cheaper elsewhere. We show here some of the items available from DJ Sportscars.

As became obvious in the previous chapters, there is no such thing as a typical kitcar, and the options open to the prospective builder are virtually endless. Choices such as whether to use the donor engine as it is, to rebuild it or to replace it (and then with a reconditioned or new unit – and in what state of tune?) will have a big bearing on the cost, so it is necessary to make a few arbitrary decisions in order to provide figures to work with. If the calculated cost is too high, perhaps economies can be made. If it's well within budget, there might be scope to add a few luxuries or more extravagant detailing.

Things are confused still further by as yet unknown factors, such as the condition of the donor vehicle; but if you assume that, for example, the wheelbearings will need replacing and in the event they don't, the saving will almost certainly compensate for an underestimation made in another area. Certain components – brake parts, for example – should be replaced as a matter of course, so they can more be more accurately budgeted for.

Before cataloguing all the parts required, you will need the relevant

prices and here, once again, it pays, literally, to do your homework. At one time kitcar manufacturers left customers very much to their own devices once they'd supplied the kit itself, but many can now supply everything required for the build, which is more convenient for the customer and, it must be said, more profitable for the company.

It is often possible to under-cut the kitcar firms, however, particularly on items like wheels, seats, tyres, instruments, which bigger, specialist suppliers can buy in bulk, and usually in greater variety. The kitcar magazines carry advertisements for a number of companies that have set themselves up as suppliers, specifically aiming at the kitcar builder (Speedex, Part-X, Merlin and Europa to name four), and their prices are generally keen. *Exchange and Mart* lists dozens of companies, but when shopping for larger items such as engines and gearboxes, do ask for a written specification because standards vary as much as prices and, of course, you generally get what you pay for.

You might decide that a local supplier, although perhaps his prices are not quite so keen, can provide a better service, and will save you hours of phoning around and collecting parts. If the firm already knows you, there's a still better chance of discount.

'Getting it Trade' is the aim of everyone who has to buy parts for his car, and a good number of private customers seem to do just that through a friend, or a friend of a friend. However, if you choose to buy most of your parts through the one local factor, the chances are you will be spending quite a bit of money there, and some form of discount can probably be negotiated in your own right.

Finally, most manufacturers use a great many production car components and where they offer the parts on their own price lists they are usually competitive, through the economies of scale. However, if you have a particularly competitive source, it is worth trying to find out the part number. For various reasons, however, the kitcar company may be reluctant to part with the information, and again the owners' club might be able to help.

So, with lists of kitcar parts and of component prices at your side, begin a methodical list of your own. Detail all the parts required for the build and write the prices in alongside them. Again we are faced with the problems of multiple choice and a list drawn up here to cover every version of every model would just be too complicated. So the following checklist (with a few reminders along the way) should be carefully considered against the particular cars on your shortlist and amendments made accordingly. Likewise, prices also vary too much to make their inclusion here practical or useful.

Checklist

Tools and equipment (see Chapter 5, but as a general rule don't be tempted to buy low cost, poor quality tools)

Donor car workshop manual (prices don't vary much, but secondhand copies can sometimes be found).

Donor car (see the donor car chapters: going for the cheaper example can be a false economy)

Collection of donor car (hire of trailer, etc.)

Steam cleaning (price professional job against hiring equipment)

Waxoyl (other varieties of rustproofing can save money, but check specification)

Chassis treatment (primer, paint, powder coating, etc.)

Paint for mechanical components (including primer)

Brake shoes/pads (never economize on brake component quality)

Wheel cylinders (ditto)

Brake pipe set (ditto)

Brake fluid (ditto)

Master cylinder (ditto)

Handbrake cable (ditto)

Wheel bearings (discount from local factors? Try them for brake parts too)

Oil seals (money can be saved by buying seals and gaskets in one go)

Clutchplate (increased engine power? Is standard clutch up to it?)

Dampers (or shock absorbers – it might be best to go with kitcar manufacturer's recommendation, but you can try shopping around)

Track rod ends (double-check which other suspension/steering parts are supplied by kitcar company)

Rubber bushes (for – where appropriate – springs, anti-roll bar, engine and gearbox mountings)

Engine/gearbox preparation (this is the most variable of all and can range from a simple, routine service to a complete, specially prepared, high performance replacement unit: see notes at end of this list)

Radiator hoses (if special items are specified, kitcar company may be easiest supplier)

Heater hoses (ditto)

Oil filter (check if remote unit is required, and if so if it is supplied; also oil cooler, particularly with modified engines)

Oil (engine, gearbox and back axle – easily overlooked in the costings, but not cheap)

Antifreeze/coolant (check capacity with manufacturer)

Hire of engine hoist (better to hire a good quality one than to buy a cheapie)

Basic kit (often listed as body/chassis package but usually including other components unique to car)

Collection of kit (or delivery charges – hiring a pick-up is often cheaper, but care must be taken)

Other kit parts (unique to kit but not supplied by manufacturer in basic kit – see also 'Accessories' below)

Windscreen/glass (this could be included in above, and should be part of basic kit, but often isn't – if it's lifted from production car, shop around)

Paint (preparation, materials and spraying – those using coloured gel-coat will make a big saving here)

Chroming (this is a matter of taste – we think it should be kept to a minimum)

Weather equipment (think carefully before going for cheaper option, if available)

Trim pack or trimming (if car requires professional trimming, try to speak to a company that has already done similar job)

Seats (unless they are unique to car, it pays to shop around)

Steering wheel (again, big savings can be made, but don't compromise on quality)

Wheels and tyres (a big part of the final cost, so make your choice carefully)

Accessories (this is a general term designed to cover all the bits and pieces like mirrors, badges, extra lights, etc., and could also include accurate detailing, which makes all the difference to a replica)

Wiring loom (or the cost of having the car wired professionally if you don't fancy doing it yourself)

Electrical connectors and fittings (required if you plan to do the wiring)

Nuts and bolts/self-tapping screws (literally planning every nut and bolt will save a lot of time, and money, chasing around during the build)

Sealer/grease/underseal/adhesives (again money and time will be saved by buying this in advance – a good build manual will recommend the best products for the job, but see also chapters on build)

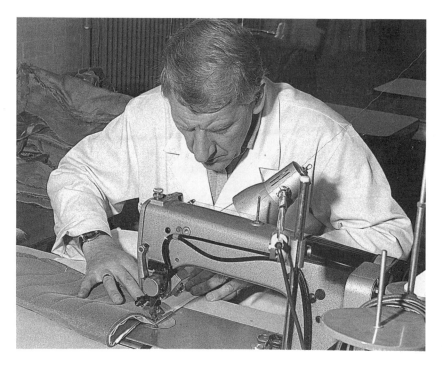

A professional trim job will look really nice, but can you afford it?

Wiper blades (even if you're not planning to take it out in the rain!)

The subject of professional builders, has been examined in Chapter 1, in the section, 'Have you got what it takes?' But if some or all the build-up work is farmed out to one of these firms, it will obviously make a big difference to the cost. Just how much depends on a number of those variables again.

It is quite common for kitcar builders to take the car along to a specialist for a particular part of the build – for the wiring or the paint, for example. The auto electrician or spray shop should be able to provide a fairly accurate estimate based on previous experience.

Things are not so easy for the build-up company, however, which may never have put together that make of kit before. The first tip, then, is to try to find a firm that does have experience of your type of car, and the manufacturer or even the owners' club should be able to provide the necessary contact.

If the company is to undertake just part of the build, make sure you know exactly how the work is to be divided, and ask for a stage-by-stage cost breakdown so that you can keep a check on things as the build progresses.

The inclusion of entries like grease and wiper blades in the 'shopping list' above will have raised a few smiles, perhaps, but such items should not be underestimated when it comes to the bottom line. Likewise, there are certain unavoidable costs that must be added to the total for a completed car before it can take to the roads.

Numberplates are obvious; and the MOT test certificate and road fund licence are straightforward enough; but kitcar insurance is a little more tricky. This and the other necessary paperwork is examined in more detail in a Chapter 15, but it can represent a considerable proportion of the overall cost – and will of course go on to account for a larger proportion each year, so it's worth some comment here.

Basically, kitcar insurance works within the same rules as any other form of motor insurance: third party cover is compulsory; 'third party, fire and theft' covers just that and does nothing to reimburse the owner in the event of an accident, etc. 'Fully comprehensive' is all-encompassing and priced accordingly.

The risk attached to individual kitcars determines their premiums in exactly the same way as it does for production cars, but you might find that some mainstream insurance companies do not have experience of your particular choice (although they will all have come across the more popular models by now) and the premium could be loaded accordingly. Generally, the best deals come from the specialist kitcar brokers who have a wider experience of the industry. They will at least recognize that most kitcars present no greater risk than their more conventional counterparts.

These specialist companies can also offer a number of unique schemes tailored to the needs of the kitcar builder. The first is designed to cover the parts, from the day they are bought, right up until the car is finally completed, with a choice of fire and theft, or accidental damage, fire and theft.

More controversial, but potentially a bigger money saver, is parts-only cover. This is a form of limited comprehensive cover (which sounds contradictory!) and works on the theory that someone who has built his own car will also be able – and indeed will want – to carry out any repairs sustained in an accident. Consequently the cover pays just for the parts, leaving the owner/builder to look after the labour, at a substantial saving on the premiums. But, the scheme's critics say, the savings should be weighed up against the scheme's limitations, and they point out a number of these, particularly that there is no cover for personal effects or personal accident. All we would say is read the fuller discussion in Chapter 15, and think carefully before making your decision. A saving on premiums now could really be false economy if you are unable, or unwilling, to carry out repairs yourself.

For those who only plan to use the car occasionally, or perhaps only in the summer, many companies now operate a limited mileage scheme, originally set up for owners of classic cars and now extended to kitcars. Policies are available with various mileage restrictions on them (3000, 5000 and 7500 being the most common), and these can be halved and applied to a six months cover period. Big savings can be

Calculating the time involved is fraught with the same problems as estimating the cost: it's a load of old variables! Yet it would be foolish to enter a project with no idea of when you are going to emerge on the other side, so the only solution is to gather as much information as possible and base your figures on those of builders who have undertaken similar projects.

The first thing to do is ignore the wildly optimistic 'Easily constructed in just a few weekends...' seen in the advertisements. Some of the discrepancy between claim and fact can be put down to the accepted 'advertising optimism quotient', and in a few cases it really is just

As this picture of the Caterham Seven clearly shows, the kit is worth a lot of money from the day you collect the parts. Some companies will insure you from the minute your trailer leaves the company gates.

had there, and it avoids paying to insure the car just to sit in the garage on axle stands.

The time is right

Some prospective builders' first reaction to the question of how long the build will take would be that they did not know, or particularly care. Their attitude is that they will spend a few hours here and there, a whole weekend when it suits them, leisurely putting the thing together: a sort of automotive therapy, with a finished car at the end of it. It sounds great. Unfortunately, a good many professional kitcar builders make their living from completing projects undertaken on just such a basis. If it works for you, then fine. Most people, however, need a realistic idea of just how long the build will take so as not to lose momentum.

The difficulty is how to determine how long it will take to do something you have never done before, and when you don't really know what it will involve until you have completed it. The answer is a device employed in the usually exact

From rotted-out MGB to a completed TD may take longer than you bargained for.

science of mathematics: the guess-timate.

deliberate deceit. More often, though, the quoted time is an amalgam of factors: the time taken by the company itself to build cars (but using already prepared components, unlimited workshop facilities, and a great deal of experience and familiarity with the kit); the claims made by previous customers (very few builders will admit to having needed twice the time the manufacturer said would be required); and the time they wished it did take to build the car.

The actual time is dependent on the variables we have mentioned: a virtually complete car, requiring just the engine to be fitted, say, in order to keep within the law, will indeed take very little time. A complete 'ground-up' build, from sourcing and reconditioning mechanical components to trimming and maybe even painting, will occupy hundreds of man-hours.

There are, however, certain guidelines that make it possible to arrive at that guesstimate. Just to put things within some sort of framework, a professional company would expect to complete a good quality, but not fanatically detailed build-up of a not too complicated kitcar in around 250–300 hours. Some cars will take more, some less time, but from experience that would seem a fairly average figure.

It must be borne in mind, however, that the professional builder is working full-time on the project. He does not have to waste time remembering where he left off, or 'getting into gear'. He will also have better workshop facilities than those available to most private builders. The private builder should perhaps allow a little extra, but working consistently through the time available, his car should be finished within 350–400 hours.

Having determined our starting place, it is now necessary to look at individual areas and how long they might take.

Mechanical components
Stripping components from a donor car, dumping unwanted bodyshell, stripping, cleaning, painting and rebuilding suspension, brakes and steering: around 75 hours.

That is a rather basic figure, which does not include rebuilding or modifying the engine. It is possible to buy complete mechanical packages taken from low mileage, crash-damaged cars and then tailored specifically to particular kitcars; although more expensive, these do dramatically cut down the time of a build-up. They are not suitable for all builds, however. Some kitcars use far more than the basic running gear and a complete car is required to donate its wiring, lights, instruments, and maybe even interior trim, exhaust (usually cut down), wheels and tyres (although these are generally replaced), and sometimes even windows, doors and other panels.

Paint and Waxoyl chassis
You can reckon on this taking around six hours, although this could be longer if you are planning a more meticulous preparation. Again, it could take less time, or none at all, if some or all of the work is carried out by the company before delivery. This would, of course, be the case where the kit includes a rolling chassis, which might be built up around components supplied by the customer or by the company itself.

Fit the main body tub
Around 12 hours. This figure will vary according to the complexity of the kit, and will almost certainly involve some assistance, so read the 12 hours as man-hours. Upmarket kits will feature mounting points and holes drilled ready for bolting. Others will require more work.

Fit ancillary components
This covers clutch, brake pipes, master cylinder, steering column wiper motor, petrol tank, heater, etc. Final specification will vary, of course, but reckon on at least 30 hours.

Fit suspension and steering
15 hours. Unless it's part of a rolling chassis package.

Wings, bonnet, boot
Some kits come with these panels fitted, and if it is offered as an option, it's worth paying extra to avoid what can sometimes be a troublesome job. If you choose to do it, expect it to take something like 20 hours. Hanging doors has been known to cause more problems than any other single stage of the build-up, except perhaps wiring.

Wiring and instruments
In fact, the thought of wiring a car is usually worse than the actual doing. Kitcar companies offer everything from a completely wired car down to nothing at all, but the average builder could expect to spend something like 25 hours.

Prepare and fit engine/gearbox
If the donor car engine/gearbox is to be used, the minimum cleaning, painting and servicing, plus renewing the clutch, etc, is likely to take around 15 hours, including the refitting. Extra time must be allowed for rebuilding or modifying the engine, and time will obviously be saved if a rebuilt unit is bought and fitted.

Trim
Again, different companies offer different packages, ranging from a complete, ready-trimmed interior to a bare shell which leaves the builder to plan and execute the upholstery. This is a deceptively time-consuming part of the work, and the impatient builder should choose the most complete package offered by the manufacturer, or pay for a professional job. The builders of more upmarket kitcars or replicas are likely to go for a high quality, professional job, either directly or through the manufacturer, but the competent amateur can achieve a simple but neat finish in around 30 hours.

Bodywork preparation and paint
Another of the kitcar builder's variable pieces of string. If the car is supplied in colour-impregnated gelcoat, it may require no more than a little cleaning up, but if it is to be painted, it will require preparation, and anything from a little flatting to extensive rebuilding and filling if modifications are planned. The time

Allow plenty of time for preparation and painting.

devoted to the painting itself again depends entirely on the standard of finish required: months can be spent applying coat after coat of colour, rubbing down between each coat, followed by numerous coats of clear lacquer. The real perfectionist might wait weeks for each coat to dry thoroughly.

The visual effect of a good paint finish is quite dramatic, and it would be criminal to spoil the car for a ha'p'orth of lacquer. If you are confident enough to carry out the work, spend the time it needs to get it right; if you are not, spend the money it takes to get someone else to do it. A good professional sprayshop can be found by speaking to local car enthusiasts, but do make sure the men there have sprayed glassfibre. Again it's well worth tapping the experience of owners' club members.

Final detailing

Completion of the jobs listed above could mean that the car is now finished. There might, however, be some detailing to be completed. This could include sourcing and fitting accessories, or installing an audio or a security system – and it all takes time.

Giving thought to these last details, and speaking to the manufacturer and other builders, should give you an indication as to the time involved. The only other remaining tasks are paperwork; the MOT, registration, road fund licence, insurance, and how long these take is largely in the hands of the authorities.

Professional builders

Throughout this chapter, we have referred to having professionals carry out parts of the build, such as the trimming and paint, and to kitcar building companies who will take on part or all of the actual kit construction.

These concerns are often recommended by kit manufacturers who might see the demand for professional help, but do not have the resources to offer it themselves. A build-up company may specialize in a particular make of kit, and may even be appointed by the manufacturers. Such a company has a stock of particular experience to offer its customers. Problems encountered by an amateur builder at home can really delay a first assembly, but once they have been overcome, the second build will be that much quicker.

Just how much of the build is farmed out, and which parts, will depend on the individual. Someone who, for example, specializes in

mechanical work might choose to have the body assembly completed professionally.

Remember, though, that it is illegal for any company – and this includes the local garage – to build a kitcar for a customer. In 'What is a kitcar?' in Chapter 1 we described how, to keep within the law, some build-up companies employ the same device as manufacturers who want to sell virtually complete cars. The car is sold complete but there is at least one major mechanical component, often the engine/gearbox unit, which the customer has to fit.

When contracting out part of the build, remember that getting to the rolling chassis stage is the easy part – it's the bodywork and trimming that take the time.

Even if you don't intend to go for a complete car, however, it is worth asking for prices, and for a breakdown of where the money goes, if the company offer such a service. It should then be possible to calculate how much of the total cost is attributable to labour; this, allowing for the skilled workers' time, familiarity with the kit and workshop facilities, should give you a realistic estimate of how long the company expects the build to take. It should also indicate how much is spent on parts and materials. But don't forget to adjust the figures for any discounts or trade prices you can get.

At some point during this research you will have decided which kit is for you. Bear in mind that there may be a wait before the kit is available (this will vary according to the stocks held by the company and the company's policy on waiting lists, but you'll have plenty to keep you busy); and the company will also require a deposit. We have known a customer put down a staggering £5000: sadly, we tend to hear about the transactions that go wrong and that particular customer lost his money when the company was dissolved. What you hand over is your decision, but a 10 per cent deposit would seem reasonable.

Chapter 5:
PREPARING FOR THE BUILD

Give me the tools and I will do the job

As we mentioned in Chapter 1, the average kitcar build does not necessitate a great deal of special equipment and tools. Your toolkit might, however, need a little supplementing, which will affect the cost calculations. Working without decent power tools, for example, or in cramped conditions, will certainly increase the time spent. The easier build will generally be the better build, and once again you will reap dividends from a little simple preparation.

The workshop

First, perhaps, we should ask whether a workshop is necessary at all. Well, given the commitment and resources, anything is possible. We have heard of kitcars being built almost entirely in a driveway, the partly built vehicle being covered or pushed under a small lean-to at the end of each session. We need hardly say that this was far from ideal; and the project completed entirely under canvas in the front garden was likewise not without its problems – but it can be

A friend built a very nice Jago Geep in this garage which had one powerpoint, a leaky roof and no doors – not what we would recommend.

done.

Given the British climate, some form of permanent and effective cover is vital. We might as well start with the ideal: a double garage that can be used solely for the build. This would provide enough space for the chassis and sub-assemblies

to be worked on, plus room for storage which is a vital aspect, easily overlooked and always underestimated. Tools and parts will all need a home, and many of them have to be easily accessible. During the build itself, the double garage will also allow space to move around the car, and room to lie out comfortably when working under it. It also enables more than one person at a time to work on the project, without tripping over one another.

That is the ideal – and we have known builders work on projects several miles from their homes in order to have that sort of space. This, too, brings with it its own problems of transporting parts, and travelling before being able to start work. It rules out 'popping out to the garage to finish off that job...'. For most builders, however, this ideal is simply impossible and they have to share the family single garage with the usual lawnmower, bikes, ladders, and other paraphernalia. If garden space allows, it might be worth investing £100 or so in a simple shed to get some of the clutter out of the way.

Having cleared the garage – and it's amazing how inspirational the imminent arrival of a kitcar can be – it's time to make a few basic improvements. Give the walls and roof space a thorough brushing or vacuuming and make good any leaks or defective panels: the last thing you need is dirt or rain dropping on to some carefully cleaned component; and the thought of going out to work in a dirty, damp garage in the middle of January can make Saturday afternoon TV irresistibly attractive.

In fact it's difficult to know where to draw the line on improving the working environment. Lining the garage walls with some form of (fireproof) board can make the whole place feel a good deal more user-friendly. Filling the gap with an insulating material will make the garage warmer and drier for the car, and easier to heat when you're working out there during those cold winter months.

Lining the walls will also make it easier to give the garage a quick coat of paint. This gives the interior a neat and tidy look, turning it into a more pleasant and comfortable, and therefore efficient, workplace. Being able to make tea there will also help in this respect and remember that you will go on benefiting from these improvements long after the build is completed.

One other measure we would consider vital is painting the floor. Cement floors are usually dusty, particularly if they were made with an overwet mix in the first place.

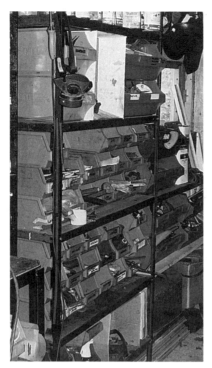

Steel storage shelves are cheap and encourage you to keep the floor space clear.

Brushing the dust off actually just removes another fine layer of cement which will redistribute itself on shelves, tools and any components lying around uncovered. The solution is a floor paint, of which there are dozens around. We have personal experience of ICI floor paint, a resin that in two coats seals the floor, fills in minor holes and leaves a smart, easy to clean, and clean to work on surface.

Having repaired and improved the fabric of the place, it's time to start fitting it out. Tools and other specialist equipment might seem the obvious prime consideration, but we would suggest that you next look at storage, and the less space available to you, the more important it is to use that space efficiently. The golden rule should be to always keep the floor space clear: which means plenty of shelving.

For practicality and cost efficiency, it's difficult to beat steel, multi-adjustable shelving units. These are so cheap that unless you have spare material you want to use up, it is not worth making shelves yourself. Lining one wall with 9 in or 1 ft deep shelves will

provide large, easily labelled areas of storage. The same supplier (check the companies in *Exchange and Mart* for the best prices we've seen) will also stock plastic storage bins, which will prove invaluable for small tools, nuts and bolts and smaller components that need a temporary home during building.

All the traditional storage containers – screw-top jam jars, ice cream tubs and cardboard boxes – have their parts to play, but labelled, stacked and easily accessed boxes take some beating. Labelling is an important part of the donor car strip-down, as we will see later on, and keeping appropriate parts together in boxes is the easiest solution. You will also need to store tools in a way that maximizes space but keeps them easily accessible: we will look at that when we talk about the tools required.

Garage roof space is a real bonus, and if there are strong A-frame steel supports, this is ideal. This space is most effectively utilized by panelling part of it to provide storage for bulky items such as seats. Long items like exhaust piping can be tied up to the roof framework. Beware of asbestos-type roof coverings, which can suffer from condensation: a lesson we learned the hard way when a pair of good seats were all but ruined by mould. Line the roof with insulation board, with polythene tacked to the side facing the asbestos to act as a moisture barrier, and the problem is solved.

The best way of maximizing limited storage space is not to have too much to store in it, so be ruthless when it comes to deciding what you should keep. Don't keep things just because they might come in handy – generally items kept to come in handy are either too big, not quite big enough, too few, or the wrong thread. So if you've got parts from past cars, past projects or sources so far in the past you can't actually identify them, get rid of them: not in the dustbin but via a boot sale, at a local school or car club, or through the small ads in the local paper, or specialist kitcar or classic car magazine. Remember, one man's junk is another man's sought-after

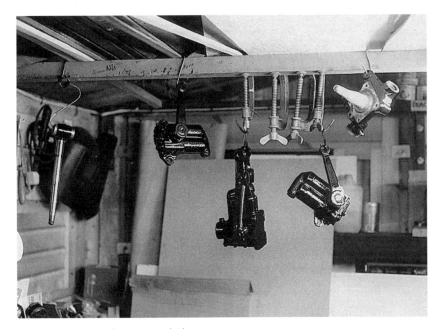

Roof space is a bonus and the beams are handy for hanging components up to dry. Do not, however, use the beams to locate an engine hoist without first providing proper support.

component.

Keeping the workshop tidy can make a huge difference to available space. You really should clear up and sweep the floor at least at the end of each work session, so leaving it clean, tidy and as spacious as possible for your return.

Tools and equipment

The easy answer to what tools and equipment are necessary to build a kitcar is 'as many as possible'. There's no doubt that the fully equipped workshop will make building a kitcar easier – just as it will make routine work on a production car that much simpler. However, buying expensive equipment just to make things easier, when it may only be used on this one project, is altogether foolish. We will examine the basic requirements, plus a few 'luxuries'. If you already have other labour-saving devices (or at least access to them – kitcar building is an ideal time to call in all your outstanding loans and favours) so much the better.

First, and rather obviously, is mains electricity. Having said that,

we know of several cars that have been built without power, using only hand tools, and without even a lead light, and the results are spectacular. The difference is made up in man-hours, patience and sheer hard work, of course; so although we are not saying it can't be done, we are saying not many would want to try.

Given that your garage has mains power, one power point in the corner feeding the electric drill, lead light, heater and kettle through a tangle of leads snaking across the

The bench does not need to be large, but it should have a decent-sized vice fitted.

garage floor is the stuff of serious accidents. In fact, that sort of behaviour amounts to negligence and some sort of disaster is almost inevitable. Far better, and relatively easy, to fit up a simple ring main with switched double 13 amp sockets on each wall, providing a convenient source of power wherever you happen to be working. Mounting them at waist height will protect them from damage (trolley jack, toolbox, hefty work boot, chassis member) and keep them within easy reach.

Good lighting, too, is vital, and besides the lead light, fluorescent tubes give less shadow and are more economical. A centrally mounted strip should prove adequate, but light over the bench is useful.

The bench is an item of equipment that can almost be considered part of the garage structure, because it must obviously be firmly fixed and can be bolted into the framework of the building. The bench need not be very big to cope with the jobs encountered during the build of a kitcar; we built and used a very effective angle iron-framed bench that measured just 13 in deep and 54 in long. It must be strong, however, and the top should be at least 2 in thick. Bolted firmly to the bench should be the biggest engineer's vice you can get hold of – with an opening of at least 6 in and at least 4 in jaws – and you should allow yourself

The Workmate is portable so that it can be taken to the job. If space is really tight it makes an excellent substitute for a fixed bench.

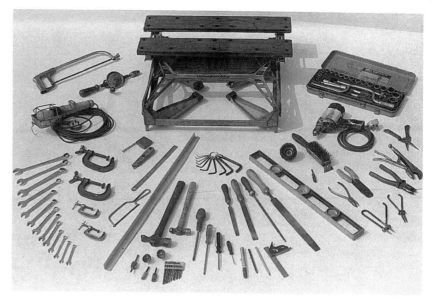

Most of the tools required to build a kitcar will probably be found in the DIY motorist's toolkit.

enough room for a hacksaw to be used properly. Don't forget that a Workmate makes an excellent back-up bench. That brings us to tools.

First a note on tool storage. We can't stress enough the importance of carefully considered tool storage, because it can save so much time and trouble. Untidy workshops are inefficient and unpleasant places to work.

The tools most frequently used – spanners, screwdrivers, drills, pliers, etc. – should be readily available, ideally mounted on pegboard or chipboard using terry clips. It is also a good idea to outline the tools on the board in black, so you can tell at a glance what goes where and what is missing.

Tools used less often can be kept in drawers or on shelves (but preferably not piled on top of each other in boxes, where they can become entangled or even damaged), and labelled for convenience. A place for everything and everything in its place may be a cliché, but it applies 100 per cent to the organization and smooth running of a workshop, particularly where space is at a premium.

The tools themselves can provide one of the best examples of false economy. Assuming you haven't already got a reasonable toolkit, getting equipped is probably going to cost a few hundred pounds; but the tools you buy will continue to be used on the car and around the house and garden for years, perhaps even generations, to come. Providing, that is, you don't skimp

on quality. Buy poor quality tools – they *can* look every bit as convincing as the good ones – and they will make the building of your kitcar more difficult, and maybe even dangerous. Poor quality spanners slip and damage knuckles; poor quality screwdrivers and sockets damage screw- and boltheads, causing inconvenience and adding time. The message is simple: don't cut corners. If you are in any doubt, get British-made tools with familiar trade names through one of the several specialist mail order companies, at your local accessory shop, or through the motor factors where you've arranged the discount.

Now to the type of tools you are likely to need, starting with the most basic and the most frequently used, and working on to the more optional.

Jack

A trolley jack is best, providing your garage allows enough space, and good quality examples can be bought for sensible money. After using it around the workshop, you'll wonder how you ever managed with a bottle or scissors jack. And, of course, you should never use a jack without axle stands.

Axle stands

Never get under the car, even during the early stages of the build, without supporting it properly, and that means on axle stands or ramps. *Never* use bricks, because they can topple and collapse all too easily. Even your helpful local parts factors don't stock spare lungs and ribs!

Always support the car on axle stands or ramps.

Spanners

Most kitcar builders will already have some spanners in their toolbox, but before buying new spanners or sockets, check in the donor car workshop manual whether you need metric or Imperial. Combination spanners – that is, with a ring

Combination spanners such as these are more versatile than the standard ring or open-ended type.

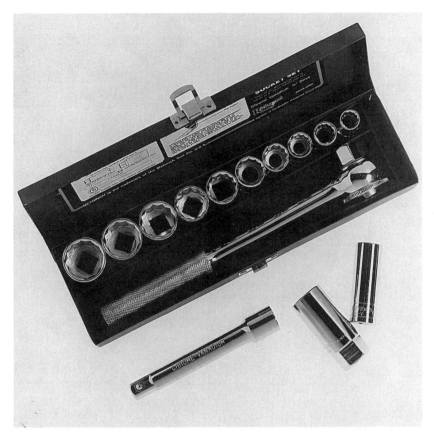

at one end and an open end at the other – are perhaps the ideal. The advantages of both types – the ring spanner is less likely to slip, the open-ended can get into more awkward places – are available on the one spanner. Because the more conventional ring or open-ended spanners have a different size at each end, however, twice the number of combination spanners are required, with the resultant extra cost. A good size range is from 10 mm to 32 mm metric or $\frac{3}{8}$ in to $1\frac{1}{4}$ in AF.

Socket set

Many people will already have one of these, but again you need to check whether it is suitable for the chosen donor car. Choose a $\frac{1}{2}$ in drive set with at least two extensions, long and short, and a universal joint attachment. Sizes should range as for the spanners.

Adjustable spanners

Generally speaking, the adjustable spanner is not to be recommended. Because there is usually some play in the jaws, they are prone to slip and can very easily chew up the head of a bolt. They are handy for odd-sized boltheads, but they should be used with care, and with regard for your knuckles.

There's a wide choice of socket sets. This $\frac{1}{2}$ in drive set by Metrinch fits both AF and metric sizes, which is useful on kits that use parts from a donor car with a mixture of both types of fastenings (there are a surprising number that do).

Torque spanner

Also known as a torque wrench, it allows you to tighten nuts and studs to a predetermined degree of 'tightness' or torque. There are two types: load-indicating and preset. The former is simpler and cheaper, and registers the torque reached on a scale. It is not as accurate as the preset type, however, which allows the user to dial in the required torque and indicates when this has been reached.

The donor car workshop manual will list the items that need to be set, and the torque required. Torque can be measured in ft/lb or kg/cm.

Electric drill

If you are buying a new drill, get one with a speed control that allows different settings for drilling

steel and glassfibre. If you already have a single-speed drill, you can buy a mechanical or electronic speed reducer. A set of high-speed steel drills could be said to be the minimum requirement, sizes ranging from $\frac{1}{16}$ in to $\frac{1}{4}$ in, plus a rose bit (countersink).

Just which accessories you will require will depend on the type of build you are undertaking. Rotary sanding tools – flapper disc, drum sander and rotary files – will prove useful, particularly if you have to work with glassfibre (more on that later). Electric saw attachments can save time when cutting glassfibre, metal or wood. Handle with care, because they can be crude as well as effective.

Hand drill

This is useful for the low-speed drilling of glassfibre, and removes the need to keep changing bits in the electric drill. For example, you can keep the rose bit in the hand drill.

Pliers

Buy a good pair of pliers, around 7 in, with insulated handles. One of the most useful tools you will buy,

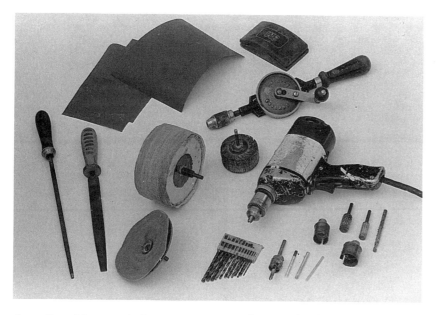

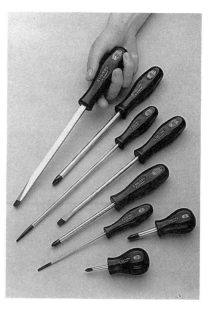

An adjustable speed electric drill, together with a selection of grinding, sanding and cutting tools will be extremely useful. Also, it is surprising how often the good old hand-driven drill is used.

so it's well worth going for the best you can find.

Hammers

Also known as the carpenter's screwdriver, the knocking stick and 'the persuader', a $\frac{1}{2}$ lb ball-pane (or pein) hammer suits most jobs. A soft-faced hammer is also useful and avoids damage to easily marked and precision surfaces.

Hack saws

Both junior and full sized hacksaws are useful, together with a full selection of blades. Using the right blade, and technique, is important, and this is discussed more fully in Chapter 6.

Files

The following selection should prove suitable for both metal and glassfibre work: 6 in round bastard file, 8 in round second cut, 8 in half-round, 6 in flat and 8 in flat.

Wire brush

The kitcar builder should never be without one: it will clean off mud, rust and old paint from donor car components, clean up threads and

castings, and polish aluminium and cast iron. It will also last for ages and can be flattened back into shape with a hammer when the bristles start to spread.

Lead lamp

No matter how well-lit your workshop might be, you'll still need a lead lamp. If you're buying one, choose the type with a clip on the back, which leaves both hands free to work (some are supplied with a hook, but there is not always somewhere to hang it). Buy a pack of spare bulbs, too: continued use and abuse in the workshop can greatly shorten the life of a lightbulb.

Screwdrivers

The temptation is to make do with a screwdriver that is really too small or too large for the job, but you need at least two sizes in Phillips and conventional slot formats; the more sizes you have, the more effective they are likely to be for the job. Likewise, don't use screwdrivers with bent and battered blades. They won't shift stubborn screws, but they will slip or damage the slot.

Clamps

Not something you'll necessarily have around the place, but to the kitcar builder working on his own they are invaluable. A couple of pairs of different-sized clamps can be as good as another pair of hands. Be careful, however, to

You will need screwdrivers of various types and sizes with blades in good condition. Avoid cheap screwdrivers; the tips blunt quickly and they don't grip the screwhead. Also, you should be aware that Phillips and Pozidrive screws are different and their drivers are not interchangeable.

spread the load with a piece of wood inside the jaws – just tightening them on to the surface can exert a great deal of force and cause damage, especially to glassfibre. See the 'Tools you can make' section below.

Self-grip wrench

Also known as a Mole grip. These wrenches, too, come in different sizes and make superb clamps, clampable adjustable spanners, something to hold cylindrical or tubular objects: they serve as a sort of general purpose, mobile vice.

Crimping tool

An all-round electrical tool, dealt with in more detail in Chapter 12.

Allen keys

These are measured by the distance across the flats and are available in both metric and Imperial. As with spanners, check the type you require. If you don't use exactly the right size, the Allen key can be a considerable instrument of destruction.

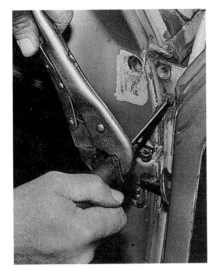

The self-grip wrench has a variety of uses. It is seen here abusing a screwdriver in an attempt to obtain some extra leverage – a bad practice which usually works, but stands a good chance of ruining the screwdriver handle.

Straight edge

For various jobs, like drawing straight lines, marking out and, in conjunction with a spirit level, ensuring levels along the length and breadth of the car.

Spirit level

If this is too small it will be susceptible to small changes in surface level, but it can be used in conjunction with a straight edge over larger distances.

Rules

A flexible 12 ft/4.0m tape is suitable for most applications. Most kit manufacturers use metric measurements, but some use Imperial, and others have been known to use both. For marking out, a 1 m steel rule is very useful.

Knife

The Stanley knife is the best known, and deservedly so. You will find it is one of the most-used tools in the workshop, so go for a Stanley with plenty of spare blades (and don't be tempted to cut corners and buy a cheap alternative!).

The staple gun and the pop rivet gun are two tools that are not strictly essential to the kitcar builder, but once you have them you wonder how you ever managed without.

Square

Invaluable when marking out and for other more unlikely jobs too. A small engineer's square will suffice, but the bigger the better. Notes on how to make one can be found in the 'Tools you can make' section below.

Markers

Do not assume there will be something around the house you can use. If you don't already have them in the workshop, buy a good soft pencil, a felt pen, a scriber and a chinagraph pencil. If you have children, keep all the markers well hidden!

Staple gun

Not something a lot of people will have in their toolkits. Although you might not buy one until you need it for part of a trimming job, for example, you will soon find numerous other uses for it. Staplers can be manual or electrically powered, and both are easy to use.

Pop rivet gun

Like the stapler, this is likely to be bought for a particular job and then used for many others: perhaps there's a good argument for buying them both in the first place. There

is more about the pop rivet gun and its use in Chapter 6, under 'Riveting'.

Blow lamp

This can be useful for applying heat to a particularly stubborn nut during the donor car strip-down, for annealing aluminium, for larger soldering jobs and various other tasks around the workshop.

Welding equipment

It shouldn't be necessary to undertake any welding during the build-up. It must, however, be said that not all builds are straightforward bolt-together affairs. If you do not already have gas- or arc-welding equipment, and the skills and confidence to use it, it could be worth making contact with a friendly local company prepared to undertake small, one-off jobs.

Goggles, mask and gloves

These are dealt with in Chapter 6, under 'Safety', but there can never be too many reminders. Always wear goggles, mask and gloves when working with glassfibre, the mask when spraying, and the goggles when grinding, using a wire brush, etc. If you're unwilling to give safety its due consideration, think of the inconvenience and lost building time of a trip to the doctor or hospital.

Tools you can make

Once you have finally decided to

build a kitcar, there is generally a frustrating period before you actually take delivery and start work. Some of it can be spent preparing the workshop as previously described, and if appropriate the donor vehicle can be sourced and stripped down. This waiting time also provides the opportunity for the builder to make some tools that will add to the satisfaction he can derive from the construction, as well as obviously saving money. The following are suggestions, but there are undoubtedly others.

Clamps

The kitcar builder's extra pair of hands, as we said earlier, but it is possible to make up your own and save considerable money. They can be tailored to specific requirements and made from studding (threaded bar) and pieces of angle iron.

Drifts

A vital part in the persuasion process. Any scrap brass, copper or mild steel bars can be used, and ends kept free from burrs by regular cleaning with a file. It's important to keep objects supported while using a hammer and drift (to avoid distortion or other damage), and do remember that a series of taps is often just as effective, and potentially less damaging, than a few hefty wallops.

Extension bars

Also known as cheaters, these are simply lengths of pipe that can be slotted over spanners and ratchet handles to increase leverage when undoing or tightening a nut. They do dramatically increase your apparent strength, however, so be careful not to strip threads or shear off the bolt.

Magnets

These are useful for holding screws and washers in inaccessible places, and for recovering dropped screws. One useful source of magnets is the strip used around old fridge doors.

Square

This was mentioned in the tools shopping list in the previous section. It can be simply made up and

A couple of trestles like this are useful for supporting the chassis while fitting the running gear.

either bolted or welded together, but it is obviously vital that the angles are accurate. You'll probably find a 45 degree square most useful, with the short sides 18-24 in long.

Test lamp/lamp and battery

These will prove very useful when wiring the car (and afterwards if you are unfortunate enough to suffer any problems). As the illustrations show, they are easily made.

Trestles

These obviously need to be strong and well-made. They are also likely to be useful after the build, so take some time over their design and manufacture. A good straight-grained clean timber is probably the easiest material to work with, but if you have welding equipment, stronger (but far heavier) angle iron can be used. Slotted angle iron would also be easy to work with, but would require extra crossbracing to avoid movement.

Trolleys

We would recommend you to build two, one for the engine and one for the back axle assembly, because these are both heavy and awkward to move around in the workshop. A strong frame can be made up from angle iron, and the timber or steel platform needs to be very strong (perhaps with crossbracing diagonally across the frame). The castors can be bought from a good ironmonger or tool shop.

Wedges

These can be useful for numerous jobs and so should be made up in different sizes. Any spare timber can be used, but hardwood wedges last longer. Do be aware of the tremendous force wedges can exert, however, and use a larger piece of wood to spread the load when working with glassfibre.

The previous two sections have dealt with most of the tools which will cover most of the jobs you are likely to perform during the course of an average build. However, when you carefully read through the workshop manual operations in advance (always advisable!), you might find that you need a hub puller or something similar. Time, then, for a quick tour through some special tools, required for particular jobs.

It wouldn't be practical to cover every specialist tool here, and if you do need them you will obviously get more information, shop around and compare prices. It is

Extension bars, a square, wedges and drifts are all tools you can make from scrap material in the workshop.

appropriate to outline the most popular ones, however, so you at least know what is available.

Special tools

Ball joint separator

The male and female parts of the ball joint are mating tapers and can be very difficult to separate. The tool works in much the same way as the hub puller, the foot being slipped between the two halves of the ball joint and, after the nut has been removed from the ball joint spindle, the bolt on the separator is screwed down until the two halves separate.

Clutch tool

This is used to align the centre of the clutch pressure plate to the centre of the clutch housing cover. If these are not accurately lined up it can be impossible to fit the gearbox. This is usually only discovered after the engine has been refitted to the car, so it's worth getting it right in the first place.

Easiout

It is to be hoped that you won't need this, but if a stud shears, and you're left with the problem of how to extract the broken stud, it is invaluable.

Spring compressors, hub pullers and ball joint splitters are all tools that can be hired.

Hub puller

As its name applies, this is used for pulling hubs and bearings from shafts. The tool consists of a central boss, with a bolt passing through its centre, and three hinged arms (each with a foot – or hand? – at the end) spaced around its circumference.

To use a hub puller, the arms are hooked behind the hub. The central bolt is screwed in so that it bears on to the centre of the shaft on which the hub is mounted. Tightening the bolt pushes on to

the end of the shaft and draws the hub from it.

Like most of these specialist tools, you shouldn't buy a hub puller until you need one (and only then if you can't borrow one – you may only need it for a few minutes). If you do buy a hub puller, choose a good one; cheap items are likely to be of poor quality and unable to cope with the forces exerted.

Spring compressors

Again the name is self-explanatory, but we should add that the springs in question are of the suspension variety – coils as used on MacPherson struts, etc. These are very powerful under compression, and if

released accidentally could cause serious injury. Do not be tempted to rig up something with bits of wire and rope! Not buying – or not hiring – spring compressors could prove to be a very dangerous economy.

As has already been mentioned, a friendly local engineering company can be a great boon, and it's worth getting the local garage interested. It might seem that they sting you for the occasional job on the family car, but they will probably be genuinely interested in a kitcar build, and might be willing to shift that obstinate nut or reposition the occasional bracket.

Finally, if you cannot contemplate

buying all these tools, you might try contacting a local kitcar club. Many of them have tools which they hire out at nominal rates. Tool hire companies, too, are worth a try for things like engine hoists. And if you know someone else who is building, or is planning to build, a kitcar, what about pooling resources, and keeping them at your place now that you've got all that shelving and storage space?

CHAPTER 6:
BASIC
TECHNIQUES

Safety

We do not feel that it is our responsibility to discuss all aspects of workshop safety in this book. The subject is very broad and to attempt to cover all eventualities would require much more space than is available here. All kitcar builders should make themselves aware of the dangers inherent in using all sharp-edged tools and electrically powered equipment. However, there are some areas that need discussion both in terms of the types of material used, and some of the tools and techniques employed in building a kitcar.

Regard for safety is a discipline that when sensibly and regularly followed becomes a habit, something that is carried out automatically, and neither irritating nor time wasting.

Glass-reinforced plastic (GRP), commonly called glassfibre, is the material from which most kitcar bodyshells are made. It has a number of advantages over traditional materials, but there are some aspects of safety you should be aware of. As we have already explained, GRP consists of strands of glass that have been saturated with resin to which a hardener has been added. The glass and resin is applied in layers to a mould until the required thicknesses are obtained. When the resin has hardened, the resultant material becomes very hard and tough.

When it is removed from the mould, the lay-up, or moulding, has a very smooth side which has been next to the mould. This is the 'cosmetic' part which will generally be on view. The other side of the material, however, can be quite rough. Some manufacturers then apply a layer of finishing tissue to the inside, or a thick mix of resin called Flocoat, and these techniques provide a smooth surface. It is still quite common, however, for the inside to have areas where the glass fibres stand proud of the surface, and when these are coated with hardened resin they become needle sharp. You only need to have one driven under a finger nail to realize how dangerous they can be.

Also, if the glassfibre moulding has been carelessly trimmed, the edges can be razor sharp: exactly at the places where your hands naturally fall when lifting or adjusting the bodyshell. To prevent injuries from splinters and sharp edges, we advise that the bodyshell should be carefully inspected and any rough areas sanded smooth with course wet and dry paper. Be careful not to remove too much material from the edges, just enough to make them smooth. When handling the heavier glassfibre panels it is advisable to wear industrial gloves, or pad the edges with cloth or stout cardboard.

Any type of dust in large quantities presents a health hazard. It causes irritation to the eyes, blocks nasal passages and generally causes respiration problems. We believe that glassfibre dust can cause additional, long-term, health problems if it is inhaled and we strongly recommend that a mask is worn on every occasion when GRP is sanded, drilled or cut. After every operation use a vacuum cleaner to collect the dust, and regularly clean the floor and horizontal surfaces.

There are number of masks available, the two illustrated are the most popular and easily obtained from DIY stores. The one on the right of the picture is merely a soft aluminium facepiece to which fits a thick filter pad. It is convenient to use, effective and very cheap. There are no condensation problems and a used filter pad can be discarded and replaced daily. To be effective the pads *must* be dry: the airing cupboard, alongside your arc welding rods, is an ideal storage place.

The rubber mask on the left is

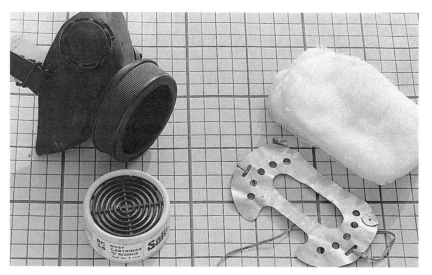

Face masks are cheap and effective against dust particles; always wear one when sanding, cutting or grinding GRP.

more versatile; you can fit various filters depending on the type of dust being created and it is generally a more robust piece of equipment. Sometimes condensation forms in the mouthpiece, but if this becomes a nuisance it can be blown out of the exhaust valves at the side. Occasionally, but not very often with today's kitcars, you will want to lay up some glassfibre yourself. If you do, work in a well-ventilated space and either wear gloves or apply a barrier cream to your hands. Contact with resin and hardener can cause skin problems. Some people react more violently than others to skin contact and inhalation of fumes. However, there is little actual glassfibre work involved in the construction of most kits, so this is unlikely to be a problem.

Eyes should always be protected with goggles when working under the car, grinding metal or glassfibre, cleaning with a wire brush or when working with power tools of any sort. Sometimes condensation can be a problem, but a wipe over the inside with a little washing-up liquid will usually cure the problem.

Fire is an ever-present hazard in any domestic garage. Tins of paint, cleaning fluid, petrol, oil, GRP, timber, dust and shavings combine to create a situation that would make a fire prevention officer close

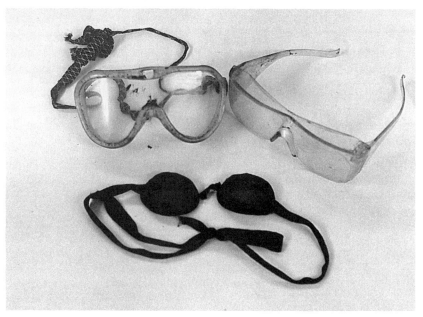

Goggles or safety glasses should be worn to prevent foreign matter from entering your eyes.

a commercial operation. It only needs a spark to start a fire that could devour your pride and joy – and even damage your car. It pays to take some precautions. We always work to the following rules:

1 No smoking in the workshop.
2 Fit two fire extinguishers: one near the door and an automatic one in the roof space.
3 Keep petrol, paraffin and all other inflammable fluids in a separate locker outside. All old oil should be ditched immediately.
4 Keep all cleaning rags in a bin – not left around waiting for a

spark from the welding set.
5 When leaving the workshop check that all appliances are switched off, and unplugged.

We realize that the average kitcar builder might think that we are taking fire prevention a little too seriously. Maybe we are, but we know from experience that one small fire can do an awful lot of damage.

Jacking up the car
Never, ever, get under a car that is supported only by a jack. The car should always be securely resting on axle stands or ramps. Don't use bricks, breeze blocks, lumps of wood or any other Heath Robinson lash-up. Such contraptions are likely to topple and the car could fall on you with fatal results. Not only that, a pile of bricks or wood is difficult to position properly and takes up an inordinate amount of space.

The best advice we can give on safety is 'Think before you act'. Any accident, from a grazed knuckle to a serious fire, can be prevented by thinking through the consequences of your actions. Do that and you won't have a silly accident to spoil your leisure activity.

Working with metal

Some superb vehicles have been

constructed by people with little experience or knowledge of cars or engineering. Starting from scratch has its own rewards, and although the learning curve will be steep and difficult to climb, the results will be very satisfying. Every step will mean learning a new technique or skill and the process of building will necessarily be slow; but with care and persistence the task can be accomplished.

At the other end of the scale, the professional mechanic, or the experienced do-it-yourselfer who is used to fixing anything from a leaking bathroom tap to changing the big-end bearings on the family car, may well breeze through building a kitcar without experiencing any problems at all.

This chapter is not written for either of these types of people. It would not be appropriate to attempt to teach a full range of skills to the novice; and the experienced person already has the necessary knowledge. In between these two extremes is the average person who knows a bit about cars, but has little experience of the techniques involved in building a kitcar. He's the man we're writing this for – but it's a pound to a pinch of rubbing compound that the other two will also find something useful in this chapter.

'Shear' force

One of the first tasks the kitcar builder may have to undertake is to strip the running gear from the donor car. In some instances the parts required have never been removed from the car since the day it rolled off the production line, so undoing some of the nuts and bolts can be a headache. Here are a few tips.

First clean the head of the nut or bolt, and the area around it, with a wire brush. Then soak the thread and the head with penetrating oil, leave it for a couple of hours and repeat the treatment. Wait another couple of hours, or even longer, before attempting to undo the nut: overnight is ideal.

Penetrating oil is specially formulated to 'creep' into all the little rusty nooks and crannies, and

loosen the bond formed by rust and dirt. WD40 has the same effect. A cheap and effective alternative is to mix equal amounts of old engine oil and paraffin. A small trigger pressure spray bottle, like those used for garden pesticides, makes an ideal applicator. Place a rag under the bolt to catch the drips and save your garage floor from getting soaked in oil – if it isn't already.

Make sure your spanner, or socket, is a snug fit on the bolthead so that it won't slip and crunch your knuckles, a condition known in the trade as 'spanner rash'. If the nut still won't move, try using an extension bar on the spanner or socket handle, but be very careful because it is easy to strip the thread. Having said that, if the bolt is easily replaced and the nut is proving difficult to remove, you may decide that the easiest course is to continue to apply enough force to shear the bolt right off – brutal, but quick and effective.

If that approach offends your sensibilities, or is not practical, try heating the nut with a blow lamp, or welding torch. Be careful not to apply heat near the petrol and pipes, or any other inflammable material. Work the nut back and forth to loosen the bond, and gradually move it down the thread. Use plenty of lubricant once the nut is moving, and the heat is dissipated.

It sometimes helps to hit the end of the bolt squarely and sharply with a hammer, while holding another heavy hammer against the bolthead. This shock treatment often loosens the bond of the threads between nut and bolt. Be careful not to burr over the end of bolt by careless use of the hammer. Either use a copper-faced hammer or protect the bolt with a piece of metal.

A stubborn nut can be cut through with a sharp chisel, or a specialist tool called, appropriately enough, a nut splitter. Used carefully, both the nut splitter and chisel can cut through the nut without damaging the thread of the bolt. Apply many light taps of the hammer when using the chisel, rather than a few hefty wallops that

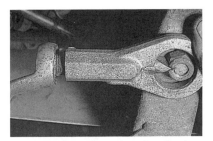

A nut splitter may be the final solution.

may damage or distort the bolt or the fitting through which it passes.

If all else fails, the head of the bolt, or the nut, can be cut off with a hacksaw.

How tight is tight?

Having spent some time looking at how to undo a stubborn nut and bolt, let's now consider the apparently simple task of doing one up.

Most people overtighten small nuts and bolts, and undertighten larger ones. Even some experienced mechanics make the mistake of thinking that they can feel when a nut is correctly torqued up. Mostly, it is merely inconvenient if a nut comes undone, or the bolt is sheared, or weakened, as the nut is being tightened. Sometimes, though, it can have serious consequences; especially if brake and suspension or steering components are involved.

Although it would be totally impractical to suggest that every nut and bolt is torqued up accurately, it is important that certain fixings are tightened to the manufacturer's specification. The only way to ensure that important nuts are tightened correctly is to use a torque wrench. The service manual will list the items that need to be set to a specific torque and the settings will be quoted in ft/lb or kg/cm, or both.

There are two types of torque wrench in popular use. The least expensive is the load-indicating type, which features a pointer on a scale near the handle. Like most things in life, you get what you pay for, and although this type is better than nothing, it does leave a lot to be desired in accuracy and ease of use.

The ratchet-type torque wrench is

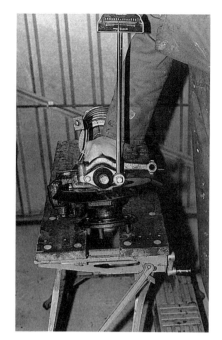

A load-indicating torque wrench in use.

best. This features a scale which is set by rotating an inner sleeve in the handle until the correct setting is obtained. In use, a ratchet in the head of the wrench will give an audible click when the torque has been reached.

Removing sheared studs

You may be unfortunate, or clumsy, enough to shear a stud and be left with the stub firmly embedded in the component. If you are lucky, there may be enough of the stud protruding from the threaded hole for you to be able to remove it. It may be possible to saw a screwdriver slot in the top, or file flats in the side for a spanner, and wind out the offending stud.

Usually, however, Murphy's Law takes over and there isn't enough metal showing to be of any use. One option is to try using a stud extractor. This little gadget has a tapered left-hand thread at one end and flats to take a spanner machined in the other. The idea is to drill a hole in the broken stud and wind the extractor into the hole. Because it has a left-hand thread, the extractor is supposed to wind out the broken stud at the same time as it winds itself into the hole.

It's great in theory, but we have

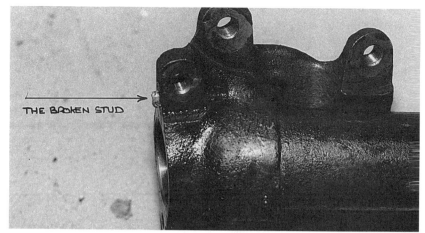

THE BROKEN STUD

This picture sequence shows an Easiout in use. Care must be taken not to shear off the tool in the already broken stud – this just adds to your problems.

not had much success with this little beast and invariably end up breaking the tool in the hole and thus presenting ourselves with a further problem. So we are telling you about the tool, but also warning you of its perverse little ways.

In the long run, we find it is better to drill out the stud and retap the hole one size larger, if we have the latitude to do so. If not, it is possible to fit a threaded insert so that the original size of stud can be used, but this requires a special tool and is best left to your local machine shop.

Cutting holes in metal

Drilling holes in metal is one of the most frequent operations undertaken by a kitcar builder. The task is a straightforward one, but there are one or two points that are worth mentioning.

It may seem like stating the obvious to say that drill bits should be sharp. Yet it is surprising how many people continue to use a drill that is wearing, rather than cutting, its way through the metal. A drill-sharpening tool is a good investment: around £15 buys you a set of stones and a jig which is driven by your electric drill. In return for this modest outlay you will have correctly sharpened drills for evermore.

Always mark the centre of the hole to be drilled with a centre punch, which will ensure that the drill tip does not wander over the surface of the material before starting to bite. A piece of masking tape over the working area will prevent the drill from slipping and scratching a finished surface.

If it is important that the hole is drilled accurately, use a square to keep the bit at right angles to the work, or ask an assistant to tell you if you are holding the drill upright. Drill speed is important, too; use a slow speed for larger holes and a faster speed for smaller ones. Clearly, a variable-speed drill is a big help, but it is possible to buy speed reducers for fixed-speed drills. The average fixed-speed drill rotates at about 2500 revs, which is too fast for all but the smallest drills (under $\frac{1}{8}$ in diameter).

Use a lubricant when drilling or cutting steel; this speeds up the process and keeps the cutting edge sharper for longer. You can buy proprietary brands of lubricants, or use engine oil. If you are drilling a hole with a diameter of more than $\frac{1}{4}$ in, use a smaller drill as a pilot first; this ensures the accuracy of the hole and it is faster, despite having to drill more than one hole. For very large holes use successively bigger drills. In sheet metal don't attempt to drill a hole larger than about $\frac{5}{16}$ in because you are likely to finish up with one that is not cut cleanly, or anywhere near circular.

Instead, use a hole saw, tank cutter or fly cutter. For larger holes mark out the circumference with a pair of dividers or a compass, then

A piece of tape covering the area to be drilled prevents the drill bit from slipping, and protects the finish.

so always clamp sheet metal in a vice or down to the bench.

Straight and curved tin snips are useful for cutting sheet metal, and

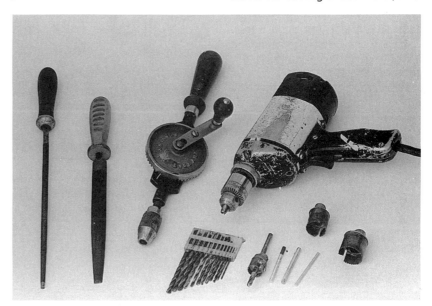

A selection of tools for making holes in metal, wood or GRP.

drill a number of holes inside the boundary. You can then cut the webs of metal linking the holes with a chisel or a thin blade and finish to the correct size with a half-round file.

A word of warning: never hold a piece of sheet metal with your hand when drilling because the flutes of the drill will pick up the material as it breaks through and spin it around. There is a good chance that it will cut your hand,

This fly cutter from Jabus Engineering is set up to cut washers.

These thin, circular blades cut this material very quickly and need to be used carefully to make an accurate cut.

laminates, but they can prove an expensive buy if you don't intend to use them often. A cheap and effective way of cutting holes and curves in metal is to use a circular blade in your hacksaw. Shaped like a flexible, thin parallel file, the blade is fixed to the hacksaw frame using a pair of special clips. Various grades of blades can be purchased with fine teeth for thin sheet and coarser teeth for thicker material.

Lastly, there are a number of tools that can be used in your electric drill. Rotary files of various grades, flapper discs, hole saws and nibblers are items that can be added to your toolkit as the need arises, and the pocket allows.

Thread cutting

Although most manufacturers ensure that all the necessary mounting points and brackets are supplied with the kit, the builder may occasionally need to cut threads. Earth points for the electrical system, additional brackets for mounting accessories and recutting threads in damaged components are examples.

A tap is the tool used to cut an internal thread, and a die is employed to make an external thread. Both of these tools need to be held in a handle. The handle for the tap is called tap wrench; and

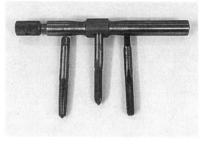

A set of taps – taper, intermediate and plug – together with a wrench.

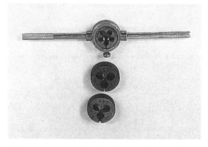

Dies and a stock. Note that the dies are split to allow for adjustment as the thread cutting proceeds.

just to confuse things, the handle for the die is called a stock.

A glance at the accompanying pictures will save us a thousand words of explanation. Suffice it to say that the tap has three cutting edges and a square shank so that it can be gripped by the wrench. The die is like a circular split nut, with hardened cutting threads. Both the tap and die have channels cut in them to allow the waste metal created in the cutting process

to escape. The split in the die allows the diameter to be reduced as the cutting process advances, and this is accomplished by adjusting the three screws in the circumference of the stock.

Just as the die is adjustable so that the cutting process can be graduated, so too is the tap. However, because it would be difficult to make the tap adjustable by expanding it, three different grades of tap are supplied for cutting each thread size.

The first grade is called the taper tap. This has no threads for part of its length and is tapered for about 10 threads before gradually increasing to full depth of thread. Because of its taper, it allows a gentle introduction of the tap in the hole and is used to start the cutting.

The second, or intermediate tap, is also tapered but only for about four of its threads, and this enables the process to be taken a step further. The final tap, the plug as it is called, completes the cutting process and allows threads to be made right to the bottom of the blind hole.

When making an internal thread with a tap, it is obvious that the diameter of the hole drilled in the material to be threaded has to be smaller than the outside diameter of the tap; so if you want to drill and tap a hole for a 9 mm bolt the hole must be smaller than 9 mm by the depth of the thread.

The reverse logic applies when cutting an external thread. The stud to be threaded must have a diameter that is the size of the external diameter of the finished thread.

To find out the exact drill and stud size for every thread there are engineer's tables. These are often given away with tool catalogues, or can be bought at good tool shops (you are unlikely to find them at your local DIY superstore) for a few pence. Because your requirements are likely to be limited to a range from about 6 to 12 mm in 2 mm steps (or the Imperial equivalents), it is worth buying individual taps and dies, together with the correct size drills, as you need them.

Threads should be cut using lubricant; oil will do fine. Make sure the

A stock and die being used to cut an external thread.

This sequence of pictures shows how a gearbox cover was made and demonstrates the versatility of sheet aluminium. First the aluminium was cut to shape and annealed using soap as a guide to the correct temperature. Next the shape was formed by bending the aluminium between two blocks of wood held in a vice. Then the sides were riveted together and the whole box covered in vinyl cloth.

tap or die is square with the work and wind it in clockwise (for a right-hand thread) for a couple of turns to get it started. Then about every $\frac{3}{4}$ of a turn wind it back about $\frac{1}{4}$ turn to clear the swarf created by cutting. Don't use excessive force. If the work isn't progressing smoothly you are either trying to force the tool into too small a hole, or over too big a stud diameter. Or, the tool may not be at right angles to the work.

It could be that you are trying to cut hard metal with a carbon steel tap or die. Carbon steel tools are fine for mild steel, brass and alloy. If you need to thread harder materials, such as stainless steel, then high-speed steel taps and dies should be used. These are obviously more expensive than carbon steel tools, and if you only have a couple of threads to cut, maybe you would be better off taking the job to your local machine shop or blacksmith.

Lastly, if you merely want to clean up a thread there are tools available to do that, and these are not nearly so expensive as a set of taps or dies. Die nuts, as their name implies, are similar to dies, but are shaped like a nut and are non-adjustable. You simply wind them gently on the damaged thread with a spanner. The same rules apply as when using a die: plenty of lubricant and a back and forth movement.

Similarly, thread-restoring files can be used for cleaning up external threads. These tools are just like a file, but thread grooves are built into the cutting edges. One tool will suit a whole range of sizes. For instance, a metric thread-restoring file could have every size in 2 mm steps from 4 to 18 mm. Obviously, one metric and one AF file will be very useful additions to the toolkit: but like all good tools they are expensive, so don't buy them until you need them.

Working with aluminium

Aluminium is light and easy to work with, and it is these qualities that make it so useful to the kitcar builder. From small brackets to large panels, aluminium will be found on most cars in some form or other. In fact, most sheet material is not pure aluminium but an alloy.

For many years the authors didn't buy aluminium. They were fortunate to work near a company that specialized in fabricating trailer bodies, and for a donation to the 'tea boat' fund had free access to the firm's offcut bin. It's worth a tour of your local industrial estate to see if you can find a similar benefactor, but if not you will just have to dig deep into your pocket and buy a couple of square feet each of, say, 16 and 12 gauge.

Aluminium is easy to bend by simply clamping it between two pieces of wood and either bending it by hand, or holding a piece of

wood along the bend line and tapping it with a hammer. Avoid hitting the metal directly with a hammer or you will end up with a series of indentations along the line of the bend. A gently radiused curve is better than a sharp bend. This can be achieved by using a piece of soft wood, with a chamfer on the top edge, as the inner face of the clamp.

If it is worked too much, aluminium alloy will tend to harden and crack. This can be avoided by annealing the metal to soften it again and this process can be carried out as many times as necessary.

Annealing is achieved by heating the metal to a certain temperature and letting it cool; for instance, mild steel is heated to a cherry red. However, aluminium does not change colour when it is heated, so some other method of judging the temperature is necessary. A simple and effective way of determining the correct temperature is to mark the area to be annealed with ordinary household soap – a big X from corner to corner will do fine. Then using a blowlamp or welding torch, evenly heat the whole area until the soap turns brown. Wait for the metal to cool and away you go.

Welding

It is not our intention to describe the various welding techniques in detail in this chapter. The subject is a complex one; but there are various books and videos available that give detailed explanations and instructions on how to weld. It should be appreciated that some practice is necessary before any degree of proficiency is obtained, and the novice welder should not attempt to carry out any structural welding on crucial parts of the car such as the chassis.

Today's kits do not usually require any welding to be carried out during the build. Some do have small jobs that need to be done and these can be economically carried out by your local blacksmith or travelling welder. That said, a small welding set can save its cost in time and money over and over again.

Each process has its limitations, as well as its advantages, so perhaps it would be as well to spend a little time examining those methods that are suitable for the home workshop, to help you decide which welding set, if any, to buy.

A word of warning: there are general safety precautions to be taken when welding, and there are specific safety rules to be followed when using each type of equipment. Read the manufacturer's instructions and make yourself aware of safety procedures.

Gas welding

Oxyacetylene, commonly called gas welding, is probably the most versatile of all types of welding. In addition to welding, the oxyacetylene set can be used for brazing, soldering, cutting, heating and forming – and it can do these almost anywhere because the equipment is portable.

Most people will be familiar with the two large gas bottles with their regulators and gauges, and the rubber hoses and welding torch. Therein lie two of the problems associated with gas welding. The system takes up a lot of room, even using the mini-gas bottles now available, and the equipment required to start is expensive. The gas bottles have to be bought in addition to the rest of the equipment. However, once the initial outlay has been met, the actual running costs are low. The amounts of gas used are quite small, and refills are not expensive. The only other consumable are the filler rods and these, too, are comparatively cheap.

The flame is almost infinitely adjustable, so it is possible to weld very thin sheet metal, as well as thick plate.

Many people are intimidated by the high pressure of the gases (oxygen around 2000 psi and acetylene 375 psi) and the apparent complexity of the equipment. However, observing basic safety precautions will ensure that accidents do not occur, and the equipment is no more difficult to understand than that of other welding systems.

Like any skill, learning to gas weld takes some time, but a basic level of competence can quite quickly be reached and further skills will come with experience. If the space needed for the equipment and its initial cost are not a problem, we would choose a gas welding outfit every time.

MIG Welding

Thanks to small MIG welders, a revolution has taken place in the DIY welding market. Metal inert gas (MIG) welders use an electrode wire which is continuously fed from a reel to emerge from the centre of the welding torch. Carbon dioxide (CO_2) is also fed from the torch and this gas surrounds the area of the weld to shield it from atmospheric contamination.

The AC mains supply is rectified to a DC electrical current and fed to the electrode wire, so that when the electrode is brought in contact with the work, and the work is connected to earth, a short circuit is caused and an arc starts. This arc melts the base metal and the tip of the electrode. As the electrode melts and drips metal into the molten puddle of base metal, it shortens itself and the arc can no longer be sustained. However, the

An industrial MIG welding set in DJ Sportscars development shop. The reel of electrode wire and CO_2 bottle can be clearly seen.

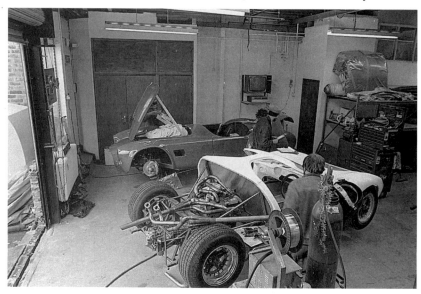

electrode is still being advanced from its reel to the tip of the torch and the arc begins again. This on/off cycle occurs about 60 times a second.

The process is easy to learn and good quality welds can be produced by the novice after a short practice session. The resultant weld is tidy and free from spatter, so there is no cleaning up to be done afterwards. Another advantage of the MIG system is that the welding can continue for as long as the reel of electrode wire lasts – no stopping to change rods.

However, although the DIY sets are fine for smaller jobs, and ideal for materials up to about $\frac{1}{8}$ in thick, for welding thicker metal a higher capacity unit, as used in professional workshops, is needed. Also, cutting, heating and forming work is not really practical with a MIG welder. To sum up: a MIG welder is easy to use, reasonably priced and comes in a neat tidy package. It needs a supply of CO_2 and 240 v power to run it, and it has some limitations in use; but it will probably do all that the kitcar builder requires.

Arc welding

An arc welder works in a similar way to a MIG welder except that the electrode carries its own flux and shielding gas in the form of a coating.

When the arc is struck, the electrode and the base metal melt into a puddle; at the same time, the coating around the rod of the electrode melts. The flux helps the rod metal adhere to the base metal, and at the same time a gas is formed which floats to the top of the weld puddle and forms a hard coating called slag. This slag forms the shield that protects the weld from contamination. When the metal is cooled the slag is chipped off to reveal the bright weld.

Small arc welders are inexpensive and, with a bit of practice, quite easy to use on heavy-gauge metal. Their limitation is revealed when you try to weld thinner material. It takes an experienced hand with the arc welder to make a decent job of joining metal that is less than $\frac{3}{32}$ in

One of JBA's engineers using an arc welder during chassis fabrication. A mask, with a specially made glass panel, must be used to prevent serious damage to the eyes and face.

thick. Welding rods are available for fine work and a heat sink can be used to conduct away some of the heat, but the novice will invariably blow holes in thinner metal. Making up your own exhaust pipe, for instance, is out of the question for most kitcar builders.

There are thousands of DIY arc welders doing sterling service in workshops all over the country. We know someone who had a £100, 150 amp arc welder and used it daily for a year before it was replaced with a larger unit.

However, smaller machines can't be used continuously and they must be rested according to their rating. For instance, a 75 per cent rated machine must be rested for $2\frac{1}{2}$ minutes in every 10.

We would put the arc welder at the bottom of our kitcar builder's shopping list because of its inability to weld fine gauge material.

Riveting

A less complicated way of joining metal is by riveting. Although this doesn't compare in strength of joint to welding, it is easier for the amateur to learn to rivet, and all types and mixtures of material can be joined. For instance, it takes special skill and materials to weld aluminium, and it is impossible to weld aluminium to steel; but in both of these cases, joining is easily accomplished by riveting.

Like most engineering processes, there is more to riveting than meets the eye, but for our purposes we can keep it simple by looking only at the type of joints the kitcar builder will want to make.

Typically, the kitcar builder will want to fix GRP or metal panels to the chassis, or to each other; he will want to fix brackets to the chassis or to GRP and maybe material, such as hood cloth, to metal tubing. Large rivets can be used to mate the bodyshell to the chassis and it is sometimes useful to employ small rivets to hold a panel temporarily in position while it is being worked on – a favourite trick of welders.

Traditionally, to make a riveted joint it was necessary to be able to have access to both sides of the material. A hole was drilled in both pieces of material to be joined and a solid rivet, usually made of the same metal as the objects to be joined, was inserted. The head of the rivet was held tight against the work by a heavy hammer, or dolly, and the tail projecting on the other side of the joint was hammered over to complete the joint. This method is still in use to make structural joints, although air- or electrically driven tools have replaced the hammer and dolly.

For our purposes, non-structural joints can be made very simply using a pop rivet gun and aluminium rivets. The rivets are hollow and have a sacrificial steel pin inserted in the hollow core. The rivet is inserted in the hole and the tail protrudes on the inside of the work. A special tool is used to grip the pin and pull it out through the rivet.

The mushroom head of the pin distorts the soft aluminium of the rivet tail, and as the tool attempts to pull the pin through the rivet core it forms a collar. The collar is pulled tight against the inner material face to make a firm joint. The pin is not designed to pull right through the rivet, but to shear off just below its outer face, the mushroom head and short shank of the pin remaining in the core of the rivet. The sheared-off part of the pin can either be left in to seal the

core, or punched out if appearance is critical.

This is a one-handed operation and only requires access to one side of the work. Thus it is possible to join material to hollow pipes, such as chassis rails, or anywhere where it is difficult to get to both sides of the work.

Various types of rivet are available in a whole range of sizes. It is not our intention here to go into the techniques involved in structural riveting (as used on aircraft, for instance), but there are now available special structural hollow rivets which can be used in ordinary pop rivet guns.

To calculate the size of rivets required you need to know the combined thickness of the materials to be joined. The diameter of the shank of the rivet should be $1\frac{1}{2}$ to 2 times the thickness of both materials, and the length of the shank of the rivet should be the thickness of the two materials plus 1 to $1\frac{1}{2}$ diameters of the rivet shank. If the rivet is too long it distorts unevenly and looks untidy, if it is too short, it won't distort enough to form a proper collar.

When designing a riveted joint, space the rivets evenly for appearance sake; and use two or three rows of rivets in preference to a single line when joining two sheets of material. If you intend to use countersunk rivet heads in thin sheet you should be aware that cutting the countersink with a rose bit will leave only a small amount of material under the rivet head, which might pull through the material. Instead, use a punch to create the countersink.

A riveted joint is much stronger in shear than in tension, and it should always be designed with that in mind. Also, when riveting GRP or other soft material, a washer should be placed under the head of the rivet to prevent it pulling through. To achieve a neat appearance in a long row of rivets it is best first to drill a single hole and insert a rivet in the middle of the line; then work outwards either side of the first rivet, drilling single holes and inserting the rivets as you go. If you drill all of the holes in one go, you are likely to find that

they gradually move out of line as the riveting process slightly distorts the material.

A good tip is to put a bead of mastic or Sikaflex adhesive between the joints. This provides sound insulation and prevents dissimilar metals from reacting with one another. It also helps to make the joint waterproof. Sikaflex markets a range of adhesives and sealers, and these should be available from your parts supplier.

Working with glassfibre

We have already included some details on the properties and makeup of GRP. Here we are looking at the material from the workshop angle, rather than through the critical eye of a buyer, and we have included a few more details than were given in Chapter 2.

Repairing chips and scratches

If possible, get a small pot of gelcoat resin and some hardener from the manufacturer when you collect your kit. (Take a jam jar with a well-fitting lid for the resin, and a smaller medicine bottle for the hardener – to save you hunting around for suitable containers.) Of course, the kit supplier may well subcontract out his glassfibre work, in which case, unless you made prior arrangements, you are going to be unlucky.

To repair a chip or gouge in the gelcoat, remove any loose material by raking out the area with a probe until you are satisfied that you are back to a sound base. Mix the resin and hardener, a couple or three drops of hardener to a tablespoon of resin will be about right, and apply the mix to the damaged area.

Carefully stick a piece of Sellotape over the repair and gently press the tape down to expel any air – this makes for a nice smooth surface. When a cure has taken place, peel off the Sellotape and allow any surface tackiness to dry. Then polish the whole area with a little T-Cut or polishing paste.

To repair a larger hole it will be necessary to fill it first with plastic padding or a resin, hardener and glass mix. Bring the filler up to just below the top of the hole (about $\frac{1}{16}$ in) and leave it to cure. Then proceed with the gelcoat repair as just described.

Larger repairs and making-up

If an accident has occurred and a wing or some other panel is in a number of pieces, it is quite easy to make an effective repair. Many companies and DIY shops sell glass-fibre repair outfits, and some kitcar manufacturers also supply the necessary materials.

Gather all of the broken pieces and fit them together as closely as possible in the original shape. Use tape on the outside surface to hold all of the pieces together in their right place. If necessary, take measurements from a similar panel, or make a template from cardboard, to ensure that the shape is accurate.

Where the broken pieces of the panel are large, or awkward to hold, tape may not be sufficient for the job, so make up some straps from aluminium. Using self-tapping screws, fix the straps to sound, undamaged material and use them to bridge the damaged area. The broken pieces of material can now either be screwed or taped to the bridging pieces which, being easily bent, can be pushed into the correct shape.

Cut a piece of glassfibre mat so that it is bigger by about 3 or 4 in than the area to be repaired. Make a resin and hardener mix, and apply the mat and resin to the underside of the damaged area. Allow time for a cure to take place and then remove the tape holding the parts together. Check that the broken parts are still in their correct position and the shape is fairly accurate. If not, break the pieces from the mat backing and start again.

When you are sure that the surface shape is as fair as you can get it, apply a further two layers of mat and resin to the underside. Now working on the outside, clean up the edges of the broken pieces, removing any loose material. Larger holes and gaps should be filled with a mat and resin mix to just below

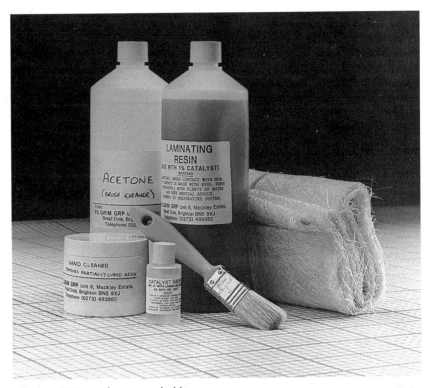

Pilgrim GRP markets repair kits for glassfibre and can supply larger quantities if required. Strand Glass also has a chain of shops throughout the United Kingdom, and supplies a series of leaflets on care and repair of GRP.

the surrounding surface level. Make up a filler, using resin and filler powder. Fill any remaining gaps with paste – finishing so that the paste is just above the level of the sound panels.

Now sand the repair until it blends in with the surrounding area with 40 grit coarse wet and dry and finishing with 600 grit fine paper in successive stages. You will be very fortunate if you have managed to get a very accurate shape with no high or low spots at the first attempt. Low spots can be filled. High spots should be ground down below the surrounding material and filled to bring them up to the required level.

The repair will, of course, have to be painted because it is not possible to obtain a gelcoat finish unless a mould is used in the construction of the laminate.

At some time in the construction of the car you may wish to extend, or make up a panel. In the

example shown here, a front light panel has been carelessly trimmed so that the diameter of the hole that accepts the headlight is much too big. We need to put back some of the glassfibre that was inadvertently removed.

First, a piece of stiff plastic sheeting is cut roughly to the size and shape of the piece to be replaced. The edges adjacent to the repair are roughed up with very coarse wet and dry paper to provide a key. Then the plastic is taped to the underside of the panel. Aluminium, cardboard or mesh would make suitable alternative backing pieces to plastic.

Then a mix of resin and finely chopped glass mat (this is available ready mixed from motor factors and DIY stores) is plastered over the plastic and pushed firmly against the surrounding area, which has been roughed up to ensure a good bond with the original material. It is made a little oversize to allow for trimming later. When the mixture has started to go off, but while it is still green (after about 20 minutes, depending on the temperature and humidity), the plastic is peeled from the back and the glass-fibre and resin mix is trimmed to shape using a sharp knife. At this stage, the surface finish of the

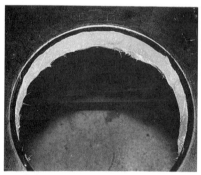

This picture sequence shows the steps involved in extending a panel. In this instance a hole for a headlight had been trimmed oversize and needed to be made up to the correct diameter. First a piece of stiff plastic was stuck to the back of the panel to support the glassfibre and give it shape, then a mix of GRP and chopped strand mat was pushed on to the plastic and the panel. The repair was finished off with a smooth coat of filler and painted.

repair is not important, providing that it is below the level finally required by about $\frac{1}{16}$ in.

The repair is reinforced with two or three layers of chopped strand mat and resin applied to the back and overlapping both the original material and the new resin mix. The final finish is achieved by trowelling on a filler mix to just above the surface level and finishing off with successive grades of wet and dry.

Bonding on fittings

Sometimes it is necessary to bond blocks of wood on to the bodyshell so that various fittings, such as trim panels, rear view mirror and sun visors, can be fitted. This is simply done using a mix of resin and chopped strand mat as an adhesive. However, there are one or two points to be aware of.

Firstly, when the resin mix hardens it can pull at the surface of a thin panel and distort it locally, so if a block of wood is bonded to the inside of, say, a door skin, it is likely that the outside of the door skin will wrinkle slightly over an area covering the size of the block.

This doesn't always happen, and it depends on the thickness of the GRP panel: obviously, the thinner the panel, the more likely it is to distort. The effect can be minimized by not using more resin mix than is necessary to achieve a satisfactory bond, and by not using too much hardener. The temptation is to increase the amount of hardener to effect a quicker curing time. This generates a lot of heat, which causes the damage.

It pays to do a trial bond of a block in an area that won't be seen, so that you can see if the skin is going to distort. Obviously, the effect of distortion is not critical on a surface that is to be painted because it will be dealt with in the pre-paint preparation. However, it can have a serious effect on self-coloured gelcoat surfaces, and there is little you can do about it once it has occurred.

Before bonding in the block, roughen the surface of the GRP panel to form a key and either cross-hatch the wooden block with a knife, or drill some holes in the back to give the resin-mat mix a grip.

Bonding-in floors and pads

It is sometimes necessary to strengthen an area that is liable to take a lot of stress: a windscreen anchorage point, for instance. Large areas of glassfibre, such as floor panels or side panels, may also need to be stiffened.

For these applications a metal or wooden pad should be bonded-in between two layers of laminate. In other words, there should be a glassfibre-pad-glassfibre sandwich.

This shows a plywood floor being bonded in. The edges are being sealed first and then the whole area will be glassed in.

The pad can be held in position temporarily with rivets or a resin/mat adhesive. The mat of glassfibre should be cut to shape, allowing an overlap of about 4 in. Cut three further pieces of glass mat, each one about 1 in smaller than the last, so that the joint can be graduated, avoiding the formation of a weak point – and it will look neater.

Apply the first layer of chopped strand mat and stipple on the resin with a stiff brush so that it thoroughly wets out the mat. Do the same with the remaining three pieces, laying them on top of the first and staggering the edges. Allow the resin to cure fully before subjecting the area to any stress.

Cutting and drilling

Glassfibre is very easy to work with, and for this reason cutting and grinding tools should be used with caution. It is very easy to remove too much material.

Most of the tools used to cut and drill metal can be employed for the same purpose on glassfibre. However, the gelcoat is very brittle and chips away from the cutting edge of a tool easily, especially when drilling or sawing from the rough side of the material. Where possible always work from the gel-coat side.

When sawing, it sometimes helps to stick masking tape over the saw line, and actually saw through the masking tape. Use a fine-toothed blade and put the pressure on the downstroke, easing off on the backstroke. If you have to cut through from the back, you can mark where the saw line is on the gelcoat side and cut through the gelcoat with a Stanley knife. Make several shallow cuts, rather than try to do it in one go. Obviously, make sure that the blade emerges on the waste side of the knife cut. This way, any chipping will be limited to the cut line.

If it is essential that you drill through from the back, first drill a very thin hole ($\frac{1}{32}$ in) to mark the location. Then from the front, on the gelcoat side, use a countersink bit to make a countersink *just* bigger than the final hole will be. Now the final size hole can be drilled with no risk of chipping, and the thin countersunk rim to the final hole makes a very neat finish. Use this technique of countersinking before drilling whenever you make a hole in glassfibre.

A cutting wheel being used to trim an oversize panel. It is very easy to take off too much material, so care must be taken. Note the use of goggles and mask. **(Picture courtesy Arnold Wilson)**

Template making

Template making is a technique that takes the pain out of producing any awkward-shaped panel for your kitcar. For dashboards, door trims, carpets, holes for heaters, petrol tanks, lights, in fact, on any occasion where an irregular shape needs to be marked out, make a template.

Corrugated cardboard is a good material to use, because it costs nothing and there is a plentiful supply behind your local supermarket or electronics dealer. Cardboard is easy to mark, cut and join; other suitable materials include hardboard, plastic, plywood and thick paper.

Let us suppose you have to make up a dash panel that has to fit an irregular recess in the GRP moulding.

First, take a piece of cardboard and cut it to a size that will be big enough to do the job, plus a bit for trimming – say 2 in bigger than required all round. You now need to transfer the outline of the recess in the GRP on to the cardboard. You can't measure it because of its awkward shape, but if the opening has well-defined edges you could press the cardboard firmly against them and you would get an accurate impression of the shape in the soft face of the board.

Unfortunately, in this instance the edges are rounded and they are not sharp enough to mark the cardboard. A way around this problem is to mark the perimeter of the opening with paint, so you can press the cardboard against the edge and then pull it away squarely without smearing the paint. The outline of the opening will then be on the reverse side of the cardboard. Do remember which side is which, or you could end up with a dashboard that will only fit if it is put in back-to-front. Wipe the paint from the lip of the opening with a rag moistened with white spirit.

Using a sharp knife or scissors, carefully cut on the waste side of the outline, checking the accuracy of the template by offering it up to the opening. In all probability it will need a little more trimming to make it exactly the right shape, but if you trim too much off, you can make up the size again using masking tape. If you really mess it up, use another piece of cardboard and start again.

When you are sure that the fit is just as you want it, you can transfer the shape to the timber blank, ready for cutting. At this stage it might be a good idea to mark out the instrument positions and glove

A dashboard template shown alongside the wooden dashboard before being fitted to the car.

box lid. You may need to juggle things around to get the best combination of practicality and appearance, and it may be an idea to make two or three templates to see which looks best.

Let us take another example. This time we need to cut out a shape in a glassfibre panel to take a sidelight. Accuracy is not too important, but you need to work to about 3 mm or so. The rubber gasket from the sidelight can be used as a tem-

plate and the required outline can be drawn with a chinagraph pencil or marker pen on to cardboard. If difficulty is experienced in keeping the gasket in place, spray paint can be used to give an accurate outline. Careful cutting will produce a male and female template. Using the female template will produce a slightly undersize outline, which would be useful if an exact fit was required. The male template will give an oversize outline and would be used where a clearance fit was needed.

There is a technique in boatbuilding called 'spiling'. It is used to copy

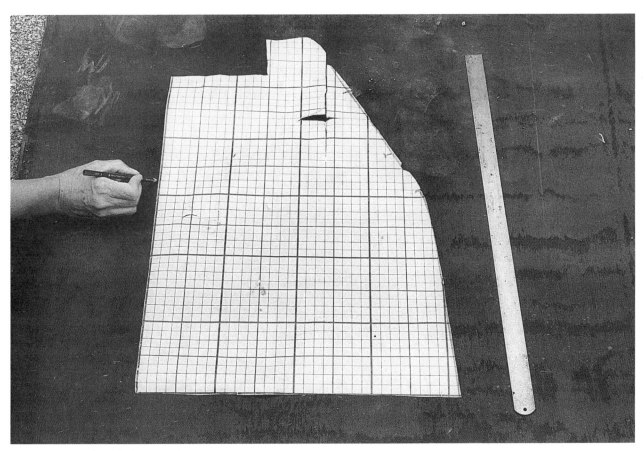

A paper template being used to mark out sheet rubber floor covering ready for cutting.

A cardboard template being used for accurate positioning of the tail light cluster on a Jago Geep.

Use spray paint to mark out the shape accurately on cardboard.

the shape of one surface on to another, usually in order to make a template.

A small gauge can be made, as illustrated, or a pair of compasses with a stiff hinge can be pressed into service.

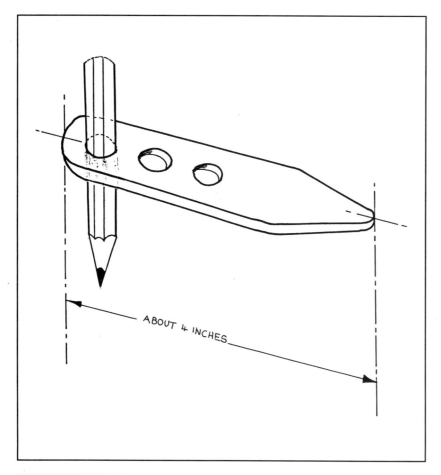

ABOUT 4 INCHES

Diagrams left: This easy-to-make gauge is useful for transferring awkward shapes on to cardboard templates.

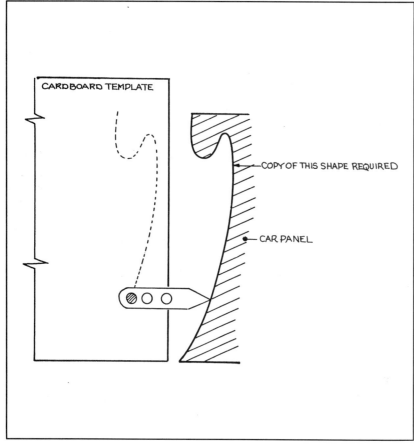

CARDBOARD TEMPLATE

COPY OF THIS SHAPE REQUIRED

CAR PANEL

CHAPTER 7:
THE PROCESS OF BUILDING

Buying a donor car

The task of buying a donor car, stripping it down and then refurbishing the various components can be time consuming, expensive and sometimes messy. So, before rushing out and buying the first rusty Cortina you clap your eyes on, take some time out to think of possible alternatives.

If your chosen kitcar uses only the mechanical components from another car, and you don't need the seats, or wiring loom, or the petrol tank, for instance, why bother to go to the trouble of buying a donor car? It is easier, and in the long run it may be cheaper, to purchase just the parts you need from a specialist supplier.

Some firms now specialize in buying low-mileage accident write-offs from insurance companies. The serviceable parts are then removed from the wreck and the components cleaned, checked and packaged to look like new. In most instances the components carry a warranty. By working closely with the kitcar manufacturers, these suppliers know exactly the components needed by the builder of a particular kit and are able to match his requirements precisely.

Alternatively, car breakers will

Some breaker's yards will supply parts that have already been removed from the car, but not many yards will look as smart as this one. **(Picture courtesy Ian Bennet)**

supply parts ready stripped from a car. These won't be checked for serviceability, and they may not even have the muck cleaned from them, but at least you are spared the inconvenience of stripping down and disposing of a donor car. Of course, no guarantee will be given either, but most breakers will happily exchange a unit if it proves to be defective.

However, that's not much consolation if the problem is only discovered after the part has been cleaned and fitted to the car. That's a chance you take and the risk can be minimized by careful inspection, testing and, if necessary, rebuilding the component before it is fitted to your car: a procedure that would have to be gone through anyway if you chose to use a donor car.

Another source of parts is through the classified columns of the kitcar magazines. Often abandoned projects are offered for sale and it is surprising what people will part with for a cash offer. Not so long ago we were able to buy every mechanical part from an MGB, together with a cherished registration number, for £250. A four-line ad in the classified column of practical car magazines could result in you obtaining the right parts for your project, really cheaply.

Having looked at the alternatives, there's a lot to be said for starting from scratch and buying a donor car. This is especially the case if you require all of the mechanical components and the trim pieces. Even if you only need a minimum of mechanical parts, there are still some compelling reasons for choosing the donor car approach.

For those working to a tight budget, buying an MoT failure can be a very economical way of obtaining the bits that are needed. Along with the obvious components, you also have a supply of odds and ends that come in very useful: a set of slave wheels and tyres that enable you to move your rolling chassis around the workshop; electrical fittings such as the interior light, fuse box and so on; all manner of nuts, bolts and self-tapping screws; various brackets and metal pieces that can be adapted for odd jobs; sound damping material and trim cloth; even the ashtray may be used.

How then do you go about choosing a donor car? What you don't do is to buy the cheapest car you can find. It is false economy to

Be wary about buying a non-runner, because it is difficult to assess its true condition.

buy a really worn out heap just because it's being virtually given away. You could spend a fortune in time and money in bringing the components you require up to a decent standard, so it is far better to spend a little more on a low-mileage vehicle.

When looking for a donor car it is, therefore, necessary to exercise the same judgement and skill as when buying any other secondhand vehicle, except that in most cases the condition of the bodywork is immaterial.

Many people pride themselves on being able to pick out a good 'un from fifty paces when buying a used car, but we have found that a structured and logical approach works best.

First double-check with the kitcar manufacturer the best donor car to obtain. For instance, the kit specification might say 'any Ford Escort Mk 1 or 2 is suitable', when in fact it is a car built after a certain date or serial number that has features that are desirable, if not essential, to have on your kitcar.

Decide what is the top limit you are prepared to pay, and only exceed that in exceptional circumstances. Start your search locally because this saves travel time and costs – first in searching for a suitable car, and then in getting your

purchase home, especially if it is not roadworthy and you have to pay the cost of transport.

If you are not successful locally and you have to search further afield, you could make use of the services of a motor engineer who will inspect the car on your behalf and report back to you. The charge for this service is around £50, but in some circumstances it could save you money and time.

It is natural to want to make a start on the project and there is a great temptation to hurry into the purchase of the donor car – but don't. Rushed decisions are often bad ones, and over-eagerness on your part is easily detected by the person selling the car and this weakens your bargaining stance. Stay cool and be clinical. The question is, where to start and what do you look for? Well, you don't buy a used car by standing ten feet away and gazing at it. Nor do you gain much by sitting behind the wheel and playing with the gear lever. The bits that you are interested in are usually encrusted with oil and mud, and either under the car or in the engine bay, so you will need to gather a few things together before you start out. You will need:

1   Something to lie on – preferably waterproof
2   A pair of overalls
3   A jack and a pair of axle stands

4 A screwdriver
5 A compression tester
6 Rag and hand cleanser
7 The checklist

In the list above, the compression tester is the only item that may require some explanation. Most people will appreciate that the compression in the cylinders of a piston engine is a reliable guide to the general health of the pistons and rings, the cylinder bores, the valves and the cylinder head.

The tool for measuring the compression is a simple pressure gauge which fits into the hole normally occupied by the sparking plug. When the engine is turned over the gauge will record the pressure in the cylinder head. A basic model costs about £12, and it is a good investment for the kitcar builder. How it is used will be described in more detail later in this chapter.

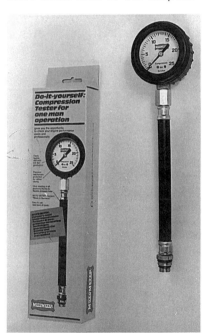

The compression tester is an invaluable part of any DIY mechanic's tool kit.

When you arrive at the car explain to the owner the tests that you would like to carry out, and ask his permission to do so. Invite him to witness the procedure and he'll probably be intrigued enough to want to do so: few people who are genuine will refuse.

Try to arrange for the car to be

BUYING A DONOR CAR - CHECKLIST		

Name of Owner ....   Year of Manufacture ....

Address ....   Engine No. ....

....   Chassis No. ....

....   Indicated Mileage ....

Telephone No. ....

Exterior Visual Inspection		**Chassis Inspection**	
Side View - Body Sag	☐	Main Members	☐
Rear Down		Out Riggers	
Front Down		Rod Locating Points	
Doors (smooth & undamaged skin)	☐	Running Gear	☐
		Attachment Points	
Rear & Front View	☐	Oil Leaks - Engine	
L/H or R/H Lean	☐	Gearbox	
Light Clusters Intact		Rear Axle	
Chrome Work Good		Rear Springs	
Wheels & Tyres (inc. spare) 1	☐	Wheel Bearings	
2	☐	Steering Linkage	
3	☐	**Road Test**	
4	☐	Engine Noise	☐
5	☐	Clutch Slip	
Interior Inspection		Hand Brake	
Doors - Bottoms	☐	Differential	
Trim		Transmission	
Window Winders		Instruments	
Seats		Wash/Wipers	
Carpets		Heater	
Fittings		Horn	
Instruments		Shock Absorbers	
Oil Pressure Warning Light		Cooling System	
Generator Warning Light		**Compression Test**	
Clutch Pedal Travel		1	☐
Brake Pedal Travel		2	☐
		3	☐
		4	☐
		Plugs 1	☐
		2	☐
		3	☐
		4	☐

standing on firm, level ground. Although we did say that you don't judge a car by gazing at it, that is just what you should do at first. Stand about 10 or 15 ft away and let your eye slowly travel over the car. Let the general impression soak in. Does it sag in the middle? Does the rear end nearly touch the ground? Walk around the car. Does it lean to one side? You should try to get the feel of the vehicle, so take your time and keep the information flow coming.

You may well wonder what the point of all this is when you are

only going to use some parts of the car. The bodyshell will be disposed of, so what does it matter if it looks old and tired? The point is, you want to start with the best possible donor car to save time, hard work and money. Sagging bodywork could well indicate broken springs; accident damage could have affected suspension geometry; and generally tatty bodywork could point towards similar neglect of the mechanical parts of the car. Be cold, be objective and above all, be aware enough to interpret the signs that are there to be read.

Now check the condition of any exterior fittings that you might be using, such as lights, door handles, windscreen wipers, indicators, doors, bumpers, and so on. Make notes about all of these things on your checklist. You probably won't buy the first car that you see, and you will require more than one copy of the checklist. So it will be an advantage to write out the parts of the list that are applicable to you and have some photocopies made.

Walk up to the car and take a close look at the wheels and tyres, even if you do not intend to use them. It is all information that is giving you a feel for the car and it will come in handy for the hard bargaining that may follow. Also, good wheels and tyres have a second-hand value that could help you offset the cost of the original purchase.

While on that subject, it is often possible to recover more than your original outlay on the donor car by selling off the parts that you don't need. A good clean engine and gearbox, complete with a set of compression figures and a test report compiled by you, could easily make a profit for you in one fell swoop.

Some kitcars use the doors from the donor car. If this applies to your kit examine each door carefully. Check the bottoms for rust and check that the exterior skin is smooth and free from corrosion. Rap the skin with your knuckles and listen for a sharp, slightly hollow sound: a dead, heavy sound indicates that body filler has been used, which could be covering a multitude of sins. Make sure that the window winding mechanism works smoothly and that the trim panels are intact.

Get in the car and sit behind the wheel. If the driver's seat is soggy, it's a fair bet that the car has covered a lot of miles. Inspect the rest of the upholstery and pay particular attention to the seats if you intend to use them.

Spend a minute or two now and review your findings up to this point. If all seems to be in order so far carry on with the inspection. On the other hand, if the messages you are getting are not good it is better

not to waste either your time, or the owner's. Politely thank him and be on your way to the next car.

Assuming all is well, make a note of the mileage and see if it corresponds with what you have found so far: record it on your checklist. Now turn on the ignition – you should have oil pressure warning light, ignition warning light and other general warning lamps showing. No oil pressure warning light could merely mean that the bulb is defective. However, it is wise to check, because it has been known for it to be disconnected so that poor oil pressure won't be detected. Start the car. It should start easily and run smoothly and both the oil pressure and ignition warning lights should go out. If the engine fails to start and you can't get it to run, then don't buy the car. With a non-runner it is impossible to check the engine, gearbox, back axle, suspension or electrics effectively, to say nothing of the heater, clutch or radiator.

While the engine is warming up check the brake and clutch pedal travel; about $\frac{1}{2}$ in free play before the pedal comes up firm is about right. Again, these are not too important for your immediate purpose, but the information all adds to the overall picture of the car.

Operate the clutch and check that you can engage gear. If the car is taxed, insured and has a current MoT, then ask for permission to take it on a test drive. The purpose of this is to enable you to test the transmission, the differential, clutch and brake operation and the engine noise.

On the road, see that the car accelerates smoothly and that the gear change is free from crunching, particularly when changing down into the lower gears: it is here that worn synchromesh will become apparent. Operate the footbrake and check that the car stops squarely and smoothly.

Listen carefully to the engine while pulling up an incline and again on the overrun – that is, when you lift your foot from the accelerator. If you can't detect any distinct engine noise in the form of a knock or rattle, the bearings are probably satisfactory.

Stop the car and apply the handbrake; engage first gear, gently lift the clutch and apply a little throttle. Again, listen for any bearing rattle. The car should not move if the handbrake is effective. There should be no initial judder from the clutch, and the engine should stall as the clutch is let out, indicating the absence of clutch slip.

To check the differential, get the car moving in top gear along a smooth piece of road at about 35 mph. Carefully listen for a rumbling noise coming from the back axle. If you have an assistant, get him to sit in the back with his ear to the rear seat squab. The thrashing noise of a worn differential is easy to detect.

After driving the car for a few minutes you will know if the gear change is smooth or not. However, it is worth checking to see if the car has a tendency to jump out of gear. Put the car into reverse, accelerate and then lift your foot off the throttle. Now do the same with the other gears. This will highlight any weakness in the gearbox.

Throughout the road test, make sure that the instruments, screen wipers, heater and light controls all operate satisfactorily.

Return to base and stop the engine. Open the bonnet and check for overheating – but do not open the radiator cap and get scalded. Hearing, feel and smell will tell you all you want to know.

If the car is unroadworthy and you are unable to test drive it, you will just have to carry out what tests you can and combine the information with the rest of your checklist. Perhaps you can find enough room off-road to check the gearbox; if so, the clutch test can be carried out, too.

Engine overheating is easy enough to detect, but the differential test will have to be tackled another way. This can be done by jacking one side of the car at the rear and gripping the rear wheel at 9 o'clock and 3 o'clock. Try to turn the wheel gently backwards and forwards; you will be able to detect some movement but this should not exceed 2 in at the rim of the wheel.

Not many kitcars use the chassis

The Citroën 2CV is one of the rare production cars still using a separate chassis. Look for corrosion in the seams on the rear horns.

from the donor car these days, but there are a few that do, such as those based on Beetle, Citroën 2CV and the Triumph Herald. So, although the following 'below stairs' inspection may not be entirely relevant, it is worth carrying out in every case. A look at the underside enables a close inspection of the suspension components and also gives you some more information about the general state of the vehicle.

Jack up the car, support it on axle stands, spread your waterproof sheet under the car, don your overalls and slide under.

Systematically inspect the chassis from front to rear, looking for signs of repair, welding, accident damage and rust. Poke about with your screwdriver, but remember that you don't own the car yet, so take reasonable care. Look for signs of fresh paint or underseal – this could indicate a cover-up job; it could also be the results of a bona fide repair.

If the vehicle has a separate chassis, it will either be the pressed-steel floorpan type as used in the Beetle and 2CV, or it may be a 'backbone', like that on the Triumph

Herald. In the Herald case, two converging main steel rails run the length of the car; these are joined by crosspieces at various intervals, and outriggers support the sides of the bodywork.

Every chassis has its weak point and the Beetle is particularly vulnerable to corrosion at the back passenger area, where the battery sits. Otherwise, it remains remarkably free from rust, thanks to there being no little nooks and crannies on the flat floor for water to sit.

The same can be said for the 2CV chassis, only in this case its weak points are the seams on the rear horns adjacent to the petrol tank. Unfortunately, the Herald chassis is subject to rust generally, especially around the outriggers. Luckily, these are easily replaced.

At the same time as inspecting the chassis, look at the suspension and steering gear to see if it is badly rusted or obviously damaged. Some surface rust must be expected. However, these are generally sturdy units and it is doubtful if rust will have advanced enough to affect their strength.

Pay particular attention to the places where the running gear is bolted to the chassis. Check the springs and dampers, too, especially leaf springs, if they are used, because broken leaves can be a nuisance to replace.

The underside inspection is a dirty job and it needs perseverance and a systematic approach, but properly carried out it can tell you a lot about the car, and possibly save you making an expensive mistake. While you're there, look for any deposits of oil. This would indicate leaky oil seals and you should make a note to take corrective action later.

Once again, pause and take stock. You have enough information now to enable you to decide whether to take the inspection another stage. If most things have appeared to be satisfactory so far, and you are beginning to warm towards the car, carry on with the final tests.

Spin each road wheel in turn and listen for a rough rumbling sound which would indicate worn bearings. At the same time, grip the wheel at 12 o'clock and 6 o'clock and try to rock it in and out. If there is a distinct movement and a slight knock, it is a sure sign of a wheel bearing defective, or out of adjustment.

Now grip the front wheels at 9 o'clock and 3 o'clock and rock again and watch the steering wheel. Any movement of the road wheel before the steering wheel moves indicates a degree of wear in the steering gear. To check the steering linkage ask someone to wiggle the steering wheel while you hold one of the road wheels. Any play in the linkage or trackrod ends will be apparent.

The final check is the compression test and this should be carried out while the engine is warm. It might seem logical to do this check immediately after the road test. It is more likely, however, that the car would be rejected because of faults found elsewhere, so it seems sensible to leave the compression test until last.

Compression pressure will vary depending on the engine make and type. Typically the 1600 cc low-compression, pushrod engine fitted to a Mk 3 Ford Cortina would have a compression pressure of 150 lb/in^2 when new, and would drop to about 135 lb/in^2 with a reasonable amount of wear.

The reading is taken with the engine turning over at crank speed, that is by the starter motor. The figure for your engine will be found in the workshop manual. However, the actual value of the compression pressure is not so important as the uniformity of readings in each cylinder.

First remove all of the sparking plugs and connect the gauge to number one cylinder. Open the throttle and turn the engine over on the starter about six revolutions and make a note of the maximum reading obtained. Carry out the same procedure on all of the cylinders in turn. All of the readings should be within 5 or 10 per cent of each other for smooth running and maximum performance.

Any variation in readings between the cylinders must be due to leakage between the cylinder head gasket, the piston rings or valves. If a low reading is recorded on two adjacent cylinders, it indicates a leaking gasket.

Any cylinder that is more than 10 lb less than the highest reading obtained from the other cylinders points to leakage past piston rings or valves. To determine which is the culprit an oil test should be carried out.

Prime each cylinder with about half an eggcup of clean engine oil. Turn the engine over half a dozen times to work the oil down the sides of the cylinder, and carry out another compression test. The oil will temporarily seal any leakage past the piston and if the compression readings increase, it indicates piston leakage. If the readings remain unaltered it shows that the pistons are fine, but the valves are leaking.

If the compression increases by 10 lb or more with the oil seal over the first reading, it is a clear case of leakage past the piston ring.

As an example, with the Cortina engine giving a normal reading of 135 lb/in^2, if one cylinder shows only 110 lb/in^2 but rises to 130 on the oil test, the condition is due to leakage past the piston. If, on the other hand, the pressure only increases by 5 or 6 lb, it suggests valve trouble.

You can now tidy everything up, analyse your compression test and enter the readings on the checklist. Now you not only have a lot of information to help you make a decision, you also have a hard bargaining tool: factual information that will help you to buy the car at the lowest possible price if you decide it's the one for you. If, however, you decide you don't want the car, you have a good yardstick to measure the next one against.

Cleaning the donor car

Having transported your donor car home you can begin the task of removing the parts that you are going to use. But before your eyes, ears and nose become gradually clogged with the dirt that rains down from above as you lie under the car trying to remove stubborn nuts and bolts, how about cleaning the underside first?

Portable pressure cleaners are quite cheap to hire and the task can be done in about a couple of hours. If possible use a steam or hot water cleaner and detergent. Failing that, a high pressure cold water cleaner works quite well. There are companies who will come to your premises and do the job for you, but our experience has been that their work has not been as thorough as we would have liked.

There are a couple of drawbacks to pressure cleaning. First, the task in itself can be quite messy. The fine mist and spray, which is inherent in the process, carries small particles of dirt and oil, so the operator can't avoid getting clothes and hair wet and dirty. Overalls are a must and an old pair of waterproof trousers and a jacket will give some protection.

The object of the exercise is to remove encrusted mud and oil from the underside of the car and the engine bay. The muck that does not end up on you will drop down on to your drive or wherever the work is being done. While this is not always a problem, if you have an immaculate drive you may not welcome it being stained.

Despite these objections, pressure cleaning is by far the quickest and easiest way to ensure decent working conditions under the car.

Whether you do the job yourself, or get someone else to do it for you, make sure that the entire area where you will be working is cleaned – not just the places around the components that you are going to remove. Encrusted dirt is everywhere, and if it is not all removed then the minute you start work anywhere under the car it will shower down on you and make life thoroughly uncomfortable.

Whether or not to clean the underside before starting to remove components will very much depend on how much gear you have to remove. For instance, if you only require the front suspension beam, then there isn't much point in spending a lot of time in making the whole underside of the car scrupulously clean.

If you decide against preparatory cleaning then take some precautions before climbing under the car. Wear a pair of goggles to protect your eyes, and a pair of overalls done up at the neck will prevent some of the muck from finding its way down your back. Some people use wide elastic bands at the wrists of their overalls – it has been known for oil to trickle quietly down the arm and form an undetected pool under the armpit.

Stripping

Some sort of mania grips people when they start stripping cars. They dive in, with the socket ratchet

The carnage only stops when there are no more bits to attack.

going like a machine gun, and nuts and bolts ricocheting off the garage walls like shrapnel. In an orgy of destruction, they shear off studs, mangle threads and hack away at innocent metal with hammer and chisel. With the excitement of the chase fuelled by a growing pile of components on the garage floor, the carnage only stops when there are no more bits to attack.

When the adrenalin stops flowing and sanity returns, the realization slowly dawns that they haven't a clue how all the parts fit together, and what bolt screws into what thread, or which bush goes where. Like shell-shocked soldiers, the unhappy destroyers stumble around listlessly picking up the odd component and looking at it in total incomprehension.

Don't let this happen to you. A little preparation and planning can save you a lot of time and trouble later.

Obtain a copy of the construction manual in advance of receiving the kit. Most manufacturers are only too happy to give you the build instructions when you place your order (assuming they actually have a construction manual, of course: if they haven't, you've no business buying the kit in the first place).

Study the manual carefully and make a note of all the components that you need to take from the

donor car. Then turn to the Haynes workshop manual and study how each part is removed. If you need special tools, buy or hire them in advance.

It really does pay to do your homework thoroughly; you can spend an hour discovering how to remove a pair of seats when a couple of minutes with a Haynes Owners Workshop Manual would have told you the procedure exactly. And it's a lot more comfortable sorting out problems while sitting in an armchair than it is lying flat on your back on a cold garage floor.

Think about the detail, too. Will you need a bonnet stay, interior light, glove box lid? When the remains of your donor car have been through the crusher it's too late to realize that half the bits you needed are now reduced to matchbox size.

Remember that some items you do not need for your build may be sold; so make a note of what you intend to save. Be realistic about this, though. While MGB and Beetle body panels in good condition will find a ready market, there's not much call for Alfa Sud door panels. Unless you have a spare barn or two, don't clutter your workshop with bits of old car that will never be used.

Collect some polythene bags: the freezer-type are best because these have a little panel on which the contents can be written. Normal practice is to replace a bolt into its

Don't forget the details when stripping the donor car; small items like the bonnet lock are easily forgotten.

concentrate entirely on the job in hand. Conversely, if you are expending half of your energy on just being there, the task is difficult to carry out satisfactorily, and becomes a chore. The moral is: make yourself comfortable.

This also applies to your state of mind. As we said earlier, building a kitcar is a leisure pursuit, and should be a pleasurable experience. It does need a certain level of commitment and dedication to see the project through, but it should not be regarded as a test of stamina.

Take your time and view each operation as a task in itself, complete it to your satisfaction, then move on to the next one. Don't feel obliged to keep going when you

correct hole, so there is no confusion when reassembly time comes. It is not always possible to do this and the bags are necessary to hold nuts, bolts and small items until they are needed. Where possible tie the bags to the main component, and always mark the contents on the outside. A note pad and pen kept handy will enable you to make notes as you go along. It is going to be some while before you reassemble the items you have removed from the donor car, and a few notes made at this stage will help you to remember how everything goes back together.

You will also need something comfortable to lie on. An old rug is better than nothing; it keeps the cold from your back and cushions the hard floor a little. Better still buy, or make, a wheeled sledge which enables you to slide effortlessly under the car. Really classy models have an adjustable headrest, but a cushion will do just as well. After half an hour of straining neck muscles, you will appreciate having your head supported at the right height.

The question of being in a comfortable working position is an important one throughout the whole project. A relaxed and unstrained posture, whether you're

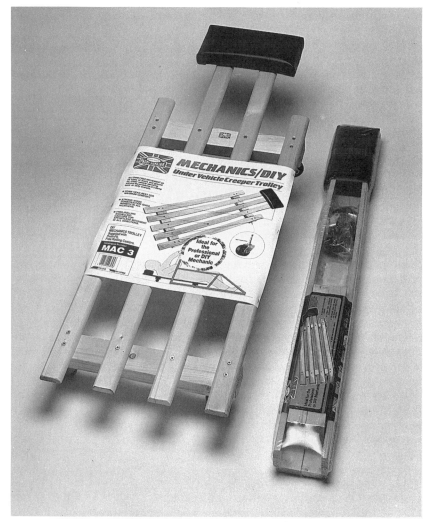

A trolley with a headrest is more than just a luxury it prevents a severe crick in the neck.

lying under the car or working in the engine bay, enables you to

feel tired or fed up. Walk away from it and go down to the pub or play a round of golf, and come back to it when you are ready. This way you will keep fresh and build a better car. 'Do it once and do it right' is not a bad motto to have on your garage wall.

It is also important to work neatly. If you don't tidy and sweep up regularly you will find yourself working in a gradually deteriorating environment, which does not encourage good workmanship. Also, you'll waste time searching for lost tools.

Back to the practicalities. You will need a can of penetrating oil and a soft brush with which to work it well into threads and crevices. You can make up your own penetrating oil a lot more cheaply than you buy it by mixing equal quantities of paraffin and old engine oil.

Another tip is to use one of the small plastic containers with a trigger spray attachment, the sort that gardeners use. Filled with the paraffin mixture this makes a handy way of soaking components with lubricant to ease the task of removal. *Be aware of a fire risk when using a spray and keep it well away from heaters or naked flame*.

One final piece of advice before we look at the actual process of stripping the car. If you haven't got one of those highly professional-looking tool cabinets on castors, buy yourself a plastic tote box – the sort divided into compartments with a handle down the middle. Think about the tools you will need for a particular job and gather them together before starting work. There's nothing more frustrating or tiring than having to make continual trips around the garage, hunting for the right tool – especially if it means sliding out from under the car every time you want something.

The first job is to disconnect and remove the battery. Then remove the doors. Although it is not strictly necessary to do this, it makes getting in and out of the car, and moving around it, a lot easier, especially if space in the garage is restricted.

Carefully remove any interior fitting you need and place small items such as door handle pins and escutcheon plates in bags. When you remove an electrical fitting, ensure the wires are clearly labelled

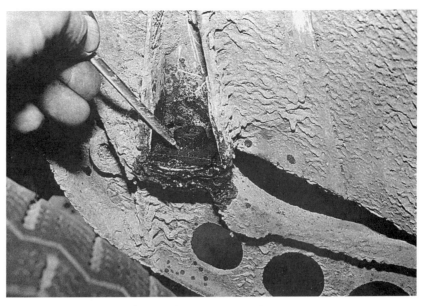

Clean the area around rusted bolts and soak overnight in penetrating oil.

by using a ballpoint pen on a masking tape sleeve.

If you haven't got one of these toolkits on wheels, a plastic tote box will do just as well.

The wiring loom

Many kitcar manufacturers offer a wiring loom as an optional extra and, in most instances, this is the sensible way to go. The cables will be the right length for the accessories to be correctly positioned and usually the loom is simpler. This is especially so with sports cars, which

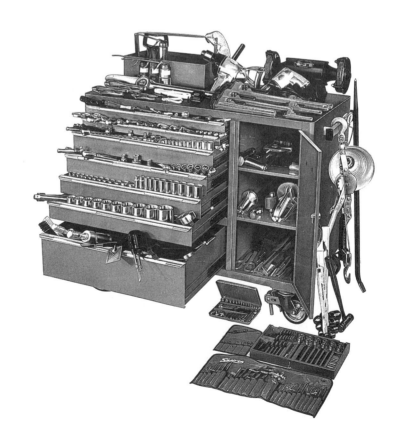

do not need the accessories found in a sophisticated family saloon.

However, if you are working on a tight budget or are building kits that use the standard electrical system from the donor car, the wiring loom will have to be re-used. Removing the wiring loom is not such a daunting task as it might at first appear.

First take out the seats and carpet from the donor car. This gives a clear and uncluttered work space and enables the wires and accessories from the instrument panel to be easily disconnected and labelled. Make sure the labelling is clear and permanent.

There are as many different electrical systems as there are cars. Some looms are split into sections, for example engine bay, cockpit and rear loom, while others are complete systems that run from one end of the car to the other. Whichever you have, the principle is the same.

Don't be put off by the appearance of the wiring system. The wires may be dirty with colours that are impossible to distinguish, but it is surprising the effect that a good wash in white spirit can have. Broken terminals and badly scuffed cables are easy to replace, and marked tie-tape can be overwound with new insulation tape.

Begin by disconnecting, not cutting, the cables to the front lights and indicator. The connections are usually via little plugs and sockets at the lampholders. Often the lights and horns are on a small loom which can be threaded through the bodywork and lifted away separately. Remove the lights and fittings from the car. Don't try and leave any fitting connected to the loom because it will become difficult to manage.

Earth cables, which are usually coloured black or brown, are connected to the bodywork at various points. These, too, should be removed.

The job of threading the wires through the bulkheads and body panels is a tedious and irritating one. The cables snag time after time as the terminals become trapped under fittings. A second pair of hands to guide the cable

The wiring loom will look something like this.

helps enormously, and you will need a little patience and perseverance.

In the engine bay, disconnect the starter, alternator, coil, distributor, water temperature sensor, oil pressure sensor, brake light switch, starter relay, control box, fuse box, and any other fitting you may have on your donor car.

At the rear of the car, remove and disconnect the rear light clusters and indicators, numberplate light and reversing lights.

Again, the components at the back of the car may be fed by a separate loom. Disconnect the fuel tank sensor, the boot and interior lights and carefully pull the loom through to the passenger compartment. It will usually be routed through the inner sill down the right-hand side of the car.

The instruments and column switches are usually connected to the loom by plugs and sockets, but sometimes the wires are connected directly to the instruments and switches. If this is the case, work methodically and label every wire; you'll be glad you did when it comes to wiring your kitcar.

Now gently pull the cables from the engine bay, if they are not connected by plug and socket, through to the passenger compartment.

There will be a big rubber grommet in the bulkhead where the cables pass through. When this has been pushed out of its hole, the cables will pass through easily.

There will now be a big untidy heap of cable in the passenger compartment – but all neatly labelled. You will also have a pile of components: horns, lights, coil and so on. Coil the loom neatly and pack it away in a box or plastic bag. Also pack the components in boxes and label them so that the contents can be seen at a glance. A trip to the back door of the supermarket will fit you up with enough apple boxes to enable you to have ready-made, matching storage units. Remove the instruments, switches and the dash panel, if appropriate, and store these items away, too.

Engine and gearbox

The removal of the engine and gearbox is usually a straightforward job which varies in detail from car to car. In the case of front engine/rear-wheel-drive cars, the two items can be removed separately or, in some instances, as a single unit. In front-wheel-drive layouts the engine and gearbox are integral and the two are removed together.

Allow yourself some time to study the workshop manual before starting work and to do some forward planning – by now you should be getting the idea of thinking ahead.

Putting that principle into practice, now is the time to loosen the wheel nuts. Sometimes they are very tight and require considerable leverage before they will move. But with the car on its wheels, and the engine and gearbox in position, it is relatively easy to put it in gear to stop it moving forwards, and use an extension bar on the wheel-brace. Try doing this when the car is jacked up and you run the risk of pulling it off its supports.

Always drain the engine and gearbox oil before removing them from the car. It is easier to do at this stage, and there is less risk of spillage. Have an engine stand, bench or trolley ready to receive these quite heavy components and make sure that you have some timber blocks ready to support the engine.

In a rear-wheel-drive car, if the engine and gearbox are being removed as a single unit, it is best to separate the two as soon as they are out of the car and stand the gearbox upright on its bellhousing with two blocks keeping the splined input drive clear of the floor. Tape some rag around the spline as further protection.

Before the big lift takes place, remove as many ancillary components from the engine, and the area around it, as possible. Items such as the starter motor, alternator, distributor, air filter and radiator are all susceptible to damage. Apart from that, their removal lightens the engine and creates more space in which to work.

For anyone who regularly works on cars, and if you are contemplating building and running a kitcar you should count yourself of that number, a mobile engine hoist is a good investment. Designed to allow the head of the hoist to be positioned right over the engine, the long, castored legs give firm support. For real ease of use go for one with a hydraulic ram lift, but a screw-jack model is just as effective and costs considerably less.

If your purse won't run to buying a crane, then hire one. At around

An engine hoist is a good investment for anyone who regularly works on cars. Alternatively one can be hired for around £10 a day.

£10 a day it is not expensive, but make sure that all your preparation work is completed before you collect it from the hire shop. This way you might be able to get away with a half-day hire charge.

We would strongly recommend that you don't try to lift heavy components using one of the small multi-part hoists that are often advertised as being suitable for this job. While they may be strong enough for the task, they rely on overhead support. This often turns out to be a structural member of the garage roof which might not be up to the job and could bring the building down about your ears.

Running gear

The car can now be placed on axle stands or trestles. Double-check the safety of this arrangement, because you are likely to be applying a lot of leverage from time to time.

The layout of each car will of course be different, but most of the kits on the market still use donor cars that have the engine at the front with the gearbox mounted directly behind it, driving the rear

wheels through a prop shaft and differential.

However, we are beginning to see the use of more modern donor cars which feature front-wheel drive and independent rear suspension. We will look at some of the more popular donor cars in greater depth later. But, while the details of stripping down each type of car will vary, the principles involved remain the same.

Some cars carry their suspension systems on subframes that can be removed complete with all components. The running gear for the Jaguar XJ6, for instance, is carried on two beams, and the front and rear systems can be removed as entire assemblies. Only four main bolts hold the MGB and VW Beetle front suspension beams, and the Cortina front end is equally simple to remove. Other cars have their components fixed to separate mounting points on the chassis and each part needs to be stripped out individually. The Ford Escort MacPherson strut front suspension is an example of this.

Working methodically from the back to the front of the car, identify the main fixings of the components you wish to remove and clean the threads with a wire brush. Lubricate the threads with penetrating oil as we have already described.

Start the stripdown by removing

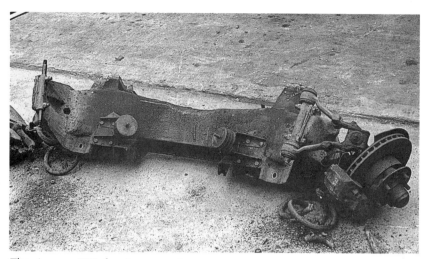

The Jaguar XJ6 front suspension beam can be removed as a complete unit.

Some rear suspension units, particularly those with a solid axle like the MGB, can be removed in their entirety.

way in.

The three main methods of springing at the rear of the car are coil springs, torsion bars and leaf springs. Treat coil springs with respect. Under compression they contain a good deal of latent energy and are quite capable of inflicting serious injury if released carelessly. Usually, lowering the rear axle on its jack will allow the spring to expand sufficiently for it to be lifted away, but if you are in any doubt, use a pair of spring compressors to keep it under control.

Leaf springs do not present any problems, but torsion bars with radius arms connecting them to the axle, as in the Beetle, need to be released with care. So follow the directions in the service manual carefully.

Disconnect the top end of the shock absorbers. You will find that two flats have been machined on the shaft at the top and you can put a spanner on these to prevent the shaft from rotating as you undo the nut above. Now remove the main fixing bolts and lower the complete assembly on to its wheels.

The front suspension is tackled in much the same way as the rear. Where the gear is carried on a

Use a spring compressor to control coil springs and torsion bars. Here a spring plate from the Beetle rear suspension is under control.

piece of tape or a blanking piece over the inlet to the rear brake cylinders will stop dirt finding its

the propshaft from the differential. If the car has a solid rear axle, support this on a trolley jack with some padding between the jack head and the differential casing. Extend the jack to take the weight of the axle but leave the wheels on the hubs.

Remove the handbrake cable assembly and disconnect the flexible brake hose. Some fluid will run out of the hose so be prepared with a container. We do not recommend the re-use of brake pipes or hoses, so no special care is needed to prevent damage to them, but a

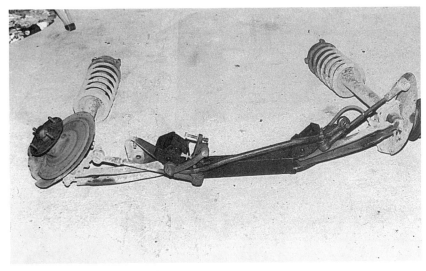

Even if the front suspension system is not self-contained, try to remove it with the uprights and steering system still connected. This MacPherson strut system can be taken to the bench and worked on.

subframe it can be removed in its entirety, supported on a trolley jack. Of course, the brake pipes and steering will have to be disconnected first.

Even where the components are not carried on a separate subframe it is still sometimes possible to remove most of the parts without stripping out every unit individually. In other words, it may be feasible to take out the uprights, steering rack, trackrods and hubs while they are still connected to one another.

To be able to do this has two advantages. Firstly, subsequent dismantling can be carried out much more easily at the bench, where everything can be seen and got at. Probably more important, however, the components can be seen in relation to one another, which makes understanding stripdown and reassembly much easier. It is so easy to forget how everything went together in the interval between dismantling the donor car and refurbishing and reassembling the parts.

Once dismantled, you may find the parts which are still connected to each other difficult to handle and store. Be careful you don't bend the trackrods; they are quite substantial but don't use them as handles. It's a good idea to make

a couple of trolleys to hold both the front and rear sub-assemblies; they can then be easily moved around the workshop.

Miscellaneous

Having removed the big components, you can now turn to any of the smaller items you may require.

The steering column, pedal assembly, brake and clutch master cylinders can be removed next but don't forget that the master cylinders may still have fluid in them. Of course, if the clutch is operated by a cable, there won't be a master cylinder. In which case the cable and its associated brackets

Drain the master cylinders and disconnect the low-level warning cables if appropriate.

should be taken off the car.

Also strip out the brake servo unit, if fitted, and the four-way brake union, which may be fitted with the brake light switch. The windscreen wiper motor, gearboxes and drive cables can sometimes be tricky to take out, and the job can be a messy one. The drive cables inside their sheaths are packed with grease, so try to avoid stripping the cables from the gearboxes. It should be possible in most cases to remove the complete unit.

Disconnect the heater controls and unbolt and remove the heater – but be careful, there may be some cooling fluid inside. Drain the fuel tank and dispose of the petrol safely. Go over the bottom of the tank with a screwdriver to check that it is sound; there is little point in removing an unserviceable tank. If it does turn out to be duff, then take out the sensor unit and locking ring. You may also need the neck and rubber connecting hose. Now go over the car and remove all of the small items you may need. Here is a reminder list:

Wing mirrors • badges • bumpers • bonnet and boot locks • door handles and catches • radio aerial • glove box lid and hinges • glove box interior moulding • interior mirror • sun visors • soundproofing material • body trim and clips • interior lights • grab handles • handbrake and cable • ashtrays • screen washer and bottle • horns

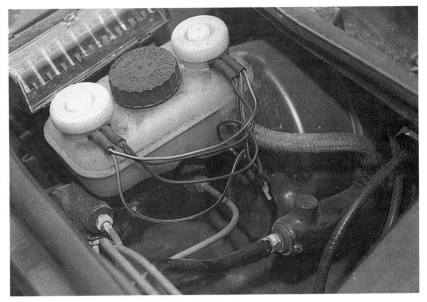

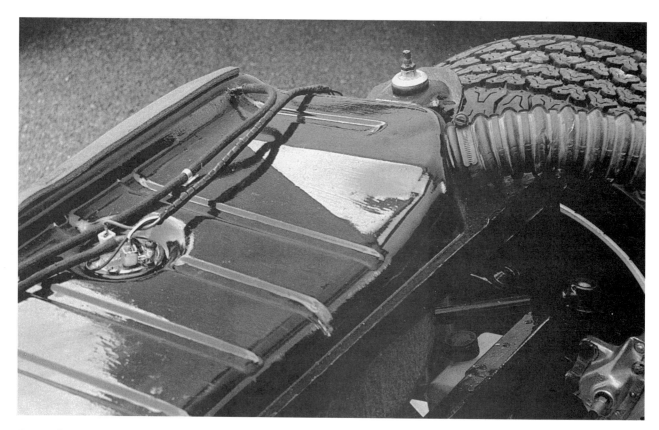

Don't forget to retain the petrol tank sensor unit and locking ring.

Labelling and storing components

We have already discussed this subject, but it does bear repeating. At the stripdown stage everything seems to be clear and you know very well that the bracket with the funny twist in it fits on the steering column and the long bolt with the slotted head goes in the third hole from the top of the bellhousing.

The head scratching starts three months later when you decide to begin rebuilding those items and you can't remember if the long bolt goes in the steering column, or if the bracket fits on the bellhousing. What's worse, you can't even remember where you put them.

A good labelling and storage system can save you a lot of time, trouble and frustration. Be methodical and where necessary identify each part with a label and store it safely in a box with the contents marked on the outside.

When storing the fuel tank don't

The unwanted donor car bodyshell can be dismantled and transported to your local tip or breaker's yard.

forget that even when empty, the fuel vapour can cause an explosion if it is ignited, so keep it well away from naked flames or sparks. Also, there is a danger that condensation will form on the inside and corrosion will start. You can prevent this

by swilling it round with some clean oil and taping up the filler neck. Write a little note to yourself on the outside of the tank reminding you to wash it out with petrol before use.

If you intend to re-use the seats, wrap them in polythene to prevent them becoming soiled or mildewed.

When you are satisfied that you have removed everything you are likely to need from the donor car then dispose of the shell. In some ways this is easier said than done. Although breaker's yards often advertise that they will call and take unwanted cars away, free of charge, they sometimes take their time about collecting the wreck.

If you have a trailer, you can transport the shell to the breaker's, and maybe you will even get a little for it. Alternatively, it is surprising how easy it is to cut a car into small pieces and carry it on a roof rack. A hammer and chisel and a hack-saw will do the job quite well. If you use a cutting torch, make sure that the petrol tank is removed and kept well away from heat and sparks; and be aware of the fire risk generally.

CHAPTER 8:
REBUILDING DONOR CAR COMPONENTS

There are some decisions to be made about quality and the standards to which you intend to work. If money, time and skill are all available in sufficient quantities, then you may decide to build your car to a standard that is as good, if not better, than a new production car; in which case you will be fitting mostly new parts.

On the other hand, you may well decide to go for a really economical build and recycle as many of the donor car parts as possible. Many people tread a middle path between the two extremes, replacing items that are vulnerable to wear and using components from the donor car that have a history of reliability.

However, what puzzles many kitcar builders is deciding how far they should go in stripping down the donor car components. Clearly, the further down the dismantling track you go, the more items you are likely to find that require replacement, and the more expensive the build is going to be.

Some builders, both amateur and professional, advocate that the minimum amount of work should be carried out on sub-assemblies. Their method is merely to clean the component, replace any obviously defective parts, spray the whole thing with a matt-black paint and fit it to the new chassis.

This is quick, cheap and any defects will show up in the first few miles of driving and can be rectified as they occur. On the other hand, subsequent faults may develop at the most inconvenient times,

The finished car will always reflect the amount of care taken over its construction – even the parts you can't see contribute to the overall quality of ride and handling. This factory-built Marlin Berlinetta looked, handled and drove like a new car.

usually on a motorway at the start of a holiday. Somehow, too this initial casual approach seems to affect the rest of the build and the whole car can end up looking tatty and incomplete.

Although we accept that people have different priorities, our method is to approach the project with two things firmly in mind. The first is that unless components are refurbished to a good standard the finished vehicle will be no better than the donor car. Secondly, the completed car is a reflection of our workmanship and we wouldn't want to be ashamed to say that we

had built it.

Consequently, our advice will always be to dismantle the donor car sub-assemblies to their component parts, replace any worn items and rebuild to an 'as good as new' standard. Later we will describe how we would go about rebuilding Jaguar and Ford running gear, which will give you an idea of what is involved.

Whatever route you choose, there are some items that should always be replaced at this stage, either because they are so cheap that the cost of fitting them is negligible compared with the time it takes to do the job once the component is reassembled; or because it is easier to do at the stripdown stage than it is later; and, perhaps most importantly, for reasons of safety.

For instance, all suspension rubbers and mounting bushes should be replaced as a matter of course. It is difficult to tell by visual inspection if they are fatigued, and they are relatively inexpensive, so it is a false economy to do otherwise – and new rubbers can transform the ride qualities of the car. Also, wheel bearings, oil seals and steering ball joints are items easily renewed when the sub-assemblies are accessible on the bench.

Never re-use brake pipes, fluid, pads or shoes. If there is any doubt about the serviceability of a brake component it should either be rebuilt using new parts or replaced.

Suspension

Perhaps the best way to explain how to go about rebuilding suspension components is to look at two of the most popular donor cars, the Jaguar XJ series and the Cortina MK 3 and 4.

Rebuilding Jaguar XJ running gear

Jaguar XJ Series running gear is a favourite choice for some of the bigger kitcars, such as Cobra replicas. It has the advantage of being of very high quality and still current, so spares are easy to

A typical Jaguar donor car.

obtain. It was designed for use on a high-performance touring car, so it is well able to cope with the requirements of a relatively light kitcar.The big Jaguar saloons weigh over 4000 lb and require a well-designed suspension system to accelerate, corner and brake such a mass; and do those things in such a way as to give a comfortable ride on good and bad road surfaces.

True, the design breaks little new ground, but it is sturdy, well put together and it works efficiently on the original car. At the front, top

The Jaguar XJ Series rear suspension and final drive fitted to a DJ Sportscars chassis.
(Picture courtesy DJ Sportscars)

and bottom wishbones keep the wheel upright while separate springs and telescopic dampers iron out the bumps. An anti-roll bar acting on the lower wishbones helps to keep the outside wheel from lifting while cornering.

At the back the differential operates two open driveshafts, which also act as a top location to stop the wheel from falling over. The lower wheel location is achieved by a bottom wishbone. Two pairs of coilover shock absorber units provide springing and damping, and on XJS models an anti-roll bar is fitted.

However, the Jaguar gear is heavy, which results in a high proportion of unsprung to sprung weight and this poses kitcar designers some problems in sorting

out ride and handling – some companies manage this better than others.

Being fully adjustable for castor and camber at the front and camber at the rear, the Jaguar suspension gives the designer and the builder a fair degree of flexibility. Both front and rear suspensions are carried on subframes which can be removed in their entirety. In fact, however, most of the kits do not use the subframes and these are discarded in favour of fitting the components directly on to the chassis. Thus the wishbones, uprights, differential and driveshafts have to be separated from the beams anyway, but this does present an ideal opportunity to carry out a refurbishing programme. Even if a particular kit did make use of the subframe, we would recommend that it was stripped down to the level we are about to describe.

Working with the appropriate Haynes Owners Workshop Manual, and with the front subframe at a convenient working height, strip out the components to the following level:

- Top and bottom wishbones
- Upper and lower balljoints
- Lower and upper inner wishbone pivots
- Stub axle carrier
- Steering arm
- Castor control shims
- Camber control shims
- Brake calipers and discs
- Trackrod ends and tie rods
- Steering box
- Hydraulic brake carrier bracket
- Anti-roll bar, saddle, keeper plates and posts
- Springs and shock absorbers
- Stub axle
- Hub, wheel bearings and seals

Note that the springs are under compression and should be treated carefully: they are quite capable of causing injury if released carelessly. To render them harmless, use spring clamps.

Different kits use a varying number of components and the

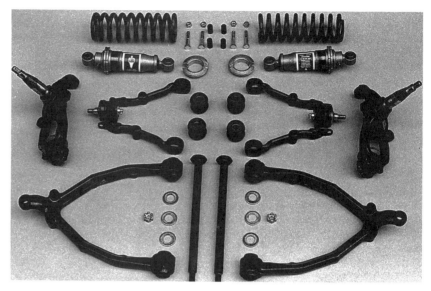

These front suspension components are ready for reassembly to the chassis. The coil/damper units are specially rated for DJ Sportscars Dax Tojeiro. **(Picture courtesy DJ Sportscars)**

above list is only quoted to give you an idea of the level of stripdown.

For instance, the Jaguar steering rack is not very often used, and sometimes the anti-roll bar is replaced with an uprated unit, or discarded altogether. Invariably, specially rated combined spring/damper units are used in place of the separate coil springs and shock absorbers of the donor car.

Hardware such as the wishbones and uprights can now be wire brushed and degreased, or shotblasted, before painting. A suitable rust-inhibiting primer, such as Finnigin's Brown Velvet, should be applied before finishing off with a top coat of black enamel or chassis paint. Be careful not to paint bearing surfaces and give the paint plenty of time to harden before handling the component.

The stub axle bearing surfaces should be inspected for wear together with the lower swivel ball joint. You will have gained some clue as to the state of these from your pre-purchase donor car inspection.

On reassembly and fitting to the chassis, we would use all new Nyloc nuts where appropriate and replace

all of the seals, bushes and rubbers. The suspension nuts should be tightened to the correct loads as quoted in the service manual, except the front fulcrum pins which should be tightened when the weight of the car is on the wheels.

No special tools are required for work on the front suspension, except perhaps for a ball joint splitter, and the task is well within the capabilities of the home mechanic, providing the procedures in the service manual are followed carefully.

Much the same procedure is adopted for the rear suspension, except that special tools are required to remove and reset the inner bearing in the hub carrier. Although it is possible to buy or borrow these tools from a Jaguar dealer, it might be best to get the firm to do the job in the workshop. The final drive unit also requires special tools and gauges, so work on this is best left to the specialists.

Many kitcars have narrower track dimensions than the original Jaguar. This poses no problems at the front end of the car, where the components are removed from the subframe and relocated on mounting points on the new chassis. All that is required is a new steering rack, together with modified steering arms, and these would normally be supplied in the kit.

It's a different story at the back. Here the track is set by the dimensions of the driveshafts, wishbones and final drive unit. To overcome

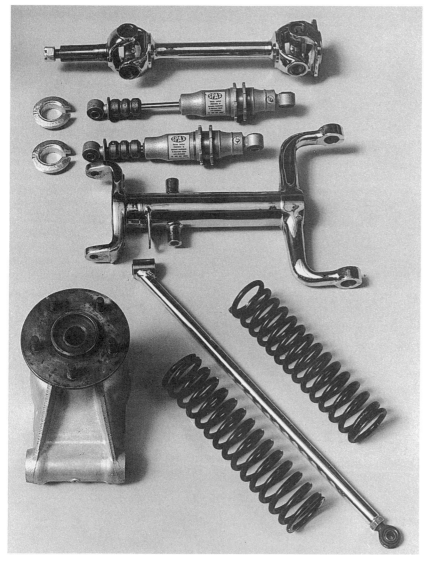

- Driveshafts
- Wishbones with inner needle rollers
- Wishbone pivot tube and rubber seals
- Pivot shafts and mountings
- Hubs and hub carriers and bearings

The lower wishbone needle roller bearings, the driveshaft universal joints and hub carrier bearings are all subject to wear and likely to be near the end of their life. Replacement at this stage is easy and we advise that new ones should be fitted as a matter of course.

Again all of the seals and rubbers should be replaced, including the front oil seal and the driveshaft seals in the final drive unit, which are easily accessible.

The large items of hardware can be given the same paint treatment as the front suspension units. Incidentally, it is a matter of personal preference which colour you paint these items. In our opinion some kitcars suffer from over-the-top paint treatment. Yellow shock absorbers, crimson wishbones and silver tie rods might please some people, but we think that black enamel paint gives a nicely understated finish.

The above brief look gives some

It is sometimes necessary to shorten rear driveshafts and wishbones to accommodate the shorter track of some kitcars. Also, the spring/damper units need to match the different weight of the kitcar. This picture shows DJ Sportscars' modified wishbones and driveshafts.
(Picture courtesy DJ Sportscars)

and the following list gives an indication of the level of stripdown:

- Differential with pinion oil seals and output shaft seals
- Brake discs and calipers

This shows the complete Jaguar front and rear suspension units fitted to a Dax chassis. Note that both front and rear Jaguar subframes have been discarded and the components fitted to pick-up points on the new chassis.

this, some kit manufacturers shorten the driveshafts and wishbones, which are either supplied with the kit or available as extras. On no account should an inexperienced welder attempt to shorten the components in the home workshop; this is a job for experts.

The remainder of the rear suspension is easy to take to pieces

idea of the work involved in rebuilding Jaguar running gear. Although XJ spares are not cheap, we feel that the cost of replacing small items at this stage represents a tiny percentage of the value of the finished car, but have a huge effect on its performance and comfort. The extra time and work involved is an investment both in terms of reliability and ultimate value.

Rebuilding Mk 3 and 4 Ford Cortina running gear

In many ways, the Ford Cortina is at the opposite end of the scale to the Jaguar. It is less expensive, it doesn't weigh as much and it is not so sophisticated. It is these qualities that, in some ways, make it a better choice for a donor car than the Big Cat. People make the mistake of thinking that if it's Jaguar, it has to be good: it is good, but not for every purpose.

As we have already indicated, most kitcars are very much lighter than their production equivalent, up to 50 per cent in some cases, and the less weighty Cortina suspension components are often more suited to these vehicles. Obviously, this brings about a favourable ratio of unsprung to sprung weight. True, a solid rear axle has its limitations, but properly located it can be very effective, as Lotus proved by using it in the Seven.

The front suspension comprises unequal-length swinging arms, coil springs and hydraulic shock absorbers. An anti-roll bar acts on the lower arms and is connected to tie bars, which can be adjusted to alter the position of the complete suspension system in a fore and aft plane. This makes it easy to control the castor angle, but the camber angle on the donor car is fixed at manufacture.

The entire suspension is carried on a beam which is easily detachable from the donor car. Some kitcars use the suspension complete with the beam, others merely have individual components bolted directly on to the new chassis.

Despite being made mainly from pressed steel components, the Cortina suspension is rugged and

Above: A typical Ford Cortina donor car.

Ford Cortina front suspension comprises coil/damper units acting on swinging arms of unequal length.

works well. With careful matching of springs and dampers, and correctly designed steering geometry, it can be made to perform much better than its origins might suggest.

There are no particular problems in stripping down the front end and

New coil/damper units replace the Ford units but otherwise the set-up remains unchanged when it is fitted to the Wildcat chassis.
(Picture courtesy JPR Cars)

there is no reason not to take apart the whole unit, replace any worn components and carry out the paint treatment as described for the Jaguar donor car. This will have to be done in any case if only the components, and not the entire beam, are used on the kitcar; and most kits specify the use of special springs and damper units, and the suspension will need to be partly stripped down to carry out the change-over. Don't forget to use the correct tool for compressing the springs, and be careful how they are handled.

The rubbers, and there are lots of them, seem to be prone to deterioration and can be badly fatigued even though they might appear to be in good condition, so change them all. We can't stress often enough what a difference new rubbers can make to the ride and handling – replacing them gives the vehicle the feel of a new car.

Check the stub axle upper and lower ball joints because now is the time to replace them if there is any doubt about their serviceability: the rubber gaiter is especially prone to cracking and splitting.

The semi-floating rear axle is a sturdily built unit capable of taking

Only the coil springs are replaced by specially rated ones when the rear axle is fitted to the Wildcat. **(Picture courtesy JPR Cars).**

a lot of abuse and it is well able to handle the power from tuned Pinto two-litre and V6 engines.

However, it is not the strength of the axle but the ratio of the crown wheel and pinion that the kitcar builder is primarily interested in. Nevertheless, the final drive cannot be looked at in isolation; the gearbox ratios have to be considered, too. Therefore it is the combined ratios of the gearbox and differential that are important. While most kitcar manufacturers have calculated these, and are able to advise the builder on the best combinations, a few companies are vague about which to go for. This is partly due to the fact that sometimes the choice of gearbox depends upon the customer and, therefore, it may be his responsibility to select the correct axle ratio.

Gearbox and final drive ratios are quoted in the form of a number such as 3.1:1. In the case of the final drive of the differential this means that the propeller shaft turns 3.1 times for every revolution of the road wheels. Similarly, for a gear in the gearbox with a ratio of 2.8:1, the engine will turn 2.8 times for every prop shaft revolution. To calculate the final effect at the road wheels of this combination simply multiply the two ratios: 2.8x3.1 = 8.689 (the overall gear ratio). The road wheels turn once for every 8.68 revs of the engine. An easy

way to calculate the road speed in any gear is to use the formula:

$$\frac{rpm \times tyre\ circumference}{overall\ gear\ ratio \times 1036}$$

The tyre circumference should be calculated using a measurement taken from the centre of the tyre to the ground, and it should be noted that this will be different from the measurement taken across the tyre with it under load.

Bear in mind that your choice of ratios should work to give you the type of performance you require from the car. Like all things on this earth, you don't get anything for nothing and a very high top speed will only be achieved at the expense of acceleration and, conversely, blistering acceleration will have the engine running out of revs very quickly and this will result in a poor top speed.

It is quite possible to change gearbox ratios, but it is not an easy job and the most sensible way to achieve the performance characteristics you want is to change the final drive ratio, and – or – the tyre size. Axle ratios on the Cortina vary from 4.11:1 on the 1300 to 3.44:1 on the 2-litre car. Kit manufacturers will, it is to be hoped, tell you which is the preferred ratio for your car. Obviously, the numerically higher ratio will produce faster acceleration through the gears, while the lower ratio will return a better fuel consumption and a higher potential top speed.

The builder using the Cortina as a donor car is fortunate in having a wide choice of final drive ratios, because in addition to having the Mk 3 and 4 range of differentials available, there is also the choice of some axles from the Escort and Zephyr/Zodiac, which are directly interchangeable with the Cortina unit.

Top and bottom radius arms each side locate the solid axle (on the Mk 2 and early Mk 3s leaf springs were used). The lower arm controls movement in a fore and aft plane and the top arm, being diagonally mounted, limits any sideways travel that may be generated during cornering. Although the system works quite well on the Ford, the rubber

Another view of the entire front suspension arrangement on the Wildcat. The tie rods, which give castor adjustment as well as locating the suspension fore and aft, can be clearly seen, as can the anti-roll bar and its mountings.

bushes have to work hard for a living and are subject to considerable wear. This of course causes a deterioration in the performance of the suspension.

Consequently, some kitcar manufacturers replace the radius arms with a five link system comprising top and bottom parallel links each side and a Panhard rod. The separate coil springs and shock absorbers used on the Cortina are replaced by coil/damper units which are usually specially rated for the car. This is a very effective treatment that results in a well-behaved back end. If the original arms are retained, all the rubbers should be replaced. Similarly, when the axle is on the bench and at a convenient height to work on, change the pinion oil seal. It is possible to strip the differential completely, but special tools are necessary to ensure that the crown wheel and pinion mesh correctly. If this is not done accurately then the back axle will sound very noisy. Generally, if your pre-purchase inspection detected no obvious faults then leave well alone.

The Steering

Most steering systems appear to be simple and straightforward, but in fact getting the steering right presents one of the biggest headaches for the kitcar designer. Steering and suspension design factors are so dependent on one another that both should be designed at the same time. However, many kitcars use the suspension system from one donor car, the steering rack from another and, maybe, trackrods from yet a third. Amalgamating all these parts to make a homogeneous whole is not easy – but that's the designer's problem. For the purposes of this book we must assume that he's got it right. From the builder's point of view, if you test the car before buying the kit, as we advise, you will know if the steering is light and sensitive with plenty of feedback. You will have checked that there is just the right amount of castor to give a comfortable self-centring action, and that excessive bump steer does not cause the car to jump about all over the road.

The reason manufacturers use such a mixture of parts is that the kitcar, especially if it's a replica, is likely to have a different track measurement from that of the donor car. Simply altering the length of the steering arms is not sufficient. For instance, lengthening the arms will slow the steering and give it a dead, insensitive feel and require more steering wheel rotation to go round the same corner – this is quite a noticeable fault on some kitcars. Shortening the arms gives quicker, more sensitive steering, but it is heavier and more difficult to control.

There are other steering systems but the rack and pinion is preferred because it is compact, reliable and very positive in operation. Illustrated here is the rack, steering arms, trackrods and ends.

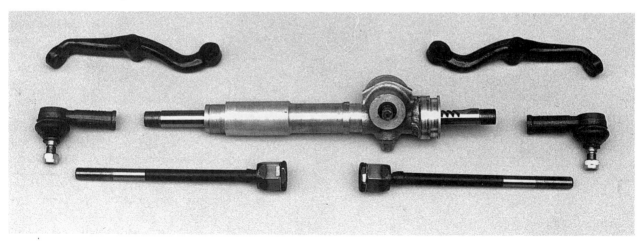

Often the steering column needs re-routing to clear obstructions in the engine bay. This is carried out by using universal joints linking one or more extension pieces. This has a side effect of giving an additional safety factor; in the event of a frontal impact the steering column is less likely to be shoved into the driver's chest.

A point to watch for is that the steering column extensions should be both splined and bolted to the universal joints for safety. Some manufacturers specify that the extensions should be welded to the universal joints. This is a cheap way of getting out of doing the job properly and should be avoided. It takes an expert to weld the casting of the universal joint satisfactorily to the mild steel extension piece, and it is not a job for the home builder.

It is becoming more common for manufacturers to supply a complete steering package either as part of the kit, or as an optional extra. Typically, this would consist of a standard rack, say MGB or Dolomite; steering arms that have been specially made to suit the track of the car, complete with ball joints; and a steering column extension and universal joints.

Laid out here is a complete steering system.

Obviously, there is no need to service or refurbish any of these items as the critical parts should all be new or rebuilt. Some kits do use some, or all, of the donor car steering parts and where this is the case, they should be carefully checked and rebuilt.

It is possible to adjust some steering boxes and the appropriate service manual will explain the procedure, but very worn units should be renewed. Look out for split and perished rubber boots and replace these where necessary. Wear in ball joints is difficult to detect when they are not connected to the steering system but your painstaking pre-purchase check will have highlighted any problems here and you can easily

The Beetle uses a worm and roller system and this has the advantage of being adjustable.

replace these at this stage if necessary.

Despite the amount of leverage involved in moving the front wheels via linkages, and what is effectively a gear train, the whole steering set-up is easily brought to a halt, or at least stiffened up drastically, by any binding in the system. So double-check that everything is free to move smoothly. We recently tested a car that was completely spoiled by dead, insensitive steering. The problem turned out to be a column bush that was ever so slightly tight. We hate to think how many customers had been put off buying the kit because of this simple fault in the steering gear of the demonstration car.

The steering components can be wire brushed and painted but make sure that the threads on the track-rod ends, adjacent to the ball joints, are free from paint and lightly greased. Finally, use new split pins on any castellated nuts, or new Nyloc nuts if these are fitted.

Photographs right: The steering rack being removed from an MGB donor car and refitted to the rebuilt front beam.

Brakes

Everyone appreciates the need to have effective and reliable brakes, yet time and again kitcar builders seem to choose to economize in this area. The easy explanation for this is that brake components tend to be expensive. We believe, however, that there is also a perverse logic that exists in people's minds and makes them wary of tackling a job that is crucial to safety. In fact, brake components are not complicated and, tackled sensibly, a complete overhaul of the system is well within the scope of the amateur mechanic.

Once again we must point you in the direction of the relevant Haynes Owners Workshop Manual. Within its pages you will find detailed procedures for every operation. It is not necessary, or practical, to attempt a step-by-step description of every job for all systems here. So

we will just give an outline of how to tackle the overhaul of a typical disc or drum layout.

First discard the brake pipes, fluid, pads and shoes but retain any T-pieces and the brake light switch. Clean all of the components with a wire brush and wipe them clean with a rag dipped in paraffin or white spirit. Keep oil and grease away from all brake components.

Some early cars were fitted with a single circuit system – the brake unit for each wheel was fed with hydraulic fluid from one source – and a leak anywhere in the line would cause all of the brakes to fail. Later cars had the much safer

dual-circuit system fitted; if a leak occurs in one line, only the brakes on two wheels are put out of action.

If your donor car has a single-circuit brake layout fitted, then we strongly recommend that you change to a dual-circuit arrangement. It means changing the single master cylinder to a tandem-type, and changing the layout of the brake pipes, but the task is a simple one (see Chapter 10). So think about this before proceeding with the brake refurbishing programme.

Inspect the brake master cylinder. This may have an integral reservoir or be attached to a servo unit. Look

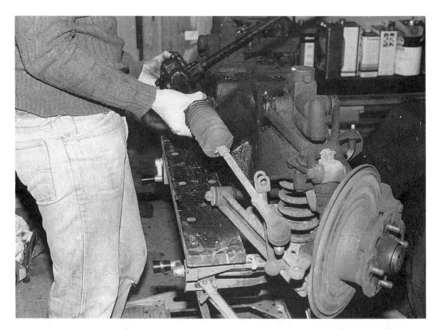

A dual circuit master cylinder with low brake fluid warning incorporated.

for fluid leaking from around the operating rod, which will tend to collect inside the rubber boot. If fluid is leaking out then you have the choice of refurbishing the unit or buying a new, or rebuilt, master cylinder. A new part will cost perhaps £40; a set of seals and springs, all boxed neatly in a kit, will set you back about £5.

Before rushing out to buy the repair kit, however, check first that the part is in good enough condition to make a rebuild worthwhile. Follow the stripdown procedure carefully in the manual. Use a note pad to sketch the way the seals fit in the barrel and make a note on the order of the way things come apart, so that you can be sure to fit them together the right way round. It is obviously important to prevent any foreign matter entering the master cylinder, or any other brake component for that matter. We always spread clean cloth over the bench, but clean newspaper will do just as well, and use lint-free cloth to wipe out the inside of the barrel.

Inspect the inside of the bore for ridges and scratches: the barrel should be completely smooth and polished. If you have any doubts at all, reject the whole unit and buy a new master cylinder. If it seems in order then go and buy a repair kit and reassemble the unit using

the new parts supplied. During the rebuild, use clean brake fluid to lubricate the parts, and nothing else. The whole job should take less than an hour.

A badly corroded or scored disc should be discarded. Discs and drums can be skimmed. We don't like the practice, but if you decide to go ahead, be sure there is enough material left to conduct the heat away. **(Picture courtesy - Arnold Wilson)**

Carry out the same procedure with the rear brake cylinders. If these show any signs of leaking, you may decide to refurbish them anyway, just to be sure that they are not going to let you down later. Inspect the discs and the rear drums for severe wear and localized grooving. During a long, hard life the faces which the pads and shoes bear on will gradually wear down and a step will form in the metal. While a small amount of wear is acceptable (anything up to $\frac{1}{16}$ in is

all right), a really badly worn surface will affect the braking. Similarly, if the brake pads or shoes have been allowed to wear down to the backing plates they are bonded to, metal-to-metal contact occurs and, again, the surface of the disc or drum will become grooved. This in turn will cause uneven wear of the brake pads and shoes.

It is possible to have some discs and drums turned down to present a new surface to the pads. Where this can be done the disc will be stamped with the minimum thickness, and the drum with the maximum allowable circumference. These dimensions should not be exceeded under any circumstances. Sufficient thickness of metal must be retained to allow the heat to be conducted away swiftly, and a thin disc or drum will simply overheat and cause brake fade.

Neither of us agrees with the practice of skimming discs and drums, and we do not recommend it. Unless it is competently carried out, not only is there a danger that too much metal will be removed, but it could result in an out of balance unit and this probably wouldn't be detected until the car is on the road.

Front calipers are expensive to replace and unless the actual housing is damaged, there is really no reason why they should not be refurbished. Like the master cylinder and rear brake cylinders, kits of parts are available to enable the seals and dust covers to be replaced at a fraction of the cost of a new unit. New pistons are available, too, so a complete rebuild of the caliper is possible.

If the car has been standing for any length of time the biggest problem is removing the pistons. Before you do anything, note the position of the cut-outs in the face of the piston. The anti-squeal shims fit into these and it is important that they are reassembled the correct way round. Sometimes it is possible to tap the sides of the caliper with a hide or copper mallet and the piston will drop out of its housing. If it does this for you, it must be your lucky day and it might be worth considering a venturesome bet. Usually, it remains

Try using Mole grips to pull the piston from its housing, or lever it out with screwdrivers. **(Picture courtesy Arnold Wilson)**

obstinately stuck in its housing.

Next, using a couple of screwdrivers with the heads taped over and with one each side, try to lever out the piston. The taped heads prevent damage to the piston sides, but still use extreme caution because it is very easy to chip pieces from the casting. If you get the feeling that it is going to take a stick of dynamite to get things moving, don't do it. Try our method instead.

Obtain a single-circuit master

cylinder and reservoir from the scrapyard, or use your donor car item. Bolt the master cylinder to a board and make up a lever about 18 in long to operate the piston of the cylinder. Blank off any unwanted outlets of the master cylinder and leave just one, which you can connect up via a piece of pipe, saved from the stripdown, to the caliper. Plumb in the reservoir and fill it with fluid.

Now pump away on your lever and watch one of the pistons start

Using a pair of clamps and two pieces of steel to prevent one piston from moving while freeing the other.

to move. Place a piece of wood between the pistons so that the first one to move does not come all of the way out, but nearly so. Work this one around a little to make sure that it is free and then push it back into its housing. This one will now come out fairly easily when the time comes; the trick is to free the other one.

Wrap a number of turns of soft wire (you may need a lot of it) around the loose piston and the body of the caliper, to stop it moving. Or, if you want to be sophisticated about it, use two strips of steel and a couple of G clamps to restrain the piston. Pump away again and watch the second piston slide from its housing. You can now remove the wire and ease out the first piston. This may sound complicated, but in fact it's easier to do than it is to describe and sometimes it's the only way to get the job done.

Of course, all this trouble could have been saved by thinking ahead when dismantling the donor car. Before removing the brake components, take out the pads from each caliper and pump the brakes. This will push the pistons further out of their housing than usual and this is enough to free them.

Wash the T-pieces and unions which were saved in the stripdown

Replacing the piston dust covers.

with brake fluid and ensure that the internal bores are bright and clean. Dry them and pack them away in a polythene bag until needed. Similarly, clean the brake light switch, which might be located either in a four-way union or on the master cylinder, and pack it away, too.

Disc brakes have an advantage over drums because they operate in an air flow and so are more easily cooled. Additionally there is a large area of metal to conduct away the heat that is generated by a relatively small contact area of the pads. The drawback is that the pads, being small, require a high

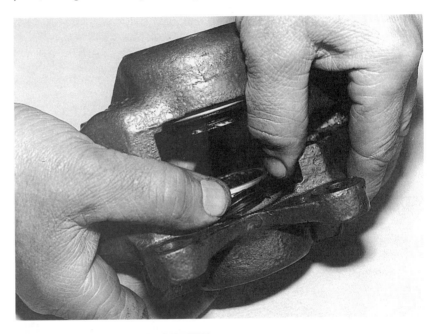

hydraulic pressure to be effective. Consequently, most production cars use servo assistance to reduce the effort necessary at the foot pedal.

Kitcars, however, are much lighter than the donor cars and less braking effort is required, so some kit manufacturers advise that the servo is dispensed with. This is because overbraking can be just as dangerous as underbraking if the wheels lock with only moderate pressure on the brake pedal.

The servo, if retained, can also be serviced but although repair kits are available, special tools are sometimes necessary and it is not always

Above: A dual circuit brake master cylinder complete with integral servo. **(Picture courtesy Arnold Wilson)**

easy to borrow them. We feel that the home builder might find the best course is either to fit a reconditioned unit, or pay a visit to the breaker's.

Maximum retardation occurs just before the wheels lock up and a skilled driver can pump his brakes to keep them on the limit when he is pressing on or in an emergency. (ABS achieves the same thing automatically for the less skilled driver.) Inevitably under some circumstances heavy application of the brakes on non-ABS vehicles will cause the wheels to lock. In these circumstances the car is easier to control if the front wheels lock up before the rear.

This can be achieved by limiting the pressure to the rear brake circuit. This is done by a pressure-limiting valve (as on the Mini and Chevette, for example) or by reducing the piston diameters in the rear wheel cylinders. Where a pressure-limiting valve is fitted, it may be incorporated in the master cylinder or fitted as a separate item in the rear wheel hydraulic circuit.

If a pressure-limiting valve is fitted, it is obvious that the different braking characteristics of the kitcar to the donor car will require the valve to be adjusted. Not all valves are adjustable, however, and kitcar manufacturers solve the problem by fitting wheel cylinders of different bore. You should be aware of this and consult the maker's construction manual or talk directly to the kitcar manufacturer. Meanwhile, just clean the valve externally and blank the inlet and outlet nipples to prevent dirt entering.

Engine and gearbox

There are so many engine and gearbox combinations available to the kitcar builder that to try to describe each one, with details on how best to tune it for performance and reliability, would be a Herculean task. Instead, the purpose of this section is to give some general advice about choosing and preparing an engine and gearbox.

Your kitcar will have been designed to accept a certain power unit and drive train. Some manufacturers offer a whole range of options; others give no choice at all and say that you must fit a certain engine; still others say that any engine and gearbox will fit into their cars.

Whatever the makers' recommendations, it makes sense to take notice of their advice. If the designer has done his job right, the car will be a harmonious blend of components that come together as a single entity, with the engine and gearbox dovetailing into the overall concept to give the car a balanced performance. Put in a big

The DJ Sportscars Supertube chassis is designed to take the big Jaguar V12 power unit, but trying to fit a similar-sized engine to a smaller car could well overpower the vehicle and unbalance it.

block V8 in place of a crossflow Ford and the whole poise of the car is likely to be spoiled. Front-to-rear weight ratios, suspension, braking and handling characteristics will all alter, and usually for the worse. What may have been a sweet car that was a delight to drive will most likely turn into a bad natured beast, a real handful to control. If you can, resist the urge to fit a bigger engine than the design calls for just for the sake of it. It's a similar story with the gearbox. We have already talked about ensuring the correct ratio match between gearbox, engine and axle. Again, unless you are experienced it is better not to experiment with combinations that are outside the manufacturer's recommendations. Straight-cut gears are fine on the race track but not suitable for normal roadwork.

It may be stating the obvious to say that you should stick with the maker's recommendations, but every company can quote instances of customers who go to great trouble and expense to fit totally inappropriate power units and gearboxes in their cars. Rarely is it a case of wanting to go smaller: bigger, more horsepower and more grunt, is invariably the cry.

If you must have more power,

Light, and very tunable, the Rover V8 is a favourite of kitcar builders.

can easily halve the cost of a good engine rebuild.

We stress the word 'good'. Beware the advertisements in the motoring press which appear to offer rebuilt engines at a cost that is less than you would pay for the parts alone. We've been down that route before – and regretted it. There is no way of telling what you are getting for your money. It is difficult to assess the quality of a rebuilt engine without stripping it down and inspecting it. Even then it isn't easy to spot mismatched pistons and inaccurate machine work. Don't be fooled by a smart paint job and new gaskets. If you intend to buy a reconditioned engine then go for a factory-built unit, or buy from a company with an established reputation.

Back to the tuning. There are a few basic rules that are so basic that they are often ignored:

1 First assess your needs. Be coldly analytical about the type of driving you really do. Don't dream, and don't be over- ambitious.

2 The law of diminishing returns applies to engine tuning. The first extra 10 hp can be had for very little outlay in terms of time or money; the next added 10 hp could cost three times as much; and the next 10 could cost 20 times as much. Do the easy things first and you will find that they are usually the most productive.

3 Seldom is the biggest, or most expensive, the best.

4 For a sensible road car, moderation is the key. In other words, aim for a moderate increase in power without losing too much traction at low revs.

5 A planned approach using components that are compatible with one another is vital.

6 The engine must be in good condition before any tuning is begun.

Many people will be quite content to fit the standard engine from the donor car, especially if the pre-

the easiest, and often the cheapest, way to get it is to fit an uprated version of the standard engine. Most GT or Sports versions weigh no more than the basic unit and give a significant increase in power output. Also, some powerful lightweight alloy engines weigh no more than a unit with a cast- iron block and head. Thus a significant increase in performance is available for no weight penalty.

That is not to say that you shouldn't try to get the best out of the standard engine. For reasons of cost, all stock power units are manufactured to tolerances that leave plenty of room for improvement. There are a whole host of books to tell you how to tune your engine and you should do some careful reading before spending any money on expensive carburettors and other go-faster goodies.

However, even if you are inexperienced, there is no reason why you should not be able to strip down, modify and rebuild an engine. With the aid of a good reference book, the right tools and a careful, methodical approach you can save a lot of money. By providing the labour and doing the easy tasks yourself, then sending out the work that needs specialist knowledge and machine tools, you

Right: Any engine looks better for a good clean and paint and any subsequent oil leaks are then easier to trace.

purchase inspection showed it to be in good condition. A straight swap from donor to kitcar is perfectly possible, but it is best to clean, paint and at least service the engine before installing it.

Before carrying out work on the engine, attend to any oil leaks that your inspection will have revealed. A quick way to spoil a lot of hard work is to fit a unit that spews oil over a pristine engine bay – to say nothing of messing up the drive or the garage floor. Usually oil leaks can be traced to faulty gaskets, such as on the sump or timing cover, but if you are unlucky it may be an oil seal, which requires a certain amount of dismantling to get at. A nuisance certainly, but fix it while the engine is out of the car and accessible.

Obviously, you should also attend to any other problems your inspection revealed, such as timing chain or water pump replacement. If you have not already done so, remove the ancillary items such as the alternator, starter motor and distributor. Get to work with a wire brush, and perhaps a toothbrush, with some proprietary degreasing agent, such as Gunk, and thoroughly clean the external casting.

If you have access to a high-pressure hose so much the better,

Above and left: The Jaguar in-line six is exactly the right engine to fit in the LR Roadsters D-Type replica.

but tape any inlets that may allow water to enter the engine and leave the plugs in place. There are some cleaning solutions that can be added to the water to bring aluminium castings up like new. Your supplier or hire shop will be able to advise you on these, but some are acid-based and you should always use these in strict accordance with the instructions. Take particular care to protect your eyes and lungs when using an atomized spray of any sort. While you have the hose out, flush the waterways with clean water.

Carry out a normal service, but don't fill the sump yet. Now is the time to carry out any modifications such as fitting the adaptors for a remote oil filter, or making up alternator brackets if you intend to reposition it. If you plan to fit electronic ignition, do this when the engine is installed and has been test run; that way you won't blame your conversion if the engine fails to run properly on the initial start. Discard all the hoses unless they really are in tip-top condition.

Paint the engine block with a high temperature, oil-resistant paint. There are plenty of proprietary brands available. Here again, you can be as adventurous as you like with your choice of colour, but if you go for one of the brighter shades just remember that you are going to have to live with it for some time.

Take your time and use masking tape if necessary to keep paint clear of machined surfaces where gaskets fit; and don't paint over everything in sight – just the block. It's a long and painstaking job, but if it is done properly it really enhances the appearance of the engine bay.

The same procedure can be carried out with the gearbox. Make sure that the spline is taped over to protect it, and stand the unit on a couple of blocks of wood to make it easy to work on. If you found oil inside the bellhousing it most likely came from a defective input shaft oil seal, and if this is the case it should be changed: the last thing you need is oil on the clutchplate.

Propeller shaft

These seemingly uncomplicated pieces of hardware sometimes cause a lot of anxiety. It's fine if the donor car item is used unmodified in the kitcar, but often manufacturers state that a shortened, or lengthened, shaft is necessary without elaborating on where to obtain one, or what length is required.

Don't attempt to modify a propshaft yourself. If it should break at 70 mph, it can be distinctly uncom-

fortable to have a couple of feet of metal knocking on the tunnel, trying to come in. It is a job for professionals: it needs to be modified properly and the shaft balanced afterwards. A glance through any practical motoring magazine, or the Yellow Pages, will give you the name and address of your local expert.

If you are unsure of the required propeller shaft length because you are fitting a non-standard gearbox or back axle, then measure from the flange on the axle to the rear face of the gearbox output shaft housing. Give this measurement to your propshaft man and tell him exactly what it is. He will also need to know the type of engine, gearbox and back axle fitted so that he can supply the correct interfaces between the units. The gearbox to propshaft connection may be made via a reverse sleeve or a spline, and the propshaft is usually connected to the back axle via a flange. All of the necessary components, such as universal joints, splines and flanges, can be supplied.

A long propeller shaft, say 50 in, would normally be supplied in two halves with a centre bearing, but most kitcars use single shafts which are less than 30 in long.

Another reason for going to a specialist is that he will take the power output of the engine into account and make the shaft out of material of the correct diameter and wall thickness. We have seen more than one propeller shaft that has been twisted like a stick of

liquorice because it was unable to handle the torque imposed by the combination of a powerful engine, wide rubber and a dry surface.

Having said all that, it is quite likely that you will be using the original item, complete with fittings from the donor car. Apart from severe corrosion of the shaft itself, the only area where mechanical problems are likely to be encountered is in the universal joints.

Trouble can be easily detected by checking for movement between the two flanges of the universal joint. Grasp the prop shaft in one hand and the outer flange of the joint in the other and try to turn your hands in opposite directions first one way and then the other. Any movement between the shaft and flange, or a clicking noise in the needle bearings, indicates wear.

Consult your Workshop Manual to see if new needle roller bearings can be fitted. In some cases this is a simple job and the manual will give a step by step guide. In others, repair is not possible and a faulty bearing will mean the replacement of the whole assembly.

If you decide to paint the propshaft, and there is no reason why you shouldn't, apply an even coat of paint and don't disturb any balancing weights. These take the form of small squares of metal which are tack welded to the outside of the tube wall.

This sight is becoming rare as Beetles are considered to be collectable.

The Beetle

In many ways the VW Beetle is unique – some would call it old-fashioned and anachronistic, and we wouldn't argue with that. But we must confess to having a soft spot for what is undoubtedly the car that started it all. The Californian beach buggy may have been the forerunner of today's kitcars but that, and fond memories, aren't the reason why we have given it its own section here. The fact is, the Beetle is still a popular donor car, with over 50 kits on the market based on its mechanical components.

There are dozens of books available describing how to modify and improve the performance of the stock Beetle – and many companies who supply the hardware to do it. Therefore we won't be covering that side of things here. Rather, we will take a brief look at the mechanics of the car and describe one or two modifications of particular interest to the kitcar builder.

The Beetle's pressed steel floorpan is remarkably corrosion-free, but it relies on the bodywork to improve its stiffness. This before-and-after shot shows what a little hard graft can do.

There are a number of reasons why the Beetle is so popular as a donor car. For a start, more Beetles were made than any other car: over 20 million in Germany and production is continuing in South America and Africa. So despite the fact that they are now being bought for restoration projects, there are still plenty of them about. The mechanics are simple and very robust, which makes them easy to work on; spares are extremely cheap and easy to obtain; and very few special tools are required when working on the car. The pressed steel floorpan is remarkably corrosion-resistant; so even if the bodywork is badly rusted and the car thrown on the scrapheap, it probably is still usable as a donor car.

The drawback – and there always is one – is that in its standard form the Beetle is certainly no burner of rubber. Reliable it is; fast it most certainly is not. Also, it does not handle particularly well, with the swing axles tending to jack up on tight corners. However, something can be done to improve these disadvantages and, on balance, the good points outweigh the bad.

Choosing a donor car

The key lies in identifying the type of suspension on a particular model. Most kitcar designers specify that torsion bar front suspension should be used. This is because the MacPherson struts used in later S-type cars will not fit under the sleeker bodywork of most of their creations.

In 1966 ball joints replaced the link-and-pin arrangement used on torsion bar suspensions; also, in late 1967 the electrics were changed from 6 v to 12 v systems, which meant that drivers could actually see where they were going in the dark. For a donor car then, choose a car registered in 1968 or later.

If maintained properly, the all-round drum brakes were effective in bringing the Beetle to a halt – even if a combination of wet roads and crossply tyres did give some interesting moments. However, 1500 cc models were fitted with disc brakes, and these are much more reassuring when used in higher performance kitcars. If you can't find a donor car with discs brakes, there are modification kits available that convert the standard drum brakes to disc, but they are expensive.

The MacPherson strut front end was introduced in 1971 on the Super-Beetle, together with a double-jointed rear axle. As we have already said, the S-types are not generally suitable for kitcars,

attempted by the inexperienced amateur.

As an aside, there was a model that featured both the torsion bar front and double-jointed rear suspension. This was the automatic or, more correctly, semi-automatic: a torque convertor replaced the clutch but there was still a gear lever that had to be shifted. These are rare and fetch very good prices, and it is unlikely that one would be used as donor car.

The front suspension

Characterized by the beefy torsion tubes and trailing arms, it is no wonder that the Beetle front suspension is a favourite choice of offroad rail designers. It is able to

Torsion bar front suspension, such as on this chassis, is more popular with kitcar designers than the taller MacPherson strut type because of the difficulty in creating a sleek, low front profile with the latter.

Right: Off-road rails use VW suspension systems because they can stand the pace, not because they are pretty. The characteristic VW front end can be seen taking punishment here.

but as these were produced concurrently with the standard model, there is no supply problem of late model stock Beetles.

It is a shame that the double-jointed rear axle was only fitted to cars with MacPherson struts, because it gave the car superior roadholding. Unfortunately the two front ends are not normally interchangeable. However, there are some companies who are able to give you the best of both worlds and graft on a torsion bar front end to a double-jointed rear axle. But this is a specialist job and not to be take a lot of punishment without cracking up, and the ride height is easily altered to suit the extreme conditions encountered in the growing sport of offroading.

By undoing four bolts and uncoupling the steering and brakes, the whole front end can be dropped out of the car in a short space of time. For kitcar building, this makes servicing and reconditioning a very easy proposition. It also makes the chassis easier to handle when the bodywork and mechanics are removed.

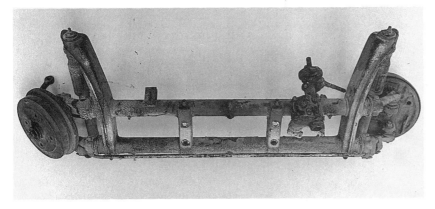

Undo four bolts and the whole front suspension can be removed.

Most kitcars are lighter than the original Beetle, with a lower centre of gravity; thus, it is likely that the ride height will need to be altered to suit. This can be achieved in a number of ways.

If you know what your requirements are going to be, then the easiest way to lower the front ride height is to take out one torsion leaf spring. This is a reasonably straightforward job, but it can be a little fiddly.

However, if you think you will need to experiment with different ride heights and damper settings until you get the right combination, then you will need to fit a modification that gives some adjustment. There are various aftermarket kits available that allow this to be done and in some cases (not all) welding is involved in fitting them. This is easily accomplished, and there is no problem in taking the very portable front suspension to your local blacksmith to have the welding done professionally.

The cheaper, and less complicated, modification kits alter the tension in the top torsion bar only. This has the effect of giving about 4 in of adjustment, but at the expense of a harsher ride. The better kits allow adjustment of both

This modification only alters the spring tension on the top torsion bar, which changes the ride height and also alters the ride quality.

the top and bottom torsion bars, and although these are a little more expensive and more trouble to fit, the end result gives a comfortable ride and more adjustment.

A word of warning here. Lowering the front suspension may cause bump steer to occur because the relationship between the tie rods and the trailing arms has altered, and this effectively alters the camber of the wheels. The remedy is to move the tie rods to mount on the steering arm from below instead of above, as they normally do. Again, a modification kit is available to do this, but a little machining is necessary in order to fit it.

Transaxle/rear suspension

A feature that contributes to the unique qualities of the VW Beetle is the transaxle. This versatile unit incorporates the gearbox and differential, the engine mounting and the suspension components. It is the combination of the way the swing axles work, and the weight of the engine hanging out behind the axle line that gives the car a tendency to be tail-happy if driven enthusiastically.

Again, torsion bars provide the springing but, unlike the front, they are solid spring steel items, which means that there is no way of removing leaves to alter the ride height. Splined into the ends of the torsion bars are two long trailing arms which carry the axles and

Here the ends of the torsion bar spline and the spring plate are being marked prior to moving the plate in relation to the torsion bar to alter the ride height.

wheel hubs at their extreme ends.

Changing the rear ride height involves removing the trailing arms from the ends of the torsion bars, and altering the relationship between the two splines by rotating the swing arm one way or the other. Moving the splines one step is equal to an alteration of about 8 degrees, or 1 in, in ride height. This is quite a coarse adjustment; perhaps too coarse for some applications.

For finer control you can do one of two things. A modified pair of trailing arms allow adjustment via a screw thread. This has the advantage of giving a range of adjustment at the turn of a screw without having to dismantle the suspension, but of course the modification kit costs money.

A cheaper way to effect fine control is to alter the relationship between the splines on the inner end of the torsion bar and the housing in the torsion tube. The secret of this is that the outer end of the torsion bar has 44 splines machined in it, but the inner end has only 40. Moving the inner end round one spline gives a movement of 9 degrees. Therefore by moving the swinging arm forward one step, and the inner spline backward one step a fine control of 1 degree is possible.

Of course, great care must be taken to mark the start position on

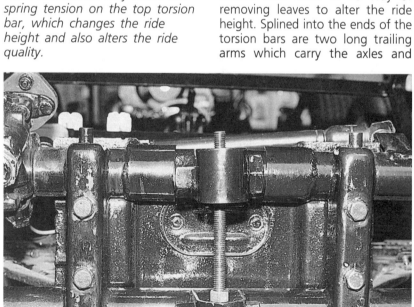

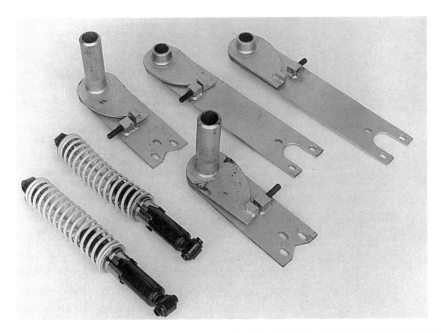

The Unique Vehicle Accessories company markets a number of kits and components to make the Beetle ride, handle and go better. Among them are these adjustable spring plates and coil/damper units.

both the torsion bar and the spline housing in the swinging arm. Don't scratch the torsion bar, because this will create a weak point. Use an indelible marker or white paint and be sure to move both sides by the same amount, otherwise the car will travel with a pronounced list.

The swing axle suspension has limitations because it produces camber changes as the wheels move up and down on uneven road surfaces. There are a number of aftermarket modifications available to correct this tendency, but you should check first that the physical dimensions of your kitcar allow room for the changes to take place. For instance, one positive step is to fit a rear anti-roll bar, a form of which was standard on production cars from 1967 onwards, but as this fits across the width of the car there may not be space enough for it on the new bodywork.

It should be appreciated that altering ride heights and springing also affects damper travel, and at the extreme settings shorter dampers may be required. Rarely can one aspect of suspension be

under kitcars, was that it was one of the few cars made after the 1960s to have a separate chassis.

By removing 32 bolts the bodyshell can be lifted from the chassis leaving a flat, uncluttered platform which, in theory, is ready to receive the new bodytub. In practice, some modification to the basic layout is usually necessary. At the least this could mean altering the pedals and seating position. At the other end of the scale, the design of the kitcar could call for the floorpan to be lowered and a chunk of metal cut from the centre of the chassis to shorten it.

The design of the floorpan readily lends itself to this type of operation. It must be remembered, however, that in its original form

This picture demonstrates the problems with the Beetle swing axles and shows the big camber changes that can take place.

looked at in isolation and alterations to one area will inevitably cause a knock-on effect elsewhere. If you contemplate carrying out modifications to your car we strongly recommend that you consult one of the specialist companies who supply aftermarket parts, such as UVA, and do some further reading.

The chassis

One reason why the VW is so popular as the basis for beach buggies, and continues to be used

the chassis relied on the bodyshell to give it extra stiffness and it was designed for the stresses imposed by 60 bhp. So if you intend to fit an uprated engine, and it is possible to mate all sorts of exotic machinery to the transaxle using special adaptor plates, some strengthening of the floorpan is essential.

Despite being described as a pan, the chassis derives its strength from a hollow backbone which fans out at webs front and rear to carry the suspension units. An open box section rail, integral with the floorpan, runs around the perimeter of the chassis and supports the extreme edges of the bodyshell; and at the same time, the bodyshell imparts some stiffness and stability to the chassis via the rail. Running inside the backbone are the clutch and throttle cables, the gearshift rod and the heater control cables. The actual floorpan contributes little in the way of stiffness and is only there to carry the seats and control pedals, and form a floor.

A common modification is to lower the seating position. The old sit-up-and-beg stance of the Beetle driver just would not fit in with most of the sportier designs of kit-cars. Also, in the case of two-seat sports cars, the driver and passenger will be sitting in the place previously occupied by the rear seat in the Beetle. The steering column will therefore have to be lengthened and the foot controls and gear change moved back.

To a person with a gas welding outfit, and the ability to use it, these modifications present no problem at all. The old floor area is cut out and a new section welded in to give the desired lower seating position. The gearshift rod can simply be cut and welded, the pedals unbolted and moved back, and the cables shortened.

Someone without welding facilities, however, will have to take the chassis to his local welding shop and have the changes made. Alternatively, most kitcar manufacturers offer a service and will do the job for you. Of course it costs money, but it does save a lot of trouble.

This is especially so when the chassis has to be altered to fit a kit with a shorter wheelbase than the

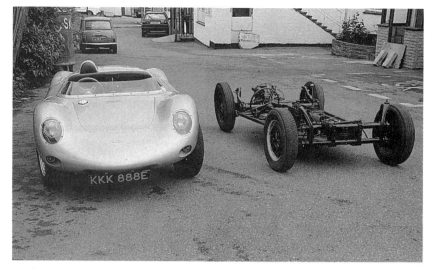

GP's Porsche Spyder replica sits on a shortened VW floorpan.

Photographs above: The stock VW engine may not be the most exciting piece of machinery in the world, but it can be modified to give much improved performance. If you really can't live with the air-cooled flat four, UVA produce a number of adaptor plates so that a variety of engines can be mounted on the VW gearbox. This picture shows a Ford Pinto engine.

original Beetle. For instance, some of the beach buggy kits, and the

GP Spyder, require shortened chassis. It sounds rather horrific to remove, say, 14 in of floorpan and tunnel from the centre section of the chassis and weld the two ends back together again , but it is quite a straightforward task. The piece to be removed is cut from the area just in front of the torsion tube, where the rear seats and battery housing used to be.

We have carried out the task using tin snips and a hacksaw to cut the metal, but a cutting torch is easier. The two remaining pieces of the chassis are overlapped and gas welded together after being accurately aligned.

An additional box section steel frame running around the perimeter of the floorpan gives the illusion of extra strength, but if the cutting and welding have been properly carried out more metalwork is not strictly necessary. It merely adds weight and does nothing to improve the torsional stiffness, which can only be achieved by bolting on a properly designed bodyshell, or adding subframes to make a three-dimensional structure.

Do not, however, let all this talk of cutting and welding put you off a Beetle-based kit. We mention it here for information only. For those wishing to carry out the task themselves, further advice and detailed instructions will be available from the kit supplier. For those who are wary of hacking a chassis about, most manufacturers are happy to supply a modified one on an exchange basis, and usually at a very reasonable cost.

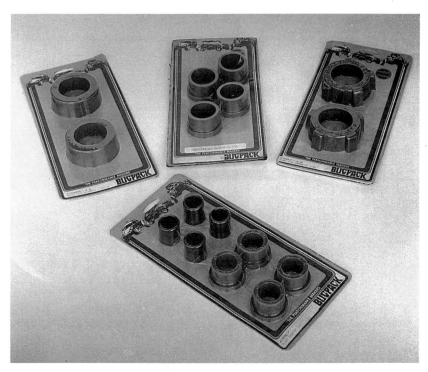

We have mentioned elsewhere the importance of renewing suspension bushes and rubber mountings, and this is no less important on Beetle-based kits. A look through the catalogues of parts suppliers will show that a number of specially made items are available, and in many cases neoprene bushes replace the stock rubber item for improved performance.

This brief look at the Beetle as a donor car will perhaps give you some idea of the versatility of the vehicle's mechanical components. Most of the modifications that are necessary to the suspension can be carried out easily and cheaply. Bear in mind, too, that most donor car

Always fit new rubbers to the suspension. These urathane bushes from UVA give improved performance and have a longer life.

suspensions, whether Ford, Jaguar or whatever, need to be modified to make them suitable for use in a kitcar – usually at a much higher cost.

So, don't be put off by uninformed remarks about the humble Beetle as a donor car. It has far more potential than many people realize and its characteristics suit some kitcars admirably.

CHAPTER 9: COLLECTING OR RECEIVING THE KIT

Whether to collect your kit or to have it delivered may or may not be your own decision. If the manufacturer does offer a delivery service the cost will obviously vary according to distance, but we would suggest that, if funds allow, it's a worthwhile investment because the company will have the responsibility of getting it to you without damage. Then it's just up to you to check it thoroughly: more on that later.

If, however, no such service is available, or for whatever reason you decide to collect it anyway (there is perhaps a certain satisfaction in having completed even this stage of the build process yourself) there are a few things to bear in mind.

Some companies offer a delivery service and this may work out to be just as economical as doing it yourself in the long run.

The means of conveyance

First is the method of transport. We have known customers to cart home complete body/chassis kits quite satisfactorily on their roofracks, but we would certainly not recommend this. Ideally, you should use – that usually means hire – a large van or pick-up, or a trailer. How large will obviously depend on the chosen kitcar. The manufacturers themselves are the best people to advise you because they will have seen cars collected by various means and will know which are suitable.

A drop-side truck or pick-up will enable the kit to be manhandled from along the length of the vehicle, and allow it to protrude up above the cab, if there is a suitable supporting framework, or from the back (but not too far!). Enclosed vans are more difficult to load, and a rather larger model will be necessary than with the other types of vehicles.

A flat car trailer is the easiest of all to load, and if the car is supplied in any state of partial completion – as a rolling chassis, for example – there is no alternative. Again trailers can be hired, and the required dimensions can be supplied by the

kitcar manufacturer. A large estate tow car is also very useful, providing space for separate panels, glass and any other components that might be supplied.

The company should also be able to provide advice on the materials needed to secure the kit for transit. A chassis or chassis/body unit can be easily secured on a car trailer; and if it is a rolling chassis, it can be tied at the axles as would a conventional car. Do check, however, that the chassis is literally rolling, i.e. that it is on wheels; and if wide wheels and tyres are part of the package, make sure the trailer is wide enough, or take along a set of skinnies, which will also make it easier to push and manoeuvre.

The complications really only arise when transporting a bare GRP bodyshell. These can be fairly floppy if not mounted on a chassis, and tying one securely could cause distortion or even cracking. Take along plenty of rope, preferably in shorter lengths so that each area can be secured separately. Pieces of soft cloth will protect the GRP against marking. If you can lay your hands on some odd lengths of timber, these too can prove useful for supporting or securing the shell. It might be less risky to hold the bodyshell in one direction with a length of timber (again using the cloth as a buffer) and then secure the wood to the trailer or pick-up.

Every kitcar is a different shape, of course, and different stages of completion will create different problems. The best advice we can give is to take along as much securing and supporting material as you can, take the advice of the manufacturer, and use your commonsense.

Kit inspection

Whether you are collecting the kit yourself, or having it delivered, there is one other important job to perform before accepting the kit: the inspection.

It might seem obvious, but if the kit is supplied damaged, or a part or parts are missing, you will save yourself a whole load of trouble if you spot it before signing on the dotted line or handing over the balance of the money.

The first job – as with model kits or self-assembly kitchen units – is to check the parts supplied against those listed in the specifications. The number of parts involved, and the variety of suppliers used by manufacturers, can cause the occasional shortage and the manufacturer might ask you to accept the kit, with the promise of the missing part or parts supplied 'soon'. Whether you accept that is your decision, and we can understand your not wanting to turn down your long-awaited kit for the sake of a couple of window frames – but we have known people get their fingers burned. We're not scaremongering, but it's well worth at least getting it in writing.

Assuming all the bits are present, you then need to check that they are correct. No reputable company is likely to try to pass on a dodgy kit, but quality control is another of those variable factors and mistakes are possible. The general principle to apply here is best covered by a computer term, wysiwyg (pronounced 'wizzy-wig' in computer circles), an acronym for 'what you see is what you get'. This, away from the world of computers, is by no means assured by the relevant

model name suffix. What you need to do, then, is check that the kit being offered to you is at least of the same quality as the one you saw at the factory (here again you see the importance of making certain the manufacturer lets you see a production kit). Although no one would expect you to sign for several thousand pounds' worth of anything without first checking the goods, there is obviously a limit to what can be done in a factory yard, or in your drive while the waiting delivery driver is reduced to reading the weather forecast.

Start with a brief check over the bodyshell, looking for flaws in the moulding; marks and scratches on the surface; and particularly damaged edges, which could have happened when it was being removed from the mould, or during storage (or delivery, if appropriate). If it's self-coloured GRP, check that the colour and shade is correct: some companies offer many different colours, and send out a great many kits. If doors, bonnet, and boot are fitted, check that they are aligned, with proper spacing (getting that right is the bother you have paid to avoid). If catches are fitted, check that they work correctly. Ensure that none of the glass, lights, etc, has been damaged (you'll be able to do all this when you check the parts off against the order), and that any chrome trim is evenly plated, and any polished aluminium not scratched.

Inspecting the chassis is tricky, because a missed hole or incorrectly aligned mounting bracket isn't going to become obvious until the build is well under way. The surface finish is worth checking – that it is as specified, and evenly applied – and if any mechanical components are being supplied fitted, obviously check that they have been.

It has been known for specifications on such items as seats, instruments, wheels, tyres, etc. to be changed between the time of ordering and the time of delivery, and for the customer not to be notified. These should therefore be checked.

If the kit is supplied in running form, the appropriate check regarding the installation and perfor-

mance of the parts should be made. A complete, turn-key car should be subjected to the same inspection as a used or new production vehicle before buying, giving additional consideration to build quality. Details will vary on any hand-built product, but any variations will need to meet your approval.

Staging and storing

Once the complete kit is in your possession, some consideration should be given to storage before the build continues. We've mentioned already that most manufacturers will supply the kit in stages, and this can make things much easier. If, as is usually the case, the build-up calls for the kit to be brought up to rolling chassis stage before the body is attached, it makes sense to take delivery first of just the chassis and any mechanical components that are part of the kit.

Having calculated when you will require the body, you can then agree a date with the manufacturer for delivery or collection, thus solving the problem of where to store the body until you need it. If the body has to come along with the chassis, you might consider covering it (primarily to prevent it getting scratched) and leaving it outside. Providing support is given to otherwise unsupported areas, it shouldn't come to any harm. As we mentioned in the section discussing workshops, roof space can also be useful for storing parts that won't be required until later in the build, as can house space such as attics and cellars.

Smaller, and particularly more fragile, items need to be stored carefully, and this is where shelving comes into its own. Try to store things in the order in which you will need them, and remember to label them. Being methodical now will save a great deal of time and anxiety later.

CHAPTER 10:
PREPARING AND FITTING OUT THE CHASSIS

Chassis design

While accepting that any car is only as good as the sum of its parts, it should be appreciated that the chassis contributes to the vehicle's character more than any other item.

It is the stiffness and rigidity of the chassis that determines whether the suspension will be able to work effectively. No matter how carefully the suspension is designed and set up, if the chassis twists then all of the painstaking work involved will have been for nothing.

As we have already discussed, there are four basic designs used in kitcars: the ladderframe, spaceframe, backbone and monocoque. In practice many designers use features from different types of chassis. It is quite common to find a basic ladderframe incorporating features from the spaceframe and backbone types, so it is difficult to hang a label on many of the kitcar chassis. What is more, most kitcars have evolved from a process of trial and error in the workshop, rather than from precise work on the drawing board. The consequence is a chassis that is overweight but apparently very strong. However,

appearances can be deceptive and the competence of a chassis should not be judged merely on the size of the steel used in its construction.

Even an expert can't tell if a chassis is any good just by looking at it. The only sensible way that the inexperienced kitcar purchaser can assess a chassis, as we have already said, is to drive the demonstration car and feel how it handles.

If you have followed our advice you will have chosen your kitcar carefully; and an important factor in your decision will have been the performance of the chassis, even if you didn't realize it at the time. It makes sense therefore, to prepare the chassis properly before fitting it out.

Most kitcar manufacturers have now woken up to the fact that their customers do not expect to have to carry out any fabrication work at all. Consequently chassis are now supplied complete with all mounting holes drilled and brackets fitted. Many are painted or have a plastic, or powder-coated, finish: all the builder has to do is to fit the running gear.

However, this is not always the case and in some instances there is work to be done before the suspen-

sion components can be fitted.

Modifications

It could be that you will buy a chassis for a special purpose, such as offroad use, intending to modify it extensively. This type of work is outside the scope of this book and we would recommend that you contact a specialist, or the manufacturers, for advice.

It is possible, however, that you may wish to incorporate additional features that would require mounting points and brackets to be welded to the chassis. For instance, your kit may not be fitted with a hoop under the dashboard, which would strengthen the scuttle area and form a mounting point for the steering column. It would be a relatively simple task to make up a hoop and weld a couple of brackets to the chassis to act as mounting points. Similarly, roll-bar mountings would be equally easy to incorporate at this stage.

Most manufacturers are happy to make up engine mountings to suit your choice of power unit, but this is a task that can easily be done at home if you change your mind

Much good work can be done with a small arc welder such as this. Its limitations are that it can't cope with welding thin metal – it just blows holes in it – and it is not rated for continuous use.

after purchase. However, we must stress that chassis members should not be reduced, or removed, without consulting the manufacturers of the kit, because this has obvious safety implications.

Any structural alterations should be carried by a competent welder,

Chassis rails should be capped, as they are on this Eagle RV chassis.

but it is surprising what can be done with a small arc or MIG welding set. The initial outlay will be saved many times over in jobs around the workshop and the home.

Some poorly designed chassis are supplied with open ends to the rails. This allows water to find its way in and corrosion begins from

Rust-preventive treatment such as Waxoyl can be injected into open-ended chassis members.

the inside. By the time the owner notices the tell-tale signs of rust coming through, it is too late for him to do anything about it. To prevent this, the rails should be sealed with plastic caps, or with a plate welded over the ends.

If moisture is sealed in, however, corrosion will still take place at an even faster rate than if the ends were left open. To prevent this too, treat the inside of the chassis members with a wax coating, such as Waxoyl, or pour a quantity of old engine oil inside before sealing the ends. Some people carry out this treatment even if the ends have already been sealed by drilling small holes in the chassis members and sealing them with rubber plugs afterwards. This allows the treatment to be repeated at a later date. However, be careful about doing this on small-gauge tubes, such as may be found on a spaceframe chassis, because the drilled holes may weaken the tubes and cause a structural failure.

Finishing the chassis

There are a number of surface treatments available both to protect

metalwork and make it attractive. As we have already said, some chassis are treated at the factory and you may be perfectly satisfied with what you are supplied with. If you don't want the standard finish, most companies are quite happy to supply a chassis in bare metal for you to complete in a finish of your own choice.

To our mind, the best possible protection is provided by hot-dipped galvanizing. This process deposits a layer of zinc on top of the steel and, if desired, this can be finished with paint to give an attractive finish. Some manufacturers offer this as a choice but mostly it is up to the individual to arrange for the galvanizing to be carried out.

If galvanizing is too much trouble, or too expensive, we would then advise a good quality enamel paint applied over a rust-inhibiting primer such as Finnigin's Brown Velvet. Paint has the advantage that it is easy to apply, inexpensive and simple to repair when the surface is damaged. Pay special attention to the top surface of the chassis rails on which the bodyshell will sit. Give this an extra coat of paint because water may remain here and corrosion begin – just at the place where it won't be noticed.

On occasions, we have been disappointed with the application of some of the more exotic finishes, such as stove enamelling, plastic and powder coating. Unless they have been properly applied, they look very impressive at first, but they don't seem to stand up to prolonged use. Stove enamelling chips easily and once the surface of plastic coating is breached water creeps under it and quietly corrodes away the metal without being detected. Powder coating just does not seem able to withstand the assault of stones, road salts and moisture to which a car chassis is subjected. So, when choosing one of these treatments, try to check that the company carrying it out has established a reputation for sound workmanship.

Underseal can be applied to the chassis and this provides effective protection, but this suffers from the same drawback as plastic coating in

This NG TD chassis was powder coated and began to deteriorate quickly when the car was in use.

that once the surface layer is breached, and water creeps under the coating, corrosion takes place undetected. Providing that this is realized and regular inspections made, undersealing the chassis is a cheap and effective way of guarding against corrosion. It can also be used to seal the small gap between the chassis and bodywork, which will prevent water lying on top of a square section chassis rail.

Fitting the running gear

As a general rule, and for reasons of accessibility, it is best to fit as many parts to the chassis as possible before the bodyshell is secured. The manufacturer's assembly manual should tell you the order in which to work, but so often these give too little detail and the instructions are sketchy, to say the least. Very often your only guidance will be the appropriate donor car workshop manual.

For each kitcar the procedure will be different, but here is a typical sequence of events for a front engine/rear-wheel-drive car which uses a Ford Cortina donor vehicle. The type of instructions and the

way they are written is fairly typical of most construction manuals.

1 Fit the front and rear suspension units first, because the slave wheels and tyres can then be attached to give the chassis some mobility.

2 Use new rubber mountings and bushes throughout – a smear of Vaseline will make them easier to fit. The original nuts and bolts can be used if serviceable, but new split pins should be employed to lock the castellated nuts. Alternatively, new Nyloc or Metaloc nuts can be used.

3 Starting at the front. Fit the tie rods and lower swinging arms directly to the mounting points on the chassis.

4 Fit the top wishbones using the original bolts if they are serviceable, or obtain new items from a Ford dealer. (Most kitcars that use Ford Cortina running gear dispense with the standard springs and shock absorbers and use purpose-made coil over damper units. Usually, these require new mountings and the kitcar manufacturer will supply modified lower spring pans or give instructions how they can be modified by the builder.)

The Pike Predator is based around a mixture of Ford components.

5   The stub axles can now be fitted and the new coil/damper units bolted in position: the upper mounting fits to a bracket on the chassis and the lower mounting to the modified spring pans. Using the original bolts and spacers, fit the anti-roll bar to the posts. Then slip the tongue of the bar clamps in the slots in the chassis rail and, using a long bolt, tighten the clamp securely over the rubber bush.

6   Bolt the steering rack to the bracket on the chassis using the new high tensile steel bolts and Nyloc nuts supplied, and fit the trackrods to the steering arms on the stub axle. This completes the fitting of the front suspension and steering.

7   Move now to the back of the car. The rear anti-roll bar is retained and is contained within the lower radius arms – the original fixings can be re-used. Fit the lower radius arms to the rear axle. Using a trolley jack, position the rear axle under the chassis

and secure the other ends of the lower radius arms to the brackets on the chassis.

8   The diagonal upper radius arms can now be fitted to the axle and the chassis using the original bolts. Insert the new, specially rated, springs into the pans on the lower radius arms and into the upper mounting on the chassis. Now bolt the new shock absorbers in position using the original bolts. This completes the fitting of the rear suspension.

In some cases, where complete suspension units are used, the transformation from a collection of parts to a rolling chassis is almost magical. The MGB front suspension beam can be fitted to a chassis in a matter of minutes by simply tightening four bolts, and the rear axle and springs are not very much more complicated to fit. In a couple of hours the rolling chassis can be trundled around on its wheels. It would be a mistake, however, to think that the body can be fitted at this stage. Before that can happen, the brakes have to be plumbed in, and maybe the engine and gearbox fitted.

The brakes

As we have already established, a single-circuit braking system is potentially dangerous and it makes sense to convert it to a tandem system. The accompanying diagrams are self-explanatory and show the component parts of both layouts. So although the arrangement will differ slightly from car to car, there is no need to explain the systems in detail.

It is possible to mix and match brake components to give the car the braking characteristics that you want, but unless you are very familiar with the principles involved we suggest that you go along with the kitcar maker's recommendations. Alternatively, there are a number of publications which, if studied carefully, will enable you to become your own brake expert. Be prepared for some heavy reading, however, because the subject gets complicated.

For now we will assume that you are going to use the donor car components. You will have noted that flexible rubber hoses make the connection between the wheels and the solid brake pipes. Sometimes a single flexible hose is used at the rear – this is usually the case with a solid axle. Independently

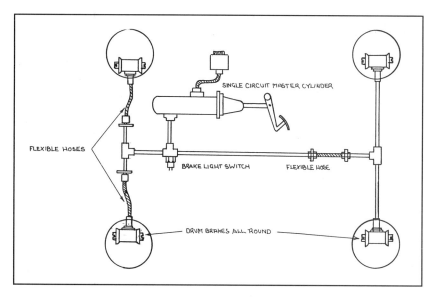

In the single-circuit brake system, a leak anywhere in the line will cause complete failure of the brakes, so we strongly recommend conversion to the dual circuit system.

your specification. When calculating the pipe run lengths remember that it is infinitely better to have a pipe that is a little too long than one that is just a tiny bit short.

Run the pipes along the vertical

face of a chassis rail so that they are protected should the car bottom out, and clip them every 9 in. Copper alloy pipes can easily be bent by hand, but take care to make gentle, shallow curves and avoid kinks. If you do inadvertently kink a pipe it must be replaced.

The unions should be just tight enough to prevent leaks; it is very easy to overtighten these fittings and actually cause a leak. To start with, engage and tighten the threads by hand. If the threads appear not to engage, don't be tempted to use a spanner on them: it is easy to cross-thread the unions. Better to realign the two parts and try again. Once the unions have been tightened by hand, a further $\frac{1}{2}$ to $1\frac{1}{2}$ turns with a spanner should be sufficient. Only tighten further if leaks are apparent on testing the circuit.

The tasks of fitting the master cylinder, the pedal box and bleeding the brakes can usually only be done when the bodyshell has been fitted. However, this is probably an opportune time to talk about bleeding the brakes, a job that causes some people to tear out their hair in frustration.

Any air in the system will be compressed when the brakes are applied and this causes the brake to feel spongy, and the brakes themselves to be ineffective. After rebuilding the components and fitting new pipes, the system will be

Clip the brake pipe to the inside of the chassis rail at 9 in intervals, using either of these types of clip.

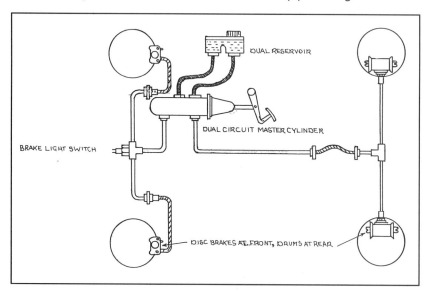

The dual-circuit brake system is safer because in the event of a failure in one part of the system, there is still braking on two of the wheels.

sprung wheels will each require a flexible hose. In all cases the hoses should be renewed.

For the solid brake pipes, copper alloy is to be preferred to steel because it is not subject to rust. Most manufacturers will supply a brake pipe kit and this will save a lot of trouble, but any garage will be willing to make up pipe runs to

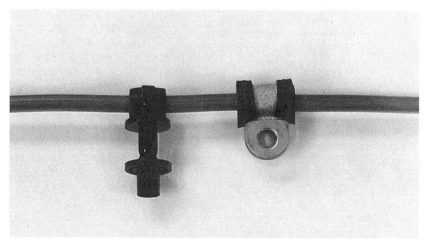

full of air, which needs to be bled out. In most cases the procedure works well and a firm brake pedal is the result of a few minutes' work. On other occasions it seems that no matter how many times you bleed the brakes, air remains trapped in the system.

Here is the way we bleed brakes. It usually works but there are a few useful tricks for the occasions when it doesn't.

There are some automatic, one-man brake bleeding systems on the market and on occasion we have seen them used effectively. However, we prefer to keep things simple – and cheap. But you will need one or two bought-in items.

First buy a one-way bleed valve, which will cost about £2 or so. You will also need a length of soft poly-thene or rubber tube that just fits over the bleed nipples on the calipers and rear drums. Be sure that there is a snug, airtight fit over the nipple. This is essential. Sometimes the nipples on the drums are a different size from those on the calipers. Be aware of this and make sure that you have a tube that fits tightly.

The tube should be long enough to reach from the bleed nipple to a wide bottom jar, which sits on the floor. Now all you need is a spanner that fits both the front and rear nipples and a litre or two of clean, fresh brake fluid.

Carefully top up the master cylinder reservoir. (Brake fluid makes a very good paint stripper, so if your car has been sprayed don't let any fluid come into contact with the paint surface.) Pump the brake pedal to get the fluid moving around the system and top up the reservoir again. Keep pumping and topping up until some resistance is felt on the brake pedal, or fluid is no longer being taken in. Don't re-use the brake fluid once it has been round the system.

Fit the one-way valve to the end of the tube, put an inch of fluid in the jar and immerse the one-way valve in the fluid. Attach the other end of the tube to the nipple on the brake that is furthest away from the master cylinder – usually the nearside rear. Crack the bleed nipple open one turn and give the

foot pedal six slow pumps, then close the bleed nipple. Keep an eye on the master cylinder and don't let the level fall below the top of the outlet pipe: if you do, you will merely be pumping air into the system. Also be sure to pour the fluid in slowly to avoid air bubbles. Go to the nipple that is furthest from the master cylinder and repeat the operation: and so on, until all four corners have been bled.

Pump the brake hard a few times and you should feel an increasing amount of resistance now. At this stage it is important to adjust the brakes mechanically. Disc brakes are self-adjusting, as are some drum brakes. Self adjusting or not, however, the rear brake shoes should now be set so that they are in contact with the drum. Operate the foot pedal again and check that the shoes are still in contact with the drum. If they're not, adjust them again.

Repeat the sequence of bleeding just described, only instead of pumping the pedal just six times, keep going until the fluid running down the tube is clear of air bubbles – all the time keeping an eye on the fluid level in the reservoir. You may have to go round each nipple a couple of times, but in the end you should have a nice firm brake pedal.

Finally, back off the rear brake shoes and adjust them according to the service manual, and top up the master cylinder. Then carefully inspect each union in the whole system for leaks. Take your time and be sure: it's important.

The above procedure should be effective on most occasions, but sometimes the brake pedal remains soft and spongy. The reason is simply that there is air still in the system. It is being drawn in either by a leaking fitting; through a loose bleed tube; or through the threads of the bleed nipple, which has been excessively loosened; or, more likely, there is still air trapped in the components.

The first thing to do then is to recheck the fittings and the tube. If the bleed nipples are the original ones and the threads are corroded, it would be worth replacing each nipple: at a few pence each, the

cost is negligible. Then, bleed the system again, looking closely for any minute air bubbles. You may have missed them first time around – perhaps you were too eager to wrap up the job.

Make sure, too, that the operating rod of the master cylinder, the one that forms the connection between the brake pedal and the master cylinder, is travelling its full distance when the brake pedal is pressed. This is especially important if the relationship between the position of the pedal box and the master cylinder has been altered. If the rod is not being pushed into the barrel of the cylinder far enough, it may not be able to move the fluid sufficiently around the system for bleeding purposes, even though it is perfectly all right for the actual braking operation.

A visual inspection will probably indicate if this is the case and the rod can be temporarily lengthened by welding or extended by a sleeve. If you do this and find that it cures the problem, then find a rod of the correct length. On no account drive the car with a welded or temporarily extended operating rod.

If the brake pedal is fairly hard, with just a little sponginess apparent, it may be advisable to let things settle down for a while. Get on with some other job and just keep pumping the pedal three or four times a day for a day or two. Then carry out the bleed procedure again. If new seals have been fitted, it can take a little while for them to form a snug, fluid tight, fit.

If the problem persists and you are becoming desperate, you can isolate the offending part of the circuit by making up a blanking piece out of a union and some pipe closed off with solder. First disconnect the union on the master cylinder which feeds one half of the circuit, say the front part, and substitute the blanking piece. Then bleed the half of the circuit which is still connected. If the pedal comes up hard then you will know that the problem is in the other part of the system. You can then carry out the same procedure on that half and isolate one wheel at a time until you have found the component that has air trapped in it.

Having found the part with air trapped in it, how do you get the air out? Well, moving the part will invariably do the trick. Unbolt it while it is still connected to the hydraulic pipes and try inverting it or tapping it with a soft-face hammer. In the case of calipers it is worth bleeding them while they are unbolted from their mounting and inverted, but make sure that you have a block of wood between the pistons.

Having said all that, it should be appreciated that some cars have softer pedal characteristics than others and for no apparent reason it is impossible to obtain a hard crisp response. This can be exaggerated by the use of a servo. If you have any doubt about what your brakes should feel like, you should have them checked out by a garage before the MOT test.

Fuel tank and piping

The position and type of tank will vary from car to car. Some tanks are fitted before the bodywork is in position and others have to be fitted afterward. Be very wary of kitcars that employ the former method if it means that the petrol tank can't be changed without removing the bodyshell: the implications are obvious, but not always appreciated at the time of purchase.

If the tank sits in a cradle, the contact side of the latter should be lined with rubber to cushion the tank and prevent rattles and chafing. Remember that a fuel tank needs to breathe. In other words there must be a system of letting air into the tank as fuel is used. Otherwise, a vacuum will form in the tank and the fuel supply will be effected. Usually, the donor car breather pipe is used: just remember to fit it.

Remember, too, that the fuel gauge sender unit should match the instrument. If you are using the gauge from the donor car there will be no problem, but a different gauge will require its own sender unit. Makers of aftermarket instruments will invariably supply units to

match, but watch that the tank fitting is compatible.

Some fuel tanks are placed tight up against the underside of the bodywork of the car, which makes work on the top of the tank difficult, if not impossible. Sometimes this can be overcome by cutting an access hatch in the bodyshell, so that the sender unit can be reached from inside the car, usually via the boot floor. But if this is not possible, then you should ensure that the wiring to the sender unit is in position before finally fitting the tank.

Use new piping from the tank to the engine, and new fuel grade hose from the tank to the fuel pipe, if appropriate. Clip the solid pipe every 9 in, and run it long the vertical face of a chassis rail or in a position where it will not be damaged if the car bottoms on rough ground.

Make sure that the tank is securely bolted down. It should not just be fastened with a couple of small bolts. These might keep it in position during normal motoring, but should an accident occur you want to be sure that the tank does not break loose. Apart from the obvious fire hazard, a tankful of fuel will weigh over 100 lb and no one wants that flying around.

The Sahara Buggy fuel tank sits in a strong steel cradle; the only problem is that it's impossible to get at with the bodywork in position.

If possible give the engine a 'test run' before the bodywork is in position. In this case the engine was fitted after the bodywork and subsequent work on the engine mountings was awkward.

On the subject of fire, if you are contemplating fitting a new tank, especially if it's purpose made, go for an Explosafe unit which is filled with a honeycomb material to prevent the fuel vaporizing and exploding in the event of an accident. The extra cost is worth the peace of mind it brings and it is a small proportion of the overall price of the finished car. Most manufac-

turers who supply purpose-made tanks offer the Explosafe as an option.

Engine, gearbox and exhaust

Depending on the type of kit, it may be advantageous to fit the engine and gearbox before the bodyshell. You may even think it worthwhile to trial-fit the engine and gearbox first. Then you remove them and refit both units after the bodyshell has been put in place. This may seem like unnecessary work but it could save a lot of frustration later.

By adopting this method you will ensure that any adjustments of the mountings can be made without the restrictions imposed by the surrounding body panels. You can check that the ancillary items will not foul the chassis and that the propeller shaft fits correctly. Even such small items as the speedo cable and reversing light switch and cables can be fitted in relative comfort.

On some kits it is possible to drive the car before the bodyshell is fitted, to check that the main mechanical components all work satisfactorily. Although this is not usually necessary, it does give some reassurance. At the same time it revives any flagging enthusiasm: there's nothing like actually firing up the engine and driving the rolling chassis around the yard to rekindle interest in the project.

Usually the engine and gearbox can be fitted as a single unit, especially before the bodywork is in position. Although this is the most convenient way to do the job, the combined unit will be heavier and more awkward to manoeuvre. So keep the size and weight down as

much as possible by fitting the ancillary items, such as the starter motor, alternator and carburettor, after the engine has been installed. Don't forget that oil will run out of the prop shaft drive housing in the gearbox, so don't fill it with oil until the shaft has been installed.

Lastly the exhaust can be fitted and this, too, is easier to do before the bodyshell goes on. The subject of removing spent gases from the cylinders quickly and efficiently, so that they do not adversely affect the performance of the engine, is a complicated one. If you are building a high-performance car it is an area that should receive special attention. So either call on the services of a specialist or, preferably, read up on the subject and become your own expert. A good start along this path is to read *Performance Tuning in Theory and Practice* by Graham Bell.

Whatever you do, don't rely on the advice of 'knowledgeable friends'. You can waste a lot

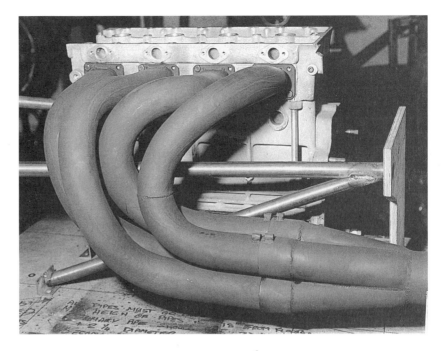

A tailor-made four-into-one exhaust system may look the part, but is it really necessary for your kitcar? **(Picture courtesy Arnold Wilson)**

of money having a special, four-branch exhaust made up which, if it is badly designed, may not be as effective as the standard pipe from the donor car. Nor should you rely on your local exhaust centre to be able to design you a system: they just do not have the knowhow.

However, don't get too carried away. For a normal roadgoing car the standard exhaust system will do a perfectly adequate job. It should be fixed to the underside of the car using flexible mountings, and kept well clear of the chassis and bodywork. During acceleration and deceleration the exhaust will move in sympathy with the engine, which may cause it to rattle on adjacent fittings.

CHAPTER 11:
FITTING THE BODY

Fitting the bodyshell is one of the landmarks in building a kitcar. So far we have dealt primarily with mechanical components which in most cases will have been stripped from the donor car, rebuilt and fitted to the chassis. Indeed, completing the rolling chassis was a big step and one that saw the outline of a car appearing from what was a collection of bits and pieces.

In a way the rolling chassis can be viewed as the skeleton of a car. Fitting the body fleshes out that skeleton and gives it form and shape. Usually the main part of the operation can be completed in a matter of hours and the transformation is both startling and exciting. Your sceptical family, friends and neighbours will look, and then look again, as they realize that you really meant it when you said you were going to build a car yourself. And you? You will find a fresh rush of energy.

Of course, some kits come with the body fully fitted; others have the panels attached to the chassis merely for transport; and some manufacturers simply provide a set of loose panels. However, the overwhelming majority of companies supply a one-piece bodytub to which the doors, boot, bonnet and other loose panels are fitted.

Preparation

As usual, there are one or two preparation jobs to be done before the exciting task of fitting the bodyshell to the chassis can begin.

All GRP panels come from the moulds with edges that need to be trimmed. Some manufacturers trim and sand the edges to a smooth finish, but mostly the panels need some attention, especially around the edges of the wheel arches, running boards, bonnet and boot.

Turn the bodyshell upside down and rest it on a couple of trestles. Using coarse wet and dry paper, take off the rough exposed edges of the glassfibre and finish off with fine wet and dry to obtain a round, smooth edge. On good quality kits there will be returns on all of the panels – in other words, the edges will be turned over, giving a neat finish and stiffening the panel. However, sometimes the returns are uneven and unless some attention is paid to this, the appearance can spoil the finish of the whole car.

Make up a little gauge using a block of wood and a pencil and mark off an even line all round the wheel arch, or whatever panel you are working on, then take back the GRP to the pencil line. A flapper

disc or sanding drum is useful for taking off larger quantities of glass-fibre, but be careful not to remove too much.

The vast majority of kitcar bodyshells are made from glassfibre and do not need protection from corrosion. Nevertheless, some barrier on the underside is desirable and a good thick coating of rubbery underseal provides a measure of sound deadening, stops drumming, and cushions the impact of small stones thrown up by the wheels, which could cause some cracking of the gelcoat. It's also a good idea to save a little underseal to cover the exposed boltheads and nuts when you have finished working on the underside of the car, and when the seats and other fittings are in place.

At least one manufacturer advises against using underseal on the non-gelcoat side of glassfibre, quoting reports received of the black colour leaching through and effecting the finish of the gelcoat. Although we have never experienced this, it might be wise to check this point with the kit supplier. Even if you decide against underseal, it is a good idea to paint the underside of the bodyshell with a matt-black paint. As well as giving a more finished look, this stops light

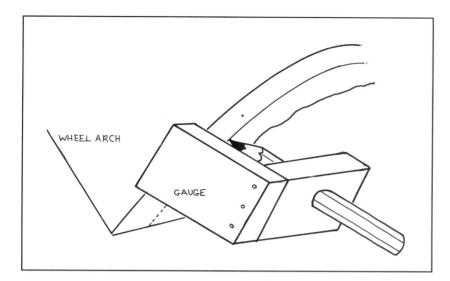

Make up a simple gauge to mark an even line for trimming wheel arch returns.

Right: Applying underseal to a bodyshell protects the underside from stone chips and enhances the appearance.

shining through the translucent laminate, which would make the fibreglass appear flimsy.

Lining up

Each manufacturer should give specific instructions about fitting the bodywork to the chassis. Some do, but others leave a lot for the builder to work out for himself. In most cases it is simply a matter of making sure that the two line up and then drilling up through the holes already bored in the chassis rails, or brackets, and through into the GRP.

Often it is necessary to level the chassis both fore and aft and side to side, so that reasonably accurate measurements can be taken. Even if this is not said by the manufacturer to be strictly necessary, it provides a useful reference point for the eye. Accurate measurement is not always possible and often the builder relies on 'eyeing up' to get a pleasing result.

Nevertheless, if the chassis is at least level, and standing on a level floor, it is possible to take measurements from the floor to the bodywork, and from the chassis to the bodywork, to help ensure that the

car will not have a permanent list to port or starboard.

Mention was made earlier of the fact that glassfibre panels can easily twist if they are not stored properly. This is likely to happen if they are supplied without bulkheads or other stiffening bonded in, or if they were still 'green' when stored. Like concrete or plaster, GRP needs time to 'go off'; it should be left in the mould for at least 24 hours at room temperature, and preferably 48 hours, before removal.

Some of the smaller manufacturers have only one mould and if they have a rush of business, the temptation is to pull out the panels before they have had time to cure. It should be noted that the more sophisticated lamination shops use a hot curing method to speed up maturing time, and this allows the laminate to be pulled from the mould much more quickly without damage. However, it's been our

experience that you won't find this system used by many kitcar manufacturers.

By storing the bodyshell flat on the floor, with any overhangs supported on timber, you should avoid any tendency for it to twist. However, if when you offer the body up to the chassis you find that it is out of kilter, all is not lost. First, using a spirit level and a straight edge, make sure that it is not the chassis itself that is out of true. If it is, return it to the manufacturer and don't be put off by any excuses.

Don't be alarmed if there is a small twist in the GRP, say up to about an inch, because this will probably pull flat as the shell is progressively bolted to the chassis. Larger misalignments can be put right by warming the glassfibre with blower heaters and gradually tightening down on overlong bolts. We took a 5-in twist out of a beach buggy bodyshell by making a polythene tent over the vehicle and installing two 3 kW fan heaters running at full blast for about five hours.

We then gradually tightened down each bolt half a turn at a time, over a period of about another three hours. We kept the heat on continuously and gave the GRP time to settle about every half an hour. There were some ominous creaks and groans but the gelcoat only cracked in one place, which was out of sight anyway. We're not suggesting here that you should put up with, and correct, a faulty bodyshell. What we are saying is

A 5 in twist was taken out of this beach buggy shell by a combination of heat and brute force. It's still left-hand-down-a-bit, but by a comparatively small amount.

that despite its strength, GRP can be made to give a little if the circumstances warrant it. One word of warning: we tried the same trick on another beach buggy and the chassis bent to meet the glassfibre rather than the other way around.

Don't expect perfection. Despite many advantages, glassfibre mouldings are not as accurate as their pressed steel counterparts – not in the car industry anyway – and the kitcar builder must be prepared for things not to fit, for body panels to require trimming and perhaps filling, for dimensions to be inaccurate and boltholes not to line up. We're not saying that this is true for every kitcar, or that it is a satisfactory state of affairs, but the fact is that most of the kits we have built exhibited some or all of those faults.

You must therefore be prepared

to innovate and to overcome problems. You may need to compromise here and there. If a bodyshell sits 1 in out of true on a chassis, then maybe you will have to move it over and accept that its going to be $\frac{1}{2}$ in out each side. Certainly strive for perfection, but don't expect a bodyshell that fits together like a precision machine.

We're making this point because it can be a great setback for kit builders when they find out that the car will not go together as easily as they expected. Especially as up to this point they are unlikely to have encountered anything more serious than a sheared-off stud. What they perceive as big problems at this stage could cause them to lose interest and abandon the project, or at least shelve it for a long time. Our advice is to press on; push a little, pull a little, and you will find that it eventually goes together.

Unless the manufacturer specifies otherwise, we always like to bed the bodytub down on to the chassis using 3M Bodymastic. This prevents any squeaks where

glassfibre meets steel, and also forms something of a seal to keep water from getting between the two. Bodymastic has the advantage over some other sealants in that it does not harden, and should the need ever arise, the body can be easily separated from the chassis.

Each manufacturer has his own preferred method of fixing the bodyshell to the chassis. Some are simply bolted together, with the bolts passing straight through the chassis rails and the glassfibre floor. Others use a mixture of bolts and rivets, and some use modern adhesives, such as Sikaflex. The only problem with using adhesives of this sort is that they are so powerful that once joined together, the bodyshell and chassis are difficult to separate. Like Bodymastic, however, they do provide a cushion between the two components which prevents squeaks.

It is worth mentioning at this point that Sikaflex markets a range of polyurethane-based adhesives and sealants that can be used for bonding in the windscreen, sealing

We use Bodymastic to bed the bodyshell on to the chassis and for ensuring a watertight joint when fitting units such as the heater or the pedal box.

joints around pipes and cable entries, bonding on rubber seals to doors, boot and bonnet, joining wooden components together, sticking down trim and carpets and so on. These products, with their tremendous adhesive properties, can be used on most materials, including GRP, aluminium, steel, glass and wood. If your local spares shop does not stock the range, you will find that most motor factors will, as do boat chandlers and some caravan and camping shops.

Fitting panels

Fitting the loose panels, such as doors, bonnet and boot, usually calls for two pairs of hands and plenty of patience. A good panel fit is very important to the overall appearance of the car and you should be prepared to take your time to achieve it. A couple of days spent fitting a door is not unusual, despite the manufacturer's claim that it is only a few minutes' job. Don't be too hasty with the grinder; it is easier to remove material than it is to put it back. Such is the versatility of GRP, however, that if you

do grind away too much glassfibre, or drill a hole in the wrong place, the mistake can always be rectified.

Final fit is important, but so is a balanced appearance. Gaps should be parallel along their length; radii should be as if they were drawn with a compass; upright lines should be dead vertical; and lines of rivets or bolts should be evenly spaced.

Holes should be clean-edged, very slightly countersunk, with no chips in the gelcoat. To achieve this, first drill a small pilot hole in the correct position (if the final hole size is $\frac{1}{4}$ in or less, you can dispense with the pilot hole). Then use a rose bit (countersink bit) in the drill to

put a counter-sunk hole in the surface just a little larger than the required size of the final hole. Then, using the correct size drill, drill out the hole to its specified size. It's worthwhile reading this again and thinking about it, for it does make sense: pilot drill, countersink, final hole.

Glassfibre panels tend to slip and slide about in their apertures when they are being offered up. As we have said, two pairs of hands makes life easier but here are two tricks of the trade that will save you becoming too exasperated if you have to work alone. Use 2 in wide masking tape to hold panels in position as you work on fitting the hinges and locks; and use dabs of plasticine in the apertures to stop the panels slipping against one another.

Use masking tape to cover the area you are drilling into. This makes marking out easier and also stops the drill tip from slipping and scratching the GRP surface. It is also a good idea to cover the exposed panels of the car with cardboard taped in position. This will protect it from the inevitable knocks and scratches which are a nuisance to remove even from a base gelcoat finish that is to be sprayed on, and still more of a nuisance if the gelcoat is self-coloured high gloss.

One last word about GRP

Use tape to hold a panel in place while it is being measured and gapped.

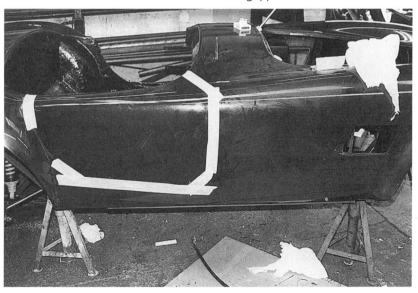

Dabs of Blu-tack or mastic in a panel aperture will prevent the panel from slipping about while being offered up.

bodytubs. The ease of working with GRP encourages modifications to the basic design – and that's fine providing the structural integrity of the shell is not compromised. For instance, it is all right to cut away an area of the bonnet to fit an air scoop, or to extend the wheel arches to take wider wheels. But don't cut large access panels in a bodytub that relies on its strength to impart some stiffness to the chassis.

Take as an example a beach buggy built on a VW chassis. The bodyshell is literally an open-ended square box bolted to the VW floor pan, and the resultant composite structure relies on the integrity of both components to give it stiffness. If you decide that it would be nice to have access to the engine from inside the car and cut a 3 x 2 ft square hole in the rear bulkhead, you will have seriously weakened the bodyshell and reduced its ability to contribute to the overall stiffness of the vehicle. So check any serious alterations to the bodyshell with the manufacturer of the kit.

CHAPTER 12: TAKING ON THE ELECTRICS

You don't have to be an auto electrician to be able to wire a kitcar, but you do need to appreciate some basic principles of electricity so that you will understand the reasons for some of the procedures described below.

In this book we have sought to avoid unnecessary technical complexities, while at the same time providing the essential insights that will allow a competent job to be done. This applies more to this chapter than any other. It is sufficiently detailed to give intelligent, non-technical people enough background knowledge for them to see that an amateur can wire a kitcar quite safely. However, if the builder intends to go into the subject more deeply, he will require a more comprehensive work of reference than can be offered in these few pages.

Which loom?

Before we start on the technicalities, perhaps it would be wise to discuss the various options available to the kitcar builder.

Undoubtedly, the easiest way to wire a kitcar is to buy a purpose-made loom, which can be supplied by the kit manufacturer or made up specially by an auto electrician. In either case you should be supplied with a properly designed layout that has all of the correct terminals in place. The cable ends should terminate in the right positions for the various electrical items; the cables should be of the correct length; and the bunches of cable protected by tape so that a very neat installation can be achieved.

One of the advantages of doing it this way is that the loom should come with step-by-step instructions, so that no knowledge of car electrics is required. Also, the correct plugs and sockets will be fitted where necessary, which means you don't have to worry about matching the connections for equipment that comes from more than one source. For instance, a typical component mix would be Ford headlights, BMC taillights and a Triumph column switch. All of these have different plugs and sockets; making your own loom, or adapting an existing one, can mean a trip to the breaker's yard in order to find matching pairs.

Disadvantages are that a ready-made loom is expensive and, unless you are prepared to carry out modifications to it, which rather negates the reason for buying a specially made item, you are restricted to using standard components.

An alternative is to use the wiring loom from the donor car. If your kit uses most of the components from the original car, then the wiring loom could almost be a straight swap. As has already been pointed out, however, most kitcars have a much simplified electrical layout compared to a production car, and you could end up not using much of it. The terminals and cables could be dirty and in bad condition, so careful inspection and restoration may be called for. However, it has been our experience that once the loom is thoroughly clean (white spirit is ideal), it takes on a new lease of life and very few cables require replacement.

One other problem associated with using the donor car wiring is that very often the position of components is different in the kitcar. The result is that the wrapping that binds the loom together has to be cut back and sometimes the cables have to be lengthened or shortened: a fiddling job, and an irritating one.

The third option is to make up your own loom. This is not so difficult as it seems at first, and certainly not so expensive. This is especially so if you reclaim some of the cables and fittings from the donor car. However, if you have never attempted anything like this before, you should carefully consider your own capabilities and experience before starting the job. It is not our intention to explain the process of making a wiring loom here: it is outside the scope of this book and further reading will be necessary if the task is to be tackled by the enthusiastic beginner.

However, even if you use a purpose-made loom, or utilize the donor car item, you will almost certainly want to wire in extras, such as a radio or driving lights. You will be able to do this with confidence if you make yourself familiar with the principles involved. You will also be easily able to find and repair any faults that occur, either during the build or later.

Safety precautions

Apart from the ignition circuit, where there may be around 20,000 v of electromotive force and special care must be taken, 12 v systems do not pose electrical shock dangers. However, the threat of electrical fires caused by overheated equipment, cables or connectors is ever-present and poses a serious danger in all cars. Fire is especially to be guarded against in cars that use GRP, timber and other combustible materials in their construction. The hazards can be avoided only by observing the following sound technical practices:

1 Use only cables in good condition and of the proper rating for the electrical load to be supplied. Where reclaimed cable is used, check that the insulation has not become brittle through ageing or heat. Bend the cable back on itself and reject it if there are any signs of cracking in the insulation.

2 Ensure that all cables are properly supported and protected against chafing, radiated or conducted heat from the engine and exhaust system, and other threats of physical damage.

3 Ensure that all connections are clean, tight and protected against

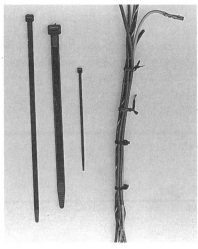

Tywraps can be used to support cables and keep them tidy. Use twists of soft garden wire to bundle cables during wiring, then when all the wires are in place substitute Tywraps for the wire.

inadvertent contact with the adjacent structure or other connections, and that water cannot get into them. A dirty or loose connection may create a sufficiently intense local hot spot to melt or ignite adjacent plastic insulators.

4 Always protect each circuit with a correctly rated fuse.

5 As far as is practicable, keep electrical installations distant from the carburettor and other places where fuel, or vapours, may be expected.

6 Always disconnect the battery connections before working on the electrical system or connecting an external battery charger. Disconnect the battery earth first and reconnect it last.

7 Disconnect all battery and alternator leads before carrying out arc welding anywhere on the vehicle.

8 Do not disconnect battery cables while the engine is running.

9 When using booster cables *be sure to connect positive to positive, negative to negative*.

In summary, the best protection

Always disconnect the battery before starting work on the electrics.

against electrical fires or inadvertent damage to equipment is through the use of good workmanship and sound materials, and by developing an engineer's eye for potential sources of danger.

Some basic principles of electricity

What is offered here has been kept simple: not so as to insult the reader's intelligence, but with those people in mind who did not take physics as a subject at school, or who have long since forgotten what it was all about.

Electricity may be characterized by whether it is direct current (DC), in which case only the supply voltage (v) is specified, or alternating current (AC), in which case both voltage and frequency must be specified (e.g. the United Kingdom domestic mains carries an alternating current of 240 v and with a frequency of 50 cycles per second, usually expressed as 50 hertz).

In an AC system the voltage varies with time at the rate determined by the frequency, and for half the time may have a negative value. A virtue of alternating current is that it can be changed by means of a transformer to give other voltages and, by use of rectifiers, converted into DC current. In kitcars, however, the only AC we encounter is produced by the alternator, and this is rectified internally and changed to DC before being fed out to the car circuits generally.

With DC circuits there are three primary quantities that we need to understand. These are Voltage (the unit is the volt and its symbol here is V); Current (the unit is the ampere, its symbol is I); and Resistance (the unit is the ohm, its symbol is R). These quantities are related by the formula:

1        $V = I \times R$

which can also be written as:

2        $I = \dfrac{V}{R}$

or:

3        $R = \dfrac{V}{I}$

Voltage and current combine to give power, or power consumption, and this is called the watt (symbol, and abbreviation, W) and this is given by the expression:

4        $W = V \times I$

which, again, can be transposed in the following forms:

5        $I = \dfrac{W}{V}$

or:

6        $V = \dfrac{W}{I}$

These six simple equations can provide an understanding of what happens in car DC electrical sys-

tems. The main concern of the kitcar builder will be to determine the current (I) flowing in each circuit so that suitable cables and fuses can be selected. Here are two examples of how the formula can be used to calculate current flowing through DC car circuits, the relevance of which will be seen later:

a) A heated rear window circuit has a resistance of 1.25 ohm. We want to know how much current it will draw.

From equation 2 above:

$$I = \frac{V}{R}$$

$$I = \frac{12}{1.25}$$

$$= 8 \text{ amp}$$

b) A headlamp is rated at 50 W. We want to know how much current it will draw.

From equation 5 above:

$$I = \frac{W}{V}$$

$$I = \frac{50}{12}$$

$$= 4.17 \text{ amp}$$

By simple ratioing it can seen that a 5 W sidelamp will draw one tenth as much current i.e. 0.417 amp.

What is an electrical circuit?

In its most basic form an electrical circuit will comprise: a power supply; a service to be operated (for example, a lamp); a means of controlling that service (usually an on/off switch); a fuse to protect the circuit; and cables to provide a path

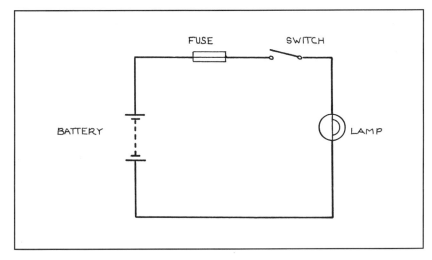

The basic electrical circuit.

along which electricity can flow.

You can see from the diagram that the circuit is a closed loop, and that there are both positive and negative cables. In the case of most production cars, where the construction is mainly of pressed steel, it is cheaper and simpler to use the steel bodyshell in place of the negative cable. In this case the negative terminal of the battery is connected directly to the steel bodywork

Here the steel bodywork of the car is providing an earth return.

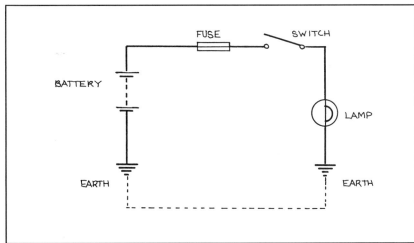

(earthed) to provide the return path. Similarly, all of the services to be powered are also earthed to the bodywork, so that only positive cables are required to complete the circuits (see diagram).

Earthing: a special note of caution

In most kitcars the bodyshell is made of glassfibre which will not conduct electricity and so can't be used as a negative return. Countless kitcar constructors have been baffled by the failure of body-mounted electrical equipment to operate, not realizing that they haven't completed the return circuit. Some other method of providing a negative return has to used. Of course, it is perfectly possible to run a wire as a negative return for each circuit, but this would be costly and time consuming.

In most cases the GRP bodyshell is mounted on a metal chassis, and this can be used in place of the negative return cables; but it will be necessary to run cables from the body mounted units to the chassis to complete the circuit. Obviously, components that are mounted on the chassis do not require a separate return, but make sure that there is a good electrical connection between the component and the chassis. This can be achieved by cleaning the paint from the chassis and the underside of the component, or by ensuring that the fixing bolts make a sound connection.

An alternative solution, which would suit a glassfibre monocoque chassis, is to run a copper-braided bus bar internally around the bodyshell. It should be connected to the negative terminal of the battery, and each circuit should be earthed to the bus bar. The cables running from the equipments to the bus bar must be at least as big as those used on the positive side of the circuit. Remember too, that the engine is mounted on rubber anti-vibration mounts and thus effectively insulated from the rest of the car. Don't forget therefore that it will require a braided earthing strap.

Where it is necessary to make earthing points on metal chassis we recommend that you use the following method:

1 Select accessible points away from any highly stressed areas of the chassis: at least 6 in (150 mm) from any suspension pick-up points or engine mountings.

2 Drill and tap 4 mm threaded holes preferably at a midpoint in a vertical chassis member.

3 Thoroughly clean a circle of about ½ in (12 mm) around the tapped hole and down to bright bare metal.

4 Attach the earthing connections with 4 mm screws (not self-tapping) secured with shake-proof washers.

5 Touch up any exposed areas with zinc-based primer.

What size cable?

As we have already said, it is important that the correct size of cable (area of cross section) is used in every circuit, and this is determined by the amount of current flowing in that circuit.

Cables used in cars are made up of a number of strands of copper wire contained in an insulating sleeve. A cable is identified by the number of strands used and the diameter of a single strand. The diameter can be quoted in either metric or Imperial measure. For instance 14/0.010 denotes a cable with 14 strands each of 0.010 in diameter. The metric equivalent would be 14/0.25, denoting a 14-strand cable with each strand 0.25 mm in diameter. Cables are also colour coded and this can help in identifying a particular circuit. However, various car manufacturers in the past had their own colour codes and it is quite common to find older vehicles with wires of a different colour from what is now standard.

Although there is a wide range of cable sizes available, for practical purposes the kitcar builder can narrow this down to those shown here.

Looking at example (a) given previously, where it was calculated that the current drawn by a heated rear window was 8 amp, it can be seen from the table that the cable required is 14/0.30. Always choose a cable that is a little too big, rather than one just under the size for your calculated current rating. Let's look at a practical example where you want to wire up two driving lights, each having a 48 watt bulb. The diagram shows a theoretical presentation of the circuit. To calculate the size of cable required use the formula in example 5 above:

$$I = \frac{W}{V}$$

$$I = \frac{2\times48}{12} \quad 8 \text{ amp}$$

From the table of wire sizes, the cable required is 14/0.30.

You will notice that the bulbs are connected in parallel, i.e. they are

There are many sizes of cable available, but the kitcar builder will find that those listed here will suit most purposes.

Table of cable sizes

METRIC	IMPERIAL	CURRENT RATING (AMPS)	APPLICATION	COLOUR
14/0.3	14/0.012	8.75	SIDE, TAIL, FOG, AND PANEL LAMPS, FLASHERS, RADIO	RED
28/0.3	28/0.012	17.5	HEADLAMPS, HORNS, HEATED REAR WINDOW	GREEN
44/0.3	44/0.012	27.5	BATTERY AND GENERATOR CIRCUITS	BROWN
65/0.3	65/0.012	35	ALTERNATOR CHARGING	BROWN
SIZES ACCORDING TO CURRENT USED BY COMPONENT			EARTH	BLACK

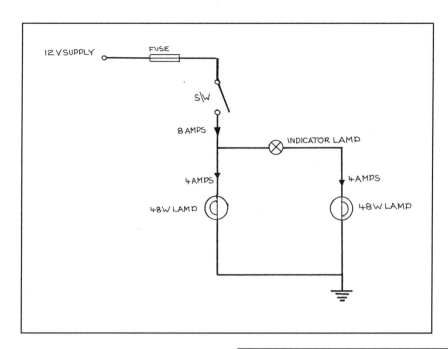

Above: The theoretical diagram for wiring two 48 watt driving lamps.

How two driving lamps would be wired in practice.

- A small electrical test meter is desirable, but not essential.

Besides the items of equipment to be installed, you will need a supply of automotive electrical cables of various current ratings (these can be bought new, or obtained from the donor car – more of that later); a range of cable plug and socket connectors (again, these can be bought new or salvaged from the donor car); a selection of crimp connections and sleeves; a selection of rubber grommets and plastic cable clips; PVC insulation tape; resin-cored solder; and a selection of bulbs and fuses.

Cable and accessories are expensive and, even if you don't intend to re-use the donor car loom, it is worth retaining it to reclaim some

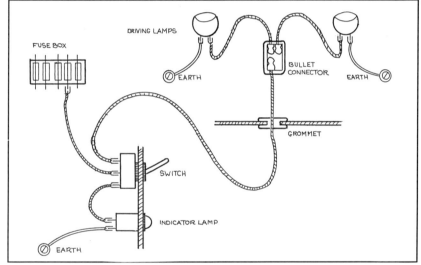

independent of each other and both draw an equal amount of current from the supply. If one should burn out, the other will continue to function.

A theoretical diagram is all very well, but people sometimes have difficulty in translating it into practice. How the lamps would actually be wired is shown in the diagram. Because each lamp draws only 4 amp, it would be possible to use smaller cable for each lamp connector, from the bullet connectors onwards. In practice you probably wouldn't bother and the same cables would be used throughout the circuit.

Tools

There aren't many special tools required for installing car electrics. The main items you will need are:

- A good pair of side-cutting pliers
- A cable insulator cutting tool
- A connector crimping tool

- A set of small metric spanners and a couple of small screwdrivers
- An electrical soldering iron
- A 12 v lamp with a crocodile clip on one leg of the cable and a test probe on the other. The cable on the crocodile clip end should be about 12-13 ft (4 m) long and on the probe end about 3 ft (1 m) long.
- A lamp and battery (a modified torch is ideal) with crocodile clips on both legs of the cable. One cable should be about 12-13 ft (4 m) long and the other around 3 ft (1 m) long.

of the cables. Once the outer wrapping has been removed from the loom it will be seen that the cables are usually in very good condition. However, carefully check the insulation of each cable for deterioration before use. Strip back a couple of inches of the outer cover at each end and make sure that the conductor strands are bright and clean.

Plugs and sockets should also be saved. Some soldering may be necessary if they are to be re-used (if you haven't soldered before, instructions are given later). By all means save bullet connector sleeves for re-use, but the metal connectors do corrode and become brittle; and this may go undetected because they are protected by rubber

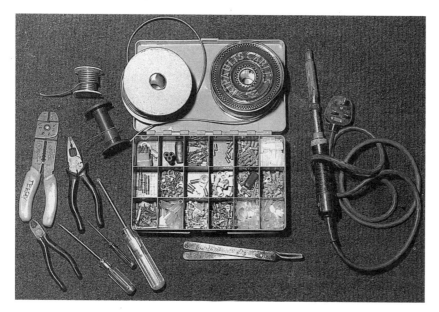

An extensive electrical toolkit is not necessary. Most of the items will be found in the DIY motorist's toolkit. About the only specialist items, apart from the wire and terminals, are the crimping tool on the left and the soldering iron on the right.

insulation. The insides can be slipped out of the sleeves and inspected.

We make it a practice to keep all of the little fittings removed from the donor car, such as the warning lights, glove box and interior lights, the fuse box, bulbs, and so on. It is surprising how many of these can be re-used, and they do not take up much storage space just for the duration of the build. (Yes, we confess to being magpies, collecting all sorts of assorted car parts we think will come in handy one day, and often do prove useful – but we don't recommend the practice.)

Good connections, good results

Most electrical failures occur ecause of bad connections. The biggest culprit is the pre-insulated crimped connector. This type is popular because no soldering is necessary; the insulation is stripped from the cable and slipped inside a metal barrel on the terminal end. The barrel is covered with a soft plastic insulated sleeve and the connection is made by crushing the sleeve and

the metal barrel on to the cable end.

A special tool is required to carry out this operation successfully. This is where the problem lies. Many people try to use ordinary pliers, or use the proper tool incorrectly. The connector must also match the cable size (they are colour coded to make identification easy). To try to economize by using one size of connector for two or three sizes of cable just doesn't work. The position of the two crimps is important, (see the diagram): one crimp to crush the metal and the insulated sleeve on to the cable to make the electrical connection, and another to allow the insulated sleeve to grip the cable insulation. This latter crimp prevents the cable insulation from creeping back and exposing bare conductors.

The crimping tool has clearly marked settings which allow the correct crimp to be made according to the size of the connector and the cable. In addition most crimping tools are designed to cut cables and strip off the insulation without damaging the conductors beneath.

In trying to explain how the system works and where it goes wrong, we have perhaps made the

The crimps must be carefully positioned to ensure that a good electrical connection is made, and that the insulation is tightly gripped to prevent it moving back and exposing bare wire.

operation sound complicated. It isn't; it's easy, and when done correctly the crimped connection is as good as any other.

Making a crimped connection

A good crimped connection takes about 30 seconds to make:

1 Select the connector to match the cable size.

2 Strip the insulation from the cable and push the cable into the connector, so that the bared cable end fully enters the barrel and the insulation of the cable butts against the end of the barrel.

3 Make two crimps in the insulated sleeve. One to make the electrical connection, and another to secure the insulated sleeve to the cable insulation.

These insulated connectors are made with many types of terminal ends to suit all applications. They are available as spade connectors, rings, open-ended, bullets, piggyback and in-line connectors. The most convenient way to obtain a variety of terminal ends is to buy a starter kit containing a selection of items and a crimping tool. Top-up packs are available from most motor spare shops. A good tip is to get hold of a catalogue from one of cables and accessories suppliers such as Ripaults, Lucas or Rists. These not only contain details of the products available, but also some hints and tips on how to use them.

Talk to any racing man and he will probably tell you that he wouldn't allow a crimped connection near his competition car and would insist on soldered connections and screw-down terminals.

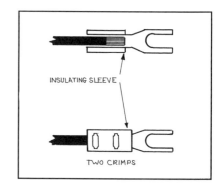

INSULATING SLEEVE

TWO CRIMPS

Pre-insulated terminals come in a wide variety of shapes and sizes.

Although this has proved to be a reliable practice, it is not worth going to the expense and trouble of fitting screw-down terminals for the average road car.

Soldered connections

It is worth considering using soldered terminals, however, for although a soldered joint is a little more trouble to make, the fittings are cheaper and a properly made joint is very reliable. The process actually causes the solder to penetrate into the pores of the metal and mix with it for a small distance beneath the surface. For this to occur there must be sufficient heat.

The second requirement is cleanliness of the metals to be joined. In the case of cables and terminals there shouldn't be too much of a problem. If the terminals are new they are usually clean and already tinned (this term is explained below). As we have already said, when the insulation is cut back from a cable, it should reveal wires that are bright and clean. Any cable that has dirty, black-grey wires should be discarded.

If the metals are not clean, they should be rubbed with emery paper, a file or a wire brush until they are bright and shiny. The next step is to tin both the parts to be joined.

Heat the soldering iron until it easily melts a piece of cored solder. (Flux is necessary to the soldering process, both to help the solder to

flow and to keep air from the joint to prevent it oxidizing. In cored solder the flux is contained within the solder itself.) Then quickly wipe the tip of the iron with a piece of rough cloth to clean it. It should be bright and silvery.

Now melt a little solder on the tip of the iron and apply the iron to the cable. At the same time hold a piece of solder to the cable. After a few seconds the solder should melt and run easily into the strands. The object is to fully coat the cable, but only use enough solder to cover the cable. Too much solder is a common failing.

Now do the same to the terminal. Again just apply enough solder to coat the metal thinly – you don't need to try to fill the tag of the terminal with solder. When both pieces have been tinned bring them together and fold over the little toothlike barbs on the terminal to hold the two together while you solder. Hold the iron under the terminal and wire just long enough to melt the solder on both surfaces. You'll easily see when this occurs: it's like a chocolate biscuit melting.

Remove the iron but keep the two items to be soldered together until the solder solidifies. The finished joint should be bright and clean, not a great blob of grey solder. If you move the two parts while the solder is setting you will see the brightness go out of the solder and it will turn dull. If this happens, make the joint again – otherwise you will have what is known as a dry joint, and this will either quickly fail or give a high-resistance connection. Lastly, where necessary, you can slip an insulating sleeve over the terminal.

Fault finding

Fault finding on some of the more sophisticated production cars, with solid state electronics and microprocessors controlling everything from fuel consumption to the interior light, is best left to the professionals. But, fortunately, on most kitcars the electrical circuits are from a different age, and very much easier to understand.

A multi-meter costing as little as

£10-£15 will enable you to check almost every function of an electrical circuit. They aren't difficult to use (like most good tools, once you have one you'll wonder how you ever managed without it). However, two simple pieces of test equipment you can make yourself (see Chapter 5) are a test lamp, and a lamp and battery. Armed with these you will be able to track down most electrical problems that occur in your kitcar.

The test lamp is used to find out if voltage is present at any point in a circuit; it can also be used to test the continuity of a circuit when power is available. The lamp and battery can be used to test the continuity of a circuit when power is not available.

Let us take a specific example. Supposing the horn fails to work and you suspect, having checked the fuse and found it to be all right, that it's the instrument itself that is at fault. To check the circuit, simply disconnect the positive wire at the horn and clip one end of your test lamp to the positive terminal and the other to an earth point. Switch on the ignition and press the horn button. If the lamp glows you know that the circuit is satisfactory and that the horn itself is at fault, or that it is not earthed properly.

If the lamp doesn't light then there is a break in the circuit somewhere. To locate the break, you could gradually work your way back through the circuit using the test lamp at the various junctions. Alternatively, a quicker way of isolating the fault would be to check the circuit at a halfway point. If the lamp doesn't light you know that the fault is in the first section of the wiring. Do the same again at the midpoint of the remaining part of the circuit, and so on, until you have pin-pointed the fault.

Clearly, there are parts of an electrical circuit that are more prone to faults than others – switches and junction points are the obvious ones – and it makes sense to check these first if they are easily accessible. Do not make the mistake of hopping from one likely fault to the next; experience has shown us that a logical approach to fault finding brings the quickest results.

Sometimes you will want to check the continuity of a circuit when power is not available. For instance, you may suspect a length of cable has a break in the core, beneath the insulation where it can't be seen; or perhaps you are not sure if a switch is working. In both of these cases a lamp and battery can be used to detect a break, or an incomplete circuit.

The procedure is simple. In the case of the wire just clip one leg of the lamp and battery to each end of the cable. If the wire is complete the lamp should light. The same procedure is used for the switch. Attach one crocodile clip to the input terminal of the switch, and one to the output terminal, close the switch and the lamp should light. Similarly, many of the circuits in the car can be tested with the wiring *in situ*, providing the lamp and battery completes the circuit. You must realize, however, that if there is a component in the circuit with a high resistance, such as a headlamp bulb or a windscreen wiper motor, the lamp will not light even if the circuit is complete.

It is also useful to have a wandering positive, or power lead. This is a hand-held lead about 12-13 ft (4 m) long with a crocodile clip at both ends. One end is clipped to the battery, which must have its negative terminal earthed to the car chassis or bus bar. With this lead you can test individual circuits as you wire them up, without connecting the whole system to the battery. Be careful, however, that you isolate the circuit to be tested and that it is not feeding other circuits via common connections.

Instruments

It is natural to want a set of instruments that complement the overall style of the car. Often the donor car instruments are totally inappropriate and the only answer is to fit new or reconditioned items, or search the breaker's yard for suitable alternatives.

There are some companies which specialize in supplying rebuilt instruments, and they will usually be able to calibrate the speedometer to

MGB instruments are not out of place on the 1930 style dashboard of the NG TD – the switches came from a boat chandler (these stores are usually a good source of brass and stainless steel hinges and plates).

your requirements and supply instructions for wiring the rev counter, which can sometimes be tricky. New units are even better, but despite assurances from companies who specialize in making and supplying new instruments, we have always found it difficult to find exactly the kind we want. This is an experience shared with kitcar manufacturers, especially those who make replicas. They tell us that it is a great headache. 'No sooner do we find a supply of instruments than the rest of the industry gets to hear about it and the source dries up' is a common cry.

It is quite possible to use instruments from a vehicle other than the donor car. Some of the older quality cars are a rich source of nice-looking clocks. This, too, has its problems because usually some of the instruments will have to be recalibrated. For instance, the speedometer will need to be adjusted if the axle ratios and tyre size is different from the donor car, and although this is not a problem it will nevertheless need the attention of a specialist (they advertise regularly in the practical car magazines).

If you do use secondhand instruments, don't forget to obtain the ancillary items that go with them: voltage stabilizer, fuel tank sender unit, oil pressure gauge pipe or sender unit, temperature sensors, and so on.

One point to watch is that in some kitcars there is very little clearance behind the facia and the panel itself is quite narrow. Some of the older instruments have big dials and require a lot of room behind the panel: before buying, just make sure they will fit your car.

There are three extra instruments that you may well decide to fit:

- *A vacuum gauge* This can be used to diagnose engine performance and for economical driving. It can be fitted by drilling and tapping the manifold, taking care not to allow metal swarf to enter the engine.

- *Oil pressure gauge* This gives an indication of engine condition. Some are electrically operated and others are operated by direct oil pressure via a tube from the engine. Fitting procedures will vary with the type used and the manufacturer's instructions should be adhered to.

- *Ammeter* With more and more electrically driven accessories becoming common it is

Speedex supplied this range of switches and instruments for the Sahara buggy built by one of the authors.

essential that the battery is kept fully charged, and that the generator/alternator is always operating at peak performance. An ammeter is simply fitted and will allow the driver to monitor the system.

Give some careful thought to the positioning of the instruments. Place the most important gauges as near as possible in the driver's line of sight. Fit switches where they can be reached without stretching, and well apart for easy operation.

The dynamo

The very name 'dynamo' conjures up visions of ancient technology akin to the accumulator and semaphore indicators, only one step on from carbide lamps. In fact, some donor cars still use the dynamo as their source of electrical power: the Triumph Herald, Morris Minor, early Minis and Marina, Ford Escort and Cortina are some examples.

The dynamo has some advantages over the more modern alternator: it is simple and easily serviced; it is very reliable, and it is separate from its control box, which means that if one part is unservice-

able you don't have to replace both items as you do in most alternators.

Its big disadvantage is that it has very low output at low engine revs. In traffic, for instance, where the engine ticks over for long periods of time, the dynamo is unable to charge the battery satisfactorily. Then if the lights and windscreen wipers are in use, the battery will gradually discharge. For this reason it makes sense to fit an alternator in place of the dynamo.

The conversion is a simple one. Choose an alternator of the modern type – the Lucas ACR series for instance – and, if possible, from the same engine series that you are using so that it will physically fit. In other words, if your engine is from an early Ford Escort choose an alter-

nator from a later Escort. This way you can use the fitting brackets as well.

If you are using the donor car's wiring loom, the best time to make the conversion is when the loom is in position but before it's finally tidied up and clipped down because access is easier. If you are wiring up from scratch then you should follow the circuit shown in the diagram. You will no longer need the dynamo and control box and these can be discarded – or sold at your next local auto-jumble.

Cut the following cables close to the wiring harness: those cables going to terminals D and F on the dynamo and the control box; the cable going to WL on the control box and the charge warning lamp. The cables from B on the control box to the ignition switch and starter solenoid can either be cut back and a new cable inserted to join the ignition switch and starter solenoid, or the terminal ends at the control box may be joined together. Now run new cables from IND on the alternator to the charge warning lamp, and +VE on the alternator to the battery side of the start solenoid.

Alternator circuits are designed to be used in a negative earth system, but at one time it was common for manufacturers to use a positive earth. If this was the case with your donor car, you will have to change

Conversion from dynamo to alternator is a simple job and worth doing at the wiring stage.

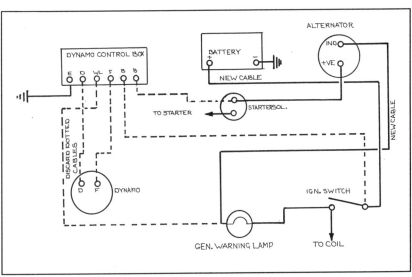

from positive to negative earth. Again, the procedure is a simple one.

Turn the battery around so that the earth strap will reach the negative terminal and swap over the coil terminals so the polarity at the sparking plug is correct; and that's all. However, if you decide to retain the dynamo but still wish to change the earth over you will need to flash the dynamo. Clamp a negative lead from the battery to the casing of the dynamo. Then take a positive lead from the battery and hold it for a few seconds on the F terminal of the dynamo. If you do this with the dynamo in the car, disconnect leads F and D on the dynamo.

Legal requirements

Vehicle lighting regulations can be confusing because the requirements differ depending on when the vehicle was registered. To complicate matters further, the Road Vehicle Lighting Regulations 1984 apply to all road vehicles, whereas the EEC Directive 76/756 applies normally to cars submitted for National or International Type Approval. The inference here is that a kitcar must comply with the Road Vehicle Lighting Regulations, but not necessarily the EEC Directive.

As far as we can ascertain, a kitcar that is registered as a rebodied vehicle, and retains the donor car numberplate, needs only to meet the regulations that were in force when the car was originally registered. However, a Q-registered car must meet all current Road Vehicle Lighting Regulations.

Look around the car park at any kitcar show and you will see numerous vehicles that do not comply with the law. Yet although they are obviously getting away with it, we strongly advise you not to follow suit. Badly positioned lights and indicators can be a safety hazard to

VEHICLE LIGHTING REGULATIONS	MAX HT FROM GROUND (mm)	MIN HT FROM GROUND (mm)	MAX DIST IN FROM SIDE OF VEHICLE	SEPARATION DIST	MAX WATTS
HEADLAMPS	1200 mm to top of lamp	500 mm to base of lamp	400 mm to centre of lamp	(Before 1969 350 mm. 1969 to 1972 600 mm.) 1–1–72 not specified	55 Dip 60 Main Beam
SIDE LAMPS	1700 mm to centre (may be increased to 2100 mm*)	N/A	400 mm	N/A	7 (diffused glass)
INDICATORS	1500 mm	350 mm	400 mm to edge of lamp	N/A	normally 21
STOP	150 mm to centre	350 mm	400 mm	600 mm	normally 21
TAIL	1500 mm to centre	350 mm	400 mm	600 mm	normally 6
FOG	500 mm to centre	250 mm	400 mm	N/A	17
Note:- if a separate switch is used a warning lamp must be incorporated.					
REVERSING	N/A	N/A	N/A	N/A	17
INDICATORS	400 mm	350 mm	400 mm	600 mm	as front
REFLECTORS	900 mm	350 mm	400 mm	600 mm	N/A

*Height of side lamps may be increased to 2100 mm if vehicle design prevents compliance with 1700 mm rule.

All category M1 vehicles (common cars) must be fitted with the following lamps:

1. Front side (position) lamps.
2. Dipped beam lamps. (Not required if the vehicle was used before 1st January 1931)
3. Main beam headlamps. (Not required if the vehicle was used before 1st January 1931)
4. Direction indicators. (Not required if the vehicle was used before 1st January 1936)
5. Hazard warning signals (Not required if the vehicle was used before 1st April 1986)
6. Rear side (position) lamps.
7. Rear fog lamp (Not required if the vehicle was used before 1st April 1980 or on vehicles whose width does not exceed 1300mm (51.18"))
8. Stop lamps. (Not required if the vehicle was used before 1st January 1936)
9. Rear registration plate lamps.
10. Rear reflex reflectors.
11. Dim Dip Device (after 1st April 1987)

Note: reversing lamps are compulsory for the EEC Directives but not for the Lighting Regulations.

The numbers correspond to the paragraphs on the subsequent pages.

Rebodied Vehicles

To the best of our knowledge a rebodied vehicle using the donor vehicle's registration number would need to meet the Regulations in force at the date of original registration. A newly registered or 'Q' suffix car must meet current Regulations.

yourself and other road users; and if you are involved in an accident, and it is found that your lights are incorrectly positioned, you could find yourself labelled as the offending party. Not only that, a kitcar attracts a lot of attention from the police as well as the general public, and it's fair to say that your car will receive more than its share of close scrutiny; a keen traffic officer may well get his tape measure out.

The table above is a précis of the current lighting regulations, but it cannot be considered to be a comprehensive work of reference. For that you will need to obtain a copy of the full regulations. Meanwhile, we are confident that if you fit your lights according to this table you won't go far wrong.

CHAPTER 13:
INTERIOR TRIM
AND FITTING OUT

Just as some people claim that a glance at a pair of shoes can tell you all you need to know about the person wearing them, so we believe that the cockpit of a car reflects the personality of both vehicle and driver.

Businesslike bare aluminium flooring, eye-level instruments and clearly labelled toggle switches tell you that here is a car with competition in mind – even if the only event it's ever entered for is the traffic light Grand Prix. On the other hand, soft seats, a rosewood dash panel and a four-track stereo system generally indicate that comfort, rather than performance, is the owner's priority. Lambswool seat covers, a clock on the top of the gear knob, and a sign in the rear window proclaiming that show dogs are in transit, tell of yet another set of priorities.

Considerable thought needs to be given to the way you finish the interior of your kitcar if it is to create the atmosphere you are trying to achieve. As much planning and organizing should to be given to this crucial area as you gave to the mechanical components or the paint job. So avoid the temptation to rush this last part of the build. We know of many builders who, in their eagerness to get on the road,

This businesslike instrument panel was obviously designed for competition purposes.

registered the car and started using it before the interior was finished. Inevitably, the task was never completed and their cars are a sad reflection of their haste.

It is easy to underestimate how long it takes and how difficult it is to trim a car. Agreed, in the case of a competition car, very little time and money need be spent on the interior to get it looking right for

the part. But a touring car with doors, a roof, floor, luggage compartment and dashboard area to trim in high quality materials can take a lot of time, money and expertise to complete to a satisfactory standard.

The first task is to decide the standard of finish you are aiming for, and then assess your own resources and skills to see if you can realistically achieve that standard by doing it yourself.

If you want a really top quality hide interior, say, for your Marcos,

Built with comfort in mind, this Merlin cockpit is both functional and very attractive.

A professionally trimmed interior could cost more than £1,000, but a car like the Marcos responds well to such treatment.

a standard that is less than perfect, but quite acceptable to most people, you can achieve very good results.

We have trimmed all but one of the cars we have built. It is our belief that patience and ingenuity can go a long way to make up for lack of skill and experience. We also accept that the way we do things would sometimes make a tradesman weep. So our intention here is not to try to give you a course in car trimming; but we can pass on some hints and tips we have found useful.

Accessories

Many parts from the donor car, or any other production model for that matter, can be used when trimming your kitcar. For instance, wooden door cappings can often be trimmed to fit and really look custom-made when revarnished. Top of the range and quality cars are a rich source of materials: anything from interior lights to edge trimming can be recycled, and a careful study of a production car interior will give you an unbelievable number of ideas for adapting existing fittings.

Just seeing how the professionals achieve a level of finish is also very instructive. Make a note of the way they hide raw edges and achieve a panelled appearance on large areas of trim; see how a panel is fitted under the dashboard to hide ugly wiring; note the use of a kickplate to protect a doorsill; check the way carpets are laid and what can be done to stop them rucking up; see how hidden fixings are used instead of visible screws; look at how sound-deadening material, not just underfelt, is utilised; see how floor carpet can be stuck to vertical surfaces to give a neat finish to footwells, and so on.

check the quality first. Women are often good at assessing the quality of upholstery materials, and they can sometimes bring traditional sewing skills to bear when trimming a car. It is surprising what effect a row of stitching can have on a bare door panel. An experienced

then a professional job by a car upholstery specialist would be your answer, providing you have the £1000 and more that it will cost. Aiming a little lower, you could have the difficult part done for you, like trimming the doors and dash-panel, and fit the carpets and after-market seats yourself.

As has already been indicated, most companies will sell you a trim kit; generally this is a good bet, but

dressmaker knows how to hide joins and raw edges and appreciates such technicalities as bias and stretch.

If you do decide to trim your kitcar yourself, be realistic about the standard you can achieve. Upholstery is a trade that takes years to learn so don't expect to be able to borrow a sewing machine and knock out a set of seats and panels in a couple of days. By aiming for

Making dashboards

Some manufacturers include a dashboard moulding with the kit and often this has a coloured gel-coat in a grained effect. There is little to be done with this except cut out the holes to take the instruments. If you don't like the colour, the GRP can be simply painted in a matt finish – upholstery paint works well.

An alternative way to finish a moulded dashboard is to cover it with vinyl or leather. A thin foam padding gives it a luxury look and feel. This is a treatment favoured by people trying to create a top quality finish, and it looks superb when it is well done. When poorly executed it looks awful: what we have seen leads us to say that this is a job we would hand over to a professional. If you do have a go at it yourself, the secret is in the neatness of the stitching along the edges and the use of thin, quite dense, foam padding.

In some ways a simple wooden dashboard is the easiest type for the DIY builder to make, but there are some pitfalls to avoid. When cutting out the holes for the instruments it is very easy splinter the wood on the face side, and this looks unsightly. To avoid this use the blade of your padsaw or fretsaw so that it cuts on the downstroke when working from the front, or face side, of the board. When working with a jigsaw, either use a laminate blade, which cuts on the downstroke, or work from the back of the board. To protect the face further we always cover it with some self-adhesive film; the type you protect book covers with is ideal.

If you need to open out the hole further, use a flapper disc in an electric drill. Make sure the adhesive film is pressed tightly against the face of the board and use only gentle pressure on the disc. Don't remove the protective film until you are ready to varnish the dash.

When fitting switches to a wooden dashpanel you will find that the threaded neck of the switch is often too short to pass right through the thick timber. This can be overcome either by fitting the switches to a brass or aluminium panel and fixing this over a cut-out on the dash, or by relieving the timber at the back of the panel enough to allow the neck of the switch to protrude through.

The interior of this Lamborghini Countach replica is spoiled by a poorly finished dashboard console

Much rubbish is talked about finishing wooden dashboards. Some people advocate using special lacquers to prevent the finish from cracking; they spend hours and

A covering of self-adhesive film protects the front of the dashboard while it is being worked on.

hours rubbing down between coats and worry about dust and flies getting on the surface and spoiling the high gloss. We used to be among them until we visited a boatshow. We were admiring the superb deep gloss of a varnished boat and wondering how many hours of labour it took to achieve such a good result, when we were let into the secret by a young boatbuilder. All

you do is to rub down the surface to remove any imperfections, then using a coarse rag rub in a grain filler across the grain. When this has dried, lightly sand smooth. Using a polyurethane varnish put on coat after coat (letting it dry between coats) until you have built up a thick covering: don't worry about dust settling on the top and

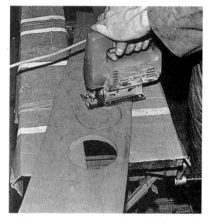

When using a jigsaw, cut from the back of the dashboard to avoid splintering the front.

don't bother to rub down between coats. With very fine wet and dry, used wet on a block, flat off the top until the whole surface has a bloom on it. Then use a rubbing compound, such as T-Cut, to bring up a high gloss surface. Building up a thick covering is essential because this allows you to cut it back; and it is important to use very fine wet and dry paper, about 800 grit, or you'll take off too much varnish.

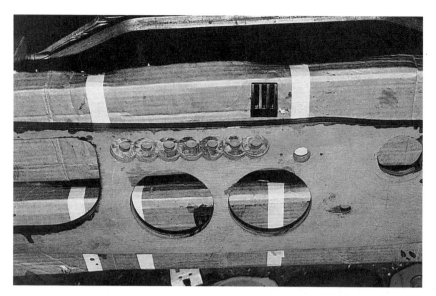

Cut wood away from the back of the dashboard to allow the threaded neck of the switch to reach through to the front.

Carpets

The choice of carpet type and quality is enormous and the final selection must always depend on personal preference and the depth of your pocket. However, do avoid using offcuts from when you last carpeted the lounge: it does nothing for the image to have a multi-coloured Axminster gracing the tunnel of your V12-powered Cobra replica.

Make templates from cardboard or thick paper to ensure an accurate fit before cutting expensive carpet, and remember to use the template face-upward. The usual layout is to make the tunnel, sill and footwell side carpets overlap the floor area by about $1\frac{1}{2}$ in, and make the floor carpet to fit snugly to the sides for a neat finish.

Compound curves cause the carpet to wrinkle and cuts must be made to remove the excess material. Careful use of the template will give you the cutting lines and you may find that it takes several templates before you get it right. Of course, the cut edges of the carpet will have to be sewn together, and the outside edges will need binding in matching leather or vinyl, which is a job for an industrial sewing machine. Some car

decking material to cover the floor of a utility vehicle that was to be used for farmwork and it proved very successful – a little imagination and you can avoid using traditional materials.

Panels

A number of kitcars of the open two-seat type do not have doors: their agile owners soon develop the technique of half vaulting and half sliding into the cockpit. This may have its drawbacks, but it does make trimming the car a lot simpler. A template of the side panel is made and a piece of foam-

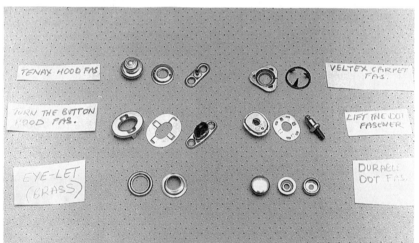

A selection of fastenings for trimming and fixing weather gear. The carpet fastener can be seen in the top right corner.

upholsterers will do this for you but in our experience they are reluctant to do so. Saddlers, on the other hand, seem only too pleased to oblige.

Purpose-made fasteners do an excellent job of keeping the carpet in place. They are almost invisible, simple to use and no special tools are necessary.

Of course, you don't have to use carpet as a floor covering. Sheet rubber is cheap, hardwearing and very easy to work with; it can be cut with scissors and glued down with contact adhesive. Sheet vinyl, the kitchen-floor type, also works well for utility vehicles providing a plain finish is chosen. We once used diamond-pattern, non-slip, boat

backed vinyl sheeting cut to size and simply glued (use a spray adhesive such as 3M 8080E) straight on to the GRP.

To cover any raw edges, cut a strip of vinyl about 1 in wide, remove the foam backing and fold the vinyl into a U shape. Then fold the strip again over the raw edge of the material and sew it into place. We use an old, ordinary domestic sewing machine for stitching vinyl and it copes – but it's entirely up to you if you want to take the risk with your machine. Alternatively, use one of the specially made finishing strips. These are usually clipped or stuck in position and can be obtained either from the donor car or your local factor.

Another way to trim the interior – and this is suitable for doors – is to make hardboard or plywood panels and cover them with vinyl or

Various edge trims and sealing rubbers are available from motor factors.

Titanfast is used to conceal raw edges of glassfibre and trim panels.

cloth. Again, a thin underlay of foam improves the appearance, and lines of stitching can be used to break up large areas. An interesting effect can be achieved by sewing in panels of different textured material: cloth and vinyl work well together.

Flocking

This technique deposits electrostatically charged nylon fibres on any surface that has been coated with a special adhesive. The result is a closely textured feltlike surface that is ideal for vehicles such as estate cars or everyday saloons. It does not make for a luxury interior; rather, it gives a hardwearing, practical finish. We applied flocking to an estate car about four years ago. It is used every day and the interior still looks good.

Be warned, however: the procedure is a messy one. The very small (0.5 mm to 3 mm) fibres are thinner than an eyelash and they get everywhere. You, the interior of the car and the workshop will be covered in a fine layer of nylon. This is because the process requires you to shoot more nylon on to the surface than will actually stick to the adhesive. A face mask is essential, as are earplugs, but goggles quickly become covered in fibres and require constant wiping.

The equipment can be hired and consists of a battery-powered gun

about the size of a large torch. A flock container is screwed into the gun and filled with fibres and an earth lead from the gun is clipped to the panel to be flocked. The panel is covered with the special adhesive and the gun held about 3 in from the surface. When the trigger is pressed the nylon fibres fly out of the gun like little arrows and stick end-on to the adhesive.

When the adhesive is dry, after about three days, the excess fibres can be vacuumed off leaving a smooth, evenly coated surface. That's the theory, anyway. In practice we found it best to paint the surface of the panel to be coated with an emulsion paint roughly the same colour as the nylon fibres, so that any thin patches won't be so noticeable. Also, despite the fact that the makers claim that non-conductive surfaces can be coated, we stick a sheet of aluminium kitchen foil behind the panel to provide a good earth.

If you do decide to flock the interior of your kitcar, we strongly advise you to practise first on some offcuts, or use a sheet of painted hardboard. It takes a while to get the technique right and once you start on the interior there is no going back, the whole panel has to be covered in one shot.

Seats

Good seats are expensive. That may sound like a rather obvious statement, but it is difficult to tell a good seat merely by its appearance and it is tempting to go for a cheap new seat, rather than a recycled donor car item. If the seat from your donor car is in good condition, and the vehicle it came from is a top of the range model, then it will usually be cheaper to have it recovered than to buy a new one of equivalent quality.

A good quality seat will provide firm lumbar and back of the thigh support, and the materials it is made from will be hardwearing so that it won't sag and lose its supporting qualities after a few months' use. A very cheap seat obviously wouldn't have these features and you could regret

It is sometimes worth having the donor car seats re-upholstered, rather than buying new.

economy in this area after a few hundred miles of motoring.

If the donor car seat is in good condition but is the wrong colour, the problem could be solved by a decent set of covers. Alternatively, if the covering is vinyl, leathercloth or some other type of plastic, upholstery paint can rejuvenate the appearance. We must admit we were sceptical about its ability to cope with the general wear and tear, but we have used it quite a lot and with excellent results.

Unfortunately, many kitcars are not designed to accept the seats from the donor vehicle. The usual problem is that they are too bulky, or too narrow, to fit into the kitcar and the only alternative is to buy new. Often, the kitcar manufacturer will source suitable seats and is able to offer a very good deal as a result of bulk buying. Alternatively, certain manufacturers and specialist supply companies stock specially made narrow seats in a variety of styles. These were not generally available until recently, when the growth in

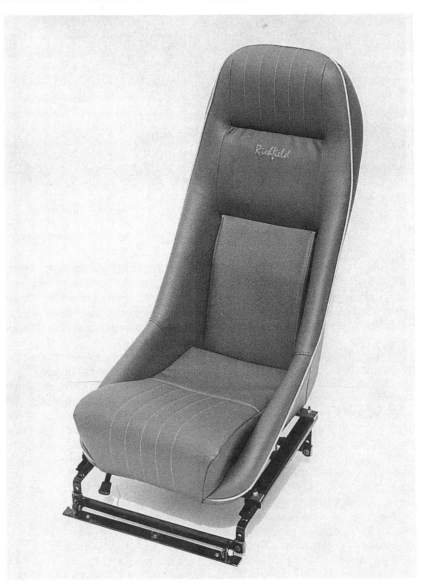

This seat was specially made for us by Richfield, a company offering a specialist service to the kitcar builder.

It is useful to have a seat frame that can be adjusted to suit almost any type of seat. This one is adjustable for height, width and rake. It also allows the seat to be tipped forward.

kitcars created the demand.

Unless a car is to be driven by one driver only, it is important to be able to adjust the seat, preferably for height, rake and reach. In some instances it also needs to be able to fold forward for access to the back of the car. Most suppliers of seats also sell suitable frames and we prefer the universal type, which can be adjusted for width, because these allow a greater flexibility in seat choice. Before shopping for seats and frames, measure carefully and be sure you know what your requirements are. Appearances are deceptive, especially with regard to seat widths.

Weather equipment

Choose a warm day to fit hoods and tonneaus. Keep the hood in the airing cupboard for a couple of days before fitting, and if necessary use heaters to bring the garage up to around 20°C (70°F). This is important because warm material becomes soft, pliable and easily stretched. Fitted cold, a hood will expand in the warmth and become loose and baggy; not only that but the material stretches in use naturally so it should be pulled as tight as possible on the initial fitting.

The construction manual should give detailed instructions for fitting weather equipment, including the measurements for stud spacing and the sequence of events to be followed. Generally the rule is to work

Some hoods come with the fastenings already in place and this makes the task of fitting that much easier.

from the windscreen back. On some systems a plastic or metal lip sewn into the front of the hood slips under a channel in the top of the windscreen frame. This not only makes a weatherproof seal but provides a very good reference and starting point.

Self-tapping screws are invariably used to fit the male part of the stud to the bodywork. Make sure to use the right sized drill. One that is too small could cause the stud to shear or, more often, will crack the gelcoat or paintwork as it is forced in.

This type of front fitting, where the plastic strip slips under a lip in the windscreen frame, is weatherproof and it eases the task of fitting the hood.

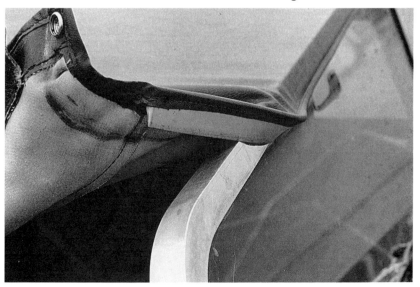

We have to say that we dislike lift-a-dot fasteners because they jam under tension and are not easy to use with cold hands. Turn-button fasteners are far preferable, but often you don't get the choice. A small hole punch is worth its weight in gold when fitting fasteners or rings. If one isn't supplied with the fittings, it is well worth buying one – poking a hole with a screwdriver is not really satisfactory.

We do not want to sound too pessimistic, but our experience has been that most kitcar manufacturers don't pay enough attention to the design of their weather equipment. More often than not we have to make modifications to render it more efficient. Each design has its different limitations, but it is surprising what can be done when the equipment is looked at with a critical eye and an innovative brain. Generally we take any sewing work to a local saddler who for a very modest charge is willing to carry out our ideas. So, don't be afraid to innovate a little in your quest for comfort.

CHAPTER 14: THE FINAL TOUCHES

Setting the suspension

It is difficult to know what to include in this chapter and how deeply to explore the subject. At one end of scale the DIY builder who has chosen a well-designed kitcar, with a clearly written instruction manual, won't require any of the following information. At the other end is the poor chap who has a badly designed car with very little in the way of instructions, and who desperately needs much more information than is available here.

We've opted for a compromise and will describe the most common characteristics of suspension and handling. In doing so we hope to be able give the novice some idea of where to look and, in some instances, what to do, if problems manifest themselves.

It is rare that problems with handling and ride can't be sorted out, but in some extreme cases a specialist's knowledge is needed. Often the keen DIY enthusiast can become his own expert by further reading. We have suffered in the past at the hands of so-called specialists and recommend a trip to the library before paying out for expensive advice.

It is a common mistake to assume that if the suspension components are refurbished and fitted correctly to the chassis, the handling and ride of the car will automatically be satisfactory. In the majority of cases the builder will experience no problems at all and the car will handle perfectly. It is not unusual, however for some aspect of the handling to be not quite right.

Dead steering, a harsh ride, bumpsteer, oversteer, understeer, uneven tyre wear, excessive bodyroll: all are examples of problems we have encountered. You also may experience one or more of these characteristics on your car. Don't despair, there is probably something you can do to eliminate or reduce the fault. Even on suspension systems that are not adjustable there is a lot which can be done to improve the car's handling and ride.

Camber

All that keeps your car on the road is the small area of tyre on each wheel about the size of the palm of your hand – the contact patches. If for any reason one tyre lifts or tilts and loses contact with the road, your car has lost a quarter of its grip. The primary function of any suspension system must be to keep all four wheels squarely in contact with the road.

One of the big problems facing the suspension designer is the fact that during cornering, under braking, when accelerating and when going over bumps, a car's wheels tend to move out of the vertical plane. In effect this tilts the tyre on its side, which reduces the contact patch.

Camber angle, the angle the tyre makes to the vertical, is built into the suspension geometry of a car with the object of keeping the maximum amount of rubber on the road under all conditions. Camber angle can be positive, where the wheel leans outward from the centre of the car, or negative where the wheels lean toward the centre.

There is an optimum angle for any car and changing that angle will result in a loss of grip. This is especially important with today's wide, flat footed tyres with their stiff sidewalls; it is easy to understand that the wider the tyre, the more effect a camber change will have.

Correct camber angle, then, is vital. Most manufacturers will have taken this into account when designing the suspension pick-up points on their chassis

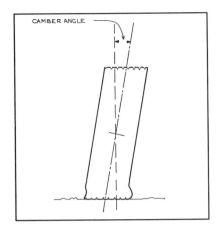

Above: Camber is the angle made by the tyre to the vertical. It must be correct if the car is to handle properly.

Right: This home-made camber gauge can give surprisingly good results.

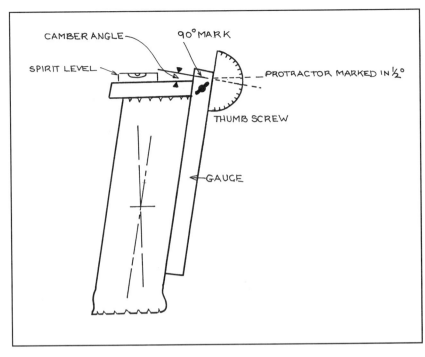

and usually no action is required from the builder. However, that might not always be the case and it may fall to the builder to make the necessary adjustments.

Ideally, the car should have zero camber in all driving conditions but, as we have already said, the camber angle is likely to change with suspension movement and some compromise is necessary. It is even possible to have different camber angles on each front wheel – more positive camber on the right front wheel (in countries that drive on the left) compensates for crowned road surfaces.

Camber adjustment is possible on many suspension systems. It is usually brought about by inserting spacers between the top wishbone, or link, and the chassis mounting point. If you suspect a camber angle problem (a car with incorrect camber angles will tend to wander and display unpredictable steering characteristics when travelling over uneven road surfaces), it is quite easy to check it using the home-made gauge illustrated. It consists of two pieces of wood and a protractor, bolted together with a coach bolt and thumbscrew. You will also need a spirit level.

To check the angle with the suspension static, place the car on level ground and set the protractor so

that the 90 degree mark is at a true right angle to the vertical leg of the gauge (this can be done by using an ordinary engineer's square). Mark the leg of the gauge so that the correct right angle position can be easily found again. Now place the vertical leg against the tyre, avoiding the bulge at the bottom, and adjust the horizontal leg until it is level. The angle of camber can now be read from the protractor.

Camber changes throughout the range of suspension travel can be checked in the same way with the suspension on full bump and full droop. This is best done with the springs removed, and although this is no problem with the spring/damper units, it would be a chore with individual springs. In the latter case a jack and some heavyweight friends should do the trick. Be sure that the suspension is not taken beyond the limits of its travel. In other words, the car body-work should not lift in bump, nor should the suspension be bottomed in droop. The road wheels should be kept on the ground throughout the check.

Castor

Castor gives the steering 'feel' and provides a self-centring effect (this

is where the wheels return to the straight ahead position after, or during, a turn if the steering wheel is released). It also has a big influence on straightline stability.

The angle made by an imaginary line drawn through the upper and lower steering pivots on the front wheels and a vertical line drawn through the centre of the hub, is called the castor angle. In positive castor the line through the steering pivots is always ahead of the tyre contact patch. When the wheel is turned the tyre contact patch moves to the left or to the right of the direction of travel of the car and the forces generated cause the wheels to return to the direction in which the car is moving.

Heavy steering at low speed can be the result of a large positive angle of castor; on the other hand, the car will be very stable at high speeds because the self-centring action will always try to move the wheels back to their original direction of travel if they are temporarily deflected by a ridge in the road surface.

Conversely, a small castor angle will give light steering at low speeds but the car will be liable to wander at higher speeds. Obviously a compromise between the two is desirable and most production cars achieve this. Clearly, with alterations

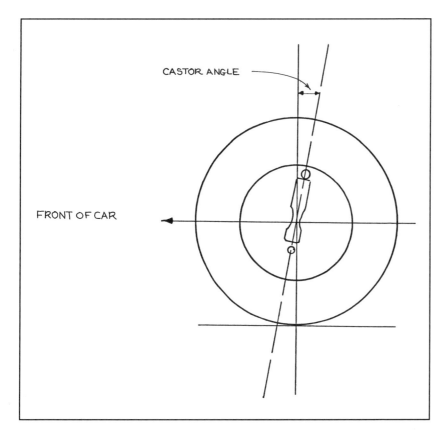

CASTOR ANGLE

FRONT OF CAR

Castor has a marked effect on the feel of the steering.

castor is adjustable and the kitcar construction manual should tell you the correct angle and how to adjust it.

The Jaguar XJ and Vauxhall Chevette systems both use shims on the upper wishbones to adjust the angle; the Ford Cortina uses a rod which acts on the lower wishbone. Angles will vary from 0 degrees up to about 7 degrees, and some cars may have a small negative angle. In general, the heavier the car, the smaller the castor angle.

It is important that both front wheels are set at the same castor angles. Competent kitcar manufacturers ensure that their chassis are accurately made, so measurement of the angle isn't necessary. However, if you do have any doubts it is advisable to have the angle measured using a special tool at a garage. Unfortunately, not many service stations, or local garages, carry such an instrument, but main dealers should be able to help you.

in weight, dimensions and geometry from the donor to the kitcar, some adjustment will be necessary to the castor angle. In the better quality kitcars this will have been taken care of in the original design – as you will have discovered for yourself during your test drives – and no action from the builder will be necessary.

Another influence on self-centring is the tyre. During a turn the tyre rubber is distorted and has a natural tendency to want to return to its original shape; thus trying to turn the wheels towards their original direction of travel. Obviously, the stiffness of the sidewall, the inflation pressure and the rubber compound used all have an effect on tyre distortion, and consequently on self-centring and feel.

Clearly the tyre contact patch and its position, have a big effect on steering feel. By fitting wide tyres and/or wheel spacers, steering characteristics can be entirely altered. We'll be talking more about tyres later but you should be aware that what you may think is a problem with castor angle may

As Martin Foster pushes the Ram D-Type replica hard into a corner the tyre rubber distorts and the forces created try to return the wheels to their original path.

well just be the size and type of tyre fitted.

On some suspension systems the castor angle is fixed and cannot be altered. In this case, it is even more important that you think twice about drastically altering the tyre specification. On other systems the

Wheel alignment

In an ideal world all four wheels will run parallel with each each other except when cornering. In practice linkage wear, 'give' in rubber bushes, road/tyre friction and wind force combine to cause the leading edge of the wheels of a rear wheel drive car to move outwards; this is called toe-out.

Because toe-out on the front wheels causes instability, initial oversteer and excessive tyre wear, it

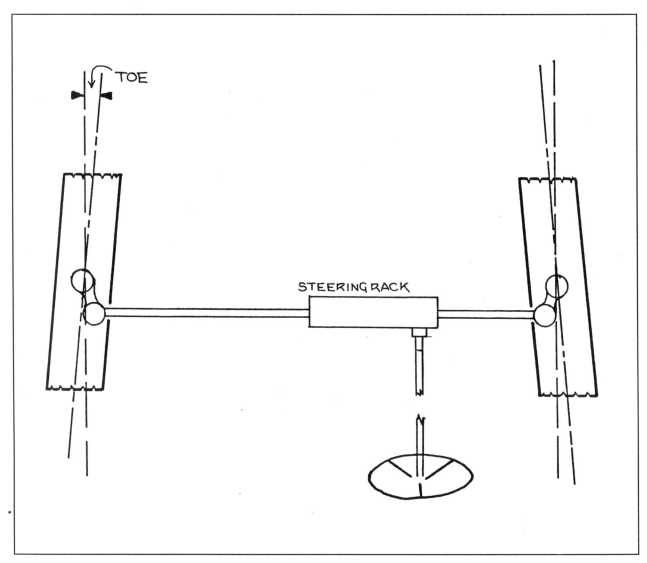

Correct toe improves straightline stability and prevents excessive tyre wear.

is necessary to adjust the wheels to have toe-in when static. This has the effect of balancing the toe-out when the car is moving at speed. The toe-in should be just sufficient to cancel the toe-out at high speed. Usually an adjustment of $\frac{1}{8}$ in is about right, but your construction manual should tell you the correct setting.

On front wheel drive cars it is a different story because the front wheels tend to toe-in under the influence of the drive shafts. In this case, the opposite corrective action is necessary and the front wheels have to be adjusted to toe-out when static. This will normally be taken into account by kitcar designers when they use front

wheel drive units in the mid-engine position. It does no harm however, to bear this in mind when setting up a mid-engined car.

Toe adjustment is made on the tie rods. It can be conveniently carried out by your tyre supplier after the tyres have been fitted and the wheels balanced; and after the camber and castor have been set.

On independent rear suspensions, the rear wheels tend to toe-in because of the driving forces. The effect of incorrect rear toe is much the same as incorrect front toe and the maker's recommendations for adjustments should be followed. In most cases the rear wheels will be set for zero toe.

Bump steer

Bump steer occurs when the toe of

the wheel alters as it moves vertically up and down on the suspension. If the steering rack and arms are badly positioned, when the wheel travels up or down over uneven road surfaces the steering arms effectively change length and cause a steering movement of the road wheels. The effect is to cause the car to dart and twitch, and become unstable.

The remedy is to alter the position of the rack or the length of the steering arms. If you suspect that you have a bump steer problem, get your main dealer (donor car) to check it with his toe gauge, with the wheels at full bump, full droop and static.

However, before you do so, you could borrow or buy copies of *'How To Make Your Car Handle'* by Fred Puhn and *'Race And Rally Source Book'* by Alan Staniforth.

At any speed above a crawl, centrifugal force overcomes the grip of the tyre and the car follows a wider path than that directed by the wheels.

By carefully studying these books you will understand what is involved and how to fix the problem. You will also learn that you can dispense with the garage or dealer and their toe gauge and make your own. In the process you will have gathered a very good knowledge of car suspension.

Oversteer and understeer

Before we can discuss oversteer, understeer or, for that matter, neutral steer we must first look at what slip angle is, and what effect it has on a car during cornering.

When cornering, centrifugal force tends to fling the car wide of its turning circle. The only thing that prevents the car from sliding sideways is the resistance of the tyre contact patches on the road surface. As the rubber clings to the road centrifugal force is trying to break its grip.

In fighting to maintain its grip the tyre distorts and creates a force which tries to overcome centrifugal force and push the car back into its intended turning circle. At any speed other than a crawl the tyre makes an effort, as it were, but it can't entirely beat centrifugal force. The result is that the car follows a path that is wider than the direction in which the wheel is trying to make it go. The difference between the wheel's planned path and its actual path is called the slip angle. This doesn't mean that the car is skidding. The tyre is maintaining its grip but in doing so it squirms over the road surface in a wider circle than the wheel would take if no centrifugal force was involved. The slower the speed, the less the centrifugal force generated and the smaller the slip angle. Also, the tighter the circle, the more the centrifugal force generated and the bigger the slip angle.

As the speed increases, or the turning circle gets tighter, the tyre has to fight harder to maintain its grip. As the battle progresses and the cornering forces begin to win, the slip angles increase and the tyre starts to lose its grip.

How quickly that situation is reached depends upon the road surface, the car's suspension and the type of tyre used as well as the speed and radius of the turn. If the car has good weight distribution and the suspension is set up properly, each wheel will develop the same slip angle and the car will drift sideways in a balanced way. This is commonly called neutral handling behaviour.

However, if a car is not balanced then the story will be different. Let's suppose that you are driving a VW-based kitcar where the engine hangs out over the back axle line. If you go into a corner too fast that heavy engine, well behind the axle line, will create much more centrifugal force than the relatively light front end. The rear tyres will be subject to much more force and the slip angles will increase. The car will therefore tend to describe a tighter circle than the driver intended. This is oversteer.

Understeer, conversely, is when the front slip angles are greater than the rear. A typical example is a front wheel drive car attempting to accelerate hard around a tight bend. The front tyres can't cope with turning and accelerating at the same time, so the car takes a wider line than the driver intended. If corrective action is not taken the car will eventually go off the road on the outside of the bend, nose first.

So far, we have talked about normal slip angles, but given a real excess of centrifugal force, these angles will suddenly increase dramatically and the tyres will loose all, or most, of their grip. You are now in a skid, and oversteer and understeer no longer apply.

Normally, of course, those limits aren't reached, but at some time or another most Beetle drivers will have had the disconcerting experience of having the back end trying to meet the front. Which is precisely why most production car manufacturers have built understeer into their cars. Whereas it may take a skilled driver to control oversteer, most people will be able to react instinctively to understeer, which makes the latter condition generally safer for the average driver. However, neither state of affairs is desirable to any great extent, and a car that exhibits excessive steering characteristics is no fun to drive. In almost every case, something can be done to improve things.

Three settings we have already mentioned effect the handling characteristics of a car: toe, castor and camber; these should be set up correctly before any other action is taken.

Having said that, adjusting the toe is a way of changing the steering characteristics, and once the base setting has been achieved it is reasonable to make small adjustments to render the handling satisfactory.

Increasing toe-in on the front will make the car understeer more and reducing it will make it understeer less. It must be borne in mind that altering toe to achieve good handling will also change the self-centring and the directional stability of the car, so a bit of juggling may be necessary before an acceptable compromise can be reached. It is also likely to alter the camber

setting, which should be rechecked.

As we have already demonstrated, excessive weight at the ends of the car can effect the way it handles. Racing drivers take a good deal of care to balance the weight on all four corners of the car but this is not a practical proposition for the average roadgoing kitcar. However, it may be possible to redistribute weight from either end of the car by moving a heavy toolbox or relocating the spare wheel – especially if the latter is hung on the boot lid.

The right tyres

Next, look at the type, size and inflation pressures of the tyres you are running on. Not many people use cross-ply tyres these days, but some older cars or replicas may be fitted with them. They have stiff sidewalls and the tread tends to distort under load, so their slip angles are greater than the more popular radial-ply tyres. Because of this you should never in any circumstances mix the two types.

A recurring problem with kitcars is that they are over-tyred. In other words people fit wider wheels and tyres than is either necessary or desirable merely because they are fashionable and look the part.

Excessively wide tyres create a number of problems that can affect handling. They will be heavier than necessary, thus increasing unsprung weight. They could be too wide for the rim size and cause the tyre to roll under cornering forces; and a wide tyre on a narrow rim could also have a rounded tread instead of sitting flat on the road. A wide tyre gives a good grip in the dry but is inferior in wet conditions, and this can give rise to hydroplaning, when all traction is lost. Wide tyres, a light car, an over-enthusiastic driver and a wet road add up to a recipe for disaster. Then, too, a wide tyre could foul the bodywork; the ride will be harsher; braking and acceleration could be affected due to the flywheel effect of heavier tyres; spacers may be necessary to enable the tyre to fit under the wheel arch, and these would affect steering geometry and place unnecessary strains on the wheel bearings.

The message is simple: stick to the maker's recommendations. If you are still unsure about tyre size, read and act on Fred Puhn's wise words in his book *How to Make Your Car Handle.* Finally, you could do worse than run on the same size rubber as the donor car used.

Tyre pressures can have a significant effect on understeer and oversteer. For road cars the golden rule is to stick to the correct tyre pressures as recommended by the company that makes them. However, there is some latitude and increasing the front tyre pressures a couple of pounds can reduce understeer, increasing the rear tyre pressures can reduce oversteer.

Anti-roll bars

A few kitcars are produced with adjustable anti-roll bars at both back and front. Some have non-adjustable bars fitted in both places; others have a fixed bar at the front only; and a few have no anti-roll bars at all. If yours has adjustable bars then it's probably designed for some type of motorsport and you will know that you can make the car understeer less by reducing the roll stiffness at the front and increasing it at the rear.

If the anti-roll bars are non-adjustable it is possible to obtain differently rated bars from specialist suppliers. We would suggest that to take this step is fairly extreme, that the kitcar manufacturer should be consulted first, and that the suspension settings should be double checked, preferably by an independent person whose expertise can be trusted.

Springs and shock absorbers

Even if our roads were perfectly smooth and level we would still need springs – and shock absorbers.

A spring has two functions. One is to try to keep the contact patch of the tyres always on the road. The other is to insulate the occupants of the car from the irregularities of the road surface.

These two cars are negotiating the same corner. Notice how weight transfer is causing the Pilgrim Bulldog (ATU 480M) to roll heavily on its soft springs, while the hard sprung Harbron Special (Q718 FRU) has a much flatter attitude.

In attempting to keep the contact patch squarely on the road the spring has to deal with the loads imposed on it by weight transfer caused by braking, acceleration and cornering, as well as those caused by the wheels reacting to uneven road surfaces.

The springs work hard for a living and if they operated in isolation each wheel would be jumping up and down kangaroo-style. This is where the shock absorber plays its part. In fact, it doesn't absorb shocks at all; 'damper' is a better name for it. The damper, as we shall call it from now on, absorbs the energy stored in the spring and prevents it reacting too quickly and violently – in other words, it dampens the action of the spring. If we now look at sprung and unsprung weight, this will give us a better idea of what the springs and dampers have to cope with.

The chassis, bodywork, engine and gearbox, car occupants, and the contents of the ashtray all rest on the springs and are considered to be sprung weight. The wheels and suspension components, in other words the running gear – the parts that go up and down – are said to be unsprung weight. It is easy to see that the ratio between sprung and unsprung weight is important and that it will have a big influence upon the choice of spring.

All things being equal, a car with a high sprung-to-unsprung weight ratio will handle better and ride better, than a car with a low ratio. The reason is that a heavy chassis and bodyshell are not affected very much by relatively light running gear bouncing up and down. The mass of the sprung weight is only slightly disturbed by the movement of the wheels and suspension components.

Despite sometimes having overweight chassis and thick GRP bodyshells, most kitcars are very much lighter than their production counterparts. If the donor car's suspension system, complete with springs and dampers were to be simply transferred to the kitcar, the ratio of sprung to unsprung weight would be low and the ride and handling unacceptable: the springs would be much too stiff.

Not a lot can be done about the sprung to unsprung weight ratio – you can't go shaving pieces off the wishbones to make them lighter. This is why the designer's initial choice of running gear is so important (and why the choice of heavy saloon car gear, such as from the XJ6, is not always appropriate for a kitcar). However, you can make sure that you don't exaggerate the effect by fitting heavier than necessary wheels and tyres, and also by ensuring that the springs and dampers match the characteristics of the car.

Most good kitcar manufacturers will have taken all this into account and will supply correctly rated springs and matched dampers with the kit. A few do not.

Sometimes the original coil springs are used but shortened in order to obtain the correct ride height. If this has been achieved by cutting coils from the spring, the effect is actually to increase its stiffness. With coil springs the stiffness is determined by the number of coils and thickness of the metal they are made from. Reducing the number of coils stiffens the spring and hardens the ride – which is usually the opposite to what you are trying to achieve.

If you must reduce the ride height and retain the original spring, the way to do it is to clamp it securely in a spring compressor and heat it to 200°C (400°F) then leave it to cool. Check the length and if necessary repeat the operation until the correct ride height is obtained. Here we must repeat our earlier warning about the latent energy stored in a compressed coil spring. A carelessly handled spring can be very dangerous, so it is important to use the proper tool.

It should be appreciated that the suspension will require freedom to move from full droop to full bump. If a coil spring has too many coils, or is too short, the coils may compress and touch one another in bump, and this will restrict the suspension movement. Conversely, in droop, the shortened spring may be free to fall out of the upper and lower spring pans.

The latter problem is easily cured by wire-locking the upper and lower coils to the pans. A spring that becomes coil-bound however, is not so easy to fix. The only remedy is to go to a suspension specialist and have a correctly rated spring supplied of the right length.

It is sometimes possible in fact to use spacers on the lower spring mounting point so that the bottom coils of the spring are actually below the spring pan or wishbone. In other words the mounting point of the spring has been lowered, which allows the original spring length to be maintained. However, we feel that experiments of this sort are probably outside the experience of most amateur kitcar builders.

Many kitcars now use combined spring/damper units where the coil springs are fitted over the damper. Most of the spring manufacturers are able to give advice to the builder about specially rated springs and dampers. We would advise you to contact these people before experimenting too much.

Some of these units, by the way, have adjustable dampers and springs. While adjusting the dampers will effect the amount of damping on the spring, adjusting the spring platform will not alter the stiffness of the spring: it merely changes the ride height.

The ride height of cars using leaf springs can be lowered by placing blocks between the axle and the spring pan. However, big changes of height may adversely affect handling and we would advise that a change exceeding 1 in should be brought about by re-arching the spring. In this operation the spring is taken apart, heated to a high temperature and bent to the new shape. This is a job for an expert and we recommend that you take your spring to a specialist.

Another method of altering ride height is to fit drop bars to the spring shackles. Some specialist accessory shops stock these, or they can be made up at home. However, while we accept that these are in common use by custom car builders, we do not recommend amateur kitcar builders to use them. In our opinion they can form a weak point and failure is not uncommon. Leaf spring stiffness can be altered by removing leaves from the spring. Removing leaves softens the spring: it also alters the ride height. It weakens the spring, too; so be sure that the weight of the rear of the kitcar really is less than that of the donor car.

Altering torsion bar suspension has been dealt with in the section devoted to Beetle-based cars (Chapter 8). Rubber springs, such as the rubber cones found on the Mini, can be softened by drilling holes (of about $\frac{1}{2}$ in diameter) in the rubber.

The exact number of holes required is a matter for experiment but probably between 20 and 30 will be needed. Altering the ride height can be achieved by taking the linkage apart and fitting shims.

CHAPTER 15: GETTING ON THE ROAD

Once the build is complete, there will inevitably be some paperwork to do before you can actually put the car on the road. This is certainly nothing to worry about; indeed some would argue that it is inadequate.

MOT, road fund tax, and insurance will be familiar to all United Kingdom motorists (although kitcar insurance has its own, unique features – more on that later). The process of registration, however, will be completely new to some people, and certain decisions do need to be made earlier on at the beginning of the build.

Registration

Before 1983, owners applying for kitcar registrations were either given a 'new' registration number (then a letter suffix) to denote the year, or were allowed to retain the number of the donor vehicle. The deciding factor was how much of the donor was used in the kitcar: if it was decided that the kit itself constituted the greater part of the new vehicle, a new number would be awarded, along with a bill for car tax.

As the kitcar movement expanded, however, this simple one-or-the-other system couldn't cope with cars in the grey area, with insufficient new parts to warrant a new plate, and not enough of the donor to keep the old number. It has to be said that there were also some rumblings of dissatisfaction about the fact that 'new' cars could be created from a £1000 worth of kit and an MOT failure. But whatever the failings of the old system, the Q plate was introduced in the name of simplification.

It has in fact simplified things. Those who set out to 'beat the system' and avoid a Q plate (because it labels the vehicle a kitcar, and is non-transferable) have to get up to all sorts of tricks, but the straightforward kitcar registration is a simple affair.

Officialdom needs definitions, of course, and it's interesting to note that what you consider to be a kitcar probably isn't officially called a kitcar at all. The official definition of a kitcar is a car built entirely from new components, supplied by one manufacturer – a kit of parts, in fact; which is logical enough. Cars in this category are the top-of-the-range models from Marcos, Caterham Cars, Midas, and so on, which these manufacturers call 'component cars'. They are also subject to car tax.

The cars which the rest of us, and the industry, call kitcars – (those that use donor car parts in conjunction with a body/chassis kit) are known as 'kit-converted vehicles' in official circles.

Again this is logical enough. Just different from the rest of the world. The relevance is that the categorization of your car will determine which numberplate you end up with.

Starting with the 'kit-converted vehicles', those that use second-hand donor car parts in conjunction with a body or body/chassis (like the Jago Geep, the Pilgrim Bulldog, the GP Spyder, etc), these are split again into two areas – and here we hark back a little to the previous system. Basically, these are the cars for which the 'Q' system was devised, but you are permitted to retain the donor car registration if the kitcar is actually built around the donor car's chassis. Most kitcars now come with their own chassis, but those using Triumph Herald/Vitesse or VW Beetle chassis would keep the original number. Shortening the chassis – as in the case of the GP Spyder, for example – is 'usually acceptable, and will be looked at separately', say the authorities. Something more radical

This GP Spyder is able to retain the original donor car number because it is classed as a rebodied VW Beetle.

like a changed wheel plan (eg, from four- to three-wheeler) would certainly result in a 'Q'. There are a few kitcars – a company called Robin Hood Engineering were first to use this system – that use the 'floorpan' of a monocoque car (in Robin Hood's case the Rover 3500 and the TR7) as the basis for a new car, the replacement body being bonded to the new base. This method of construction could also be said to use the original chassis and so would retain the original registration.

The rest of the 'kit-converted vehicles', which we would call kit-cars, will automatically receive a 'Q'-plate. Or almost certainly: we'll look later at the rather dubious methods used to get around this.

But first, how does the simple process of registering kitcar (or rather 'kit-converted vehicles') work? The first move is to complete form V5/55, officially titled 'Appli-

The Haldane 100 uses a purpose-made chassis and Ford running gear, and has to carry a Q registration unless registered as a new car.

cation for a first licence for a motor vehicle and declaration for registration'. This is available from your local Vehicle Registration Office (its address and phone number can be obtained from the telephone directory listed under 'Department of Transport').

Not all the questions on the form will be applicable to you, and will

be dependent on the taxation class required. More than likely this will be 'private', so all questions apart from 10-16 will require your attention. The form shouldn't cause any big problems, but if in doubt a call to the local VRO should clarify things.

Form V5/55 doesn't allow for the use of used parts, however, so you will also need to fill in form V627/1. Having completed them both, return them to your Vehicle Registration Office. When you hear from this office will depend very much on the work load there. Before too long, however, the VRO will contact you to arrange for an inspection of the vehicle 'at a mutually agreeable time and place' (although it doesn't pay to be too choosy if you're in a hurry). The purpose of this inspection is primarily to ensure that the stated engine and chassis numbers tally with those on the car, and it's usually conducted by a vehicle inspection officer, although police officers are called in to help out in some areas.

The examiner's (confidential) report, and the two forms you sent in, are then passed on to the VRO manager, who decides whether you retain the original number or get a Q-plate.

People's opinions of Q-plates vary. Some like the idea of having something a bit different – and having built the car, want this to be known (at least by those who recognise the significance of a Q-plate). Others, and particularly those who have built traditionally styled cars, or replicas, consider them rather ugly birthmarks.

The only legitimate way of 'Q-jumping' (apart from retaining the donor number by using its chassis) is to use all new parts, thereby qualifying for a 'new', letter-prefix registration (e.g. H123 ABC). This too will be of limited appeal to someone with a 1950s replica, but it is possible to swap it for a 'personalized' number using the normal procedure, whereas the Q-plate is,

After using mostly new components in the build, and registering the car as new, the number can later be changed for one that is more appropriate. This Ronart just wouldn't look right with a Q-plate.

as we've said, non-transferable.

The registration of an all-new car – what the authorities classify as a 'kitcar', remember – is a little simpler and involves the completion of form V5/55 and sending it with receipts, a certificate of newness from the kit manufacturer, and proof of payment of Custom and Excise duty (this is the car tax: full details from your local Customs and Excise office or from HM Custom and Excise at V1B2 (Car Tax), Knollys House, Bywater Street, London EC3R 5AY). Once the paperwork has been processed, you will be issued with a new registration number.

If the manufacturer you bought the kit from doesn't offer a complete car option, you can just buy the kit and then all the new mechanical parts from another source. It is vital, however, that you keep all the receipts.

Beating the system

If you are happy with a Q-plate, there is no problem. Simply follow the procedure outlined above and

you should experience no problems.

Those who do not want a 'kitcar label' on their car, but can't get a new number either, because they have not used all new parts, have to turn devious, and in some cases perhaps not wholly legal.

The first method really involves taking advantage of a loophole. The scheme is operated by a company that sells the plan through kitcar magazine advertisements, but, without giving anything away, it involves registering the car in Northern Ireland (the company uses a local address). The plan does have possibilities, but does perhaps need to be thought about rather carefully.

Cars registered abroad will also receive new letter prefix registrations when imported into the United Kingdom, providing the relevant foreign registration documents are available (if not, these cars too get a Q-plate). In theory, then, it means that it would be possible to register a car overseas, then import it and get a new plate. It is an expensive method, and one that only works if the kitcar complies with overseas regulations. It would, however, be worth bearing in mind if you were buying a replica overseas.

By far the most common method of avoiding the Q-plate is to retain the donor's registration document, simply changing some of the particulars. In the case of a C-type Jaguar replica, for example, the donor Jaguar's registration document would be sent back to the authorities in Swansea noting a change of seating capacity (although this isn't always noted on the registration document and can then be left blank), and a change of 'type' from 'XJ6 saloon' to 'sports'. The car would then be registered as a two-seater Jaguar, carrying the chassis numberplate and registration number of the original car, which would be scrapped.

This is a rather suspect procedure for a number of reasons. It is quite in order to give your new chassis any number you choose, but clearly it is not the XJ6 'chassis' to which the plate was originally attached. Likewise, the car is no longer a

Jaguar, even if it does look like one. The system is often further abused by either registering no changes on the document, or by registering additional changes for engine number and/or size. When the number is used on a Cobra replica, for example, which has only the front and rear suspension from the Jaguar.

There is no doubt that a great many kitcar owners do get away with this method of registration, due either to the flexibility or ignorance of the authorities. Were there no legitimate system for the registration of kitcars, anyone who was found out would have a better argument. Since there is such a system, pleading ignorance would seem to be the only chance. And ignorance of the law, as any Rumpole fan will know, is no defence.

Finally, it's worth remembering that any car registered after 1 January 1973 should use reflective numberplates. All cars with Q-plates should therefore have white ones to the front and yellow to the rear, as should any car retaining the number of a car registered after that date.

Insurance

This is an area of paperwork with which all motorists will be familiar, but as always the limitless variety of the kitcar market makes things a little more complicated for the insurer of these vehicles.

The basics are the same. Some form of motor insurance isn't just a good idea, it's a legal requirement. Before getting into the technicalities of insurance, we would warn you against ever being tempted to drive the car without it. That might seem obvious, but having spent many a wintry night building your kitcar, it can be very tempting to 'just give it a run around the block'. If during your joyride you are involved in any sort of road traffic accident, you could find yourself in immense trouble. Apart from anything else, convictions that might follow could affect any future insurance quotations.

The most basic legal requirement is third party personal injury insur-

ance, which covers injury to the third party but not damage to property. This is generally felt to be inadequate, however, and is seldom found today. One step up is third party only insurance (cover for third party injury and damage to property), which is now generally accepted as the minimum, followed by third party, fire and theft (additional cover for fire and theft as the name suggests); and fully comprehensive (cover for all parties and all property involved).

With people generally driving more expensive cars, fully comprehensive is the most common form of cover in the mainstream motor industry. In the kitcar market many specialist companies are actively discouraging anything but fully comprehensive cover.

One specialist kitcar broker explained that one reason for this trend was that third party, fire and theft policies are subject to proportionately more abuse and fraud, and there were twice as many claims for fire and theft from customers with third party fire and theft policies than from those with fully comprehensive cover. Their reasoning is simple: those who can only afford the former kind of cover are more likely to need the money. However, if they are encouraged to buy fully comprehensive cover when they cannot afford it, will they not then need the money even more?

Non-comprehensive policies are also less profitable, and higher premiums can help to absorb higher risks; anyone trying to insure a valuable kitcar is therefore unlikely to be offered any form of third party cover. Higher premiums are also a result of high performance, or of the type of car simply being unknown to the insurance company.

The first step towards keeping insurance premiums down, then, is to make sure the company is fully familiar with your car.

The companies
Traditionally, when motorists wanted cover they went to the same company as for their life and house insurance. As car ownership spread, however, and was no

longer a preserve of the wealthy – and particularly when, in the 1960s and '70s, it increased among the young – it became obvious that the old-established companies just couldn't provide what was wanted. They simply didn't understand these new, higher-risk markets. So it was that a new generation of insurance brokers grew up, specializing in the young, previously convicted, or sports car-owning drivers, who were finding it hard to get sensible quotations from the more traditional companies.

As the specialist motoring market became yet more diverse, and yet more popular, so the number of brokers increased, offering realistic quotations for custom cars, classic cars – and kitcars. (Names, addresses and the all-important quotation 'hotline' telephone numbers, can be found in the specialist kitcars press.)

Most of the brokers operating in these specialist areas today tend to cover all of these categories, but the important thing is that when you tell them over the phone that you have a kitcar, their response is likely to be a positive one. Owners of the common, popular marques of kitcars will have no difficulty with these firms because they know the cars as quantifiable risks and can classify them into categories, similar to those used by mainstream companies for production cars.

A new model will obviously require you to supply additional information, and brokers will make their own enquiries, but it will help if the car comes from an established company. Replicas are easier in that it is always possible to at least see what the original looked like, and most combinations of donor parts have been tried at one time or another.

It's important to realize that you will gain nothing by trying to keep information back. Brokers, and the insurance companies they use, take a risk when accepting a new client and car, and the premiums paid will be directly related to the size of that risk. One way of reducing the risk is to make available as much information as possible.

There are always exceptions to the rule – and there are a great

many rules in insurance for there to be exceptions to – but the big mainstream companies have now begun to catch up and are becoming increasingly familiar with the better-known kitcar makes. If you already have a good working relationship with one of these large companies, you might find you will be given a reasonable quotation to keep your business. It is always worth a try.

The cars

Some of the particular problems of insuring a kitcar have already been touched on. The kitcar owner does have some advantage over the conventional car owner, in so far as the specialist companies recognize that, having invested a great deal of time and money putting together a car, the kitcar owner will then be careful not to destroy it. Careful drivers are a better risk, and that means lower premiums. This theory is already well-known to the specialist companies, but, if you're talking to someone from one of the big firms, it's well worth mentioning. In the case of those kitcars bought virtually complete, this theory holds less water. Most companies will therefore ask you how much of the work you did yourself, if you don't volunteer the information.

The need for detailed information continues when we look at the car's technical specification. Again the better-known examples will prove no problem to the specialist brokers, providing they have been built to specification. A 1300 Marina-engined Pilgrim Bulldog, for example, is very much a known quantity; but a Lagonda replica built around Alvis running gear will not feature in the usual table of rates.

Modifications to the engine should be declared in full, as they should for any car; and if the car has a powerful engine, it's reasonable to expect the rest of the running gear to be able to cope with it. So the more modifications, the more information you can expect to be asked for – including an engineer's report in some cases.

Also in line with conventional car insurance, things will generally be easier if your kit has been built up around the running gear for which

it was designed, and more expensive if not. The premiums will also be higher the larger the engine, as you would expect. However, it's interesting that the big V8s are often rated the same once you get over 3.5-litres or so.

The insured worth of the vehicle, or 'agreed value', is very important, particularly in the case of fully comprehensive cover. Again, if the company is familiar with the car, they will know what it's worth. If your estimation of the car's value seems excessively high, or if the model is unfamiliar to the company, you will be asked to provide more information, and maybe even an independent valuation. You should hold on to all receipts in any case, and if you've kept a log of the hours spent on the machine, that too might be useful.

Finally, the form, or the voice on the phone, will ask if the car is garaged, which says something about how – or if – you look after your vehicle. Not the most reliable of gauges, perhaps, but the firm is simply trying to piece together some sort of picture of the risk they are taking on.

The driver

Whatever the advertising copy writers might have you believe, the one thing that says more about you than anything else is age. There is simply no arguing with the fact that proportionately more young people have accidents, making them a worse risk – hence the higher premiums they pay.

In fact, the old magic age barriers, after which things were supposed to get cheaper, are considered less important these days. It will still be cheaper when you're 21, and cheaper again at 25, but not as noticeably so as in the past. In addition, the loading is disproportionate, which means that while it would be cheaper for a young driver to insure a 1300 than a 5-litre V8, premiums for the latter would drop by larger amounts each year. The V8 will always be dearer, but the gap will reduce with time.

Some companies attach more importance to age than others, so it does pay to shop around. Young drivers can get cheaper insurance by having their name added to their parents' policy, but this has its problems. Adding named drivers to existing policies can be a useful way of getting the impoverished student mobile, and for couples sharing cars it's just fine. However, if the added driver intends eventually to get his or her own policy, our advice would be to do it sooner rather than later. The no-claims bonus system is the only real way of saving money on insurance, and you don't start notching up the years until it's in your name.

Your no-claims bonus gives the company information on previous convictions and accident claims, which in turn reveals something of your past track record and represents the single most important part of the process of estimating just what risk you represent. Everyone is familiar with how the system works, but it's worth remembering that if your kitcar is a second or third car, you could find yourself starting from scratch on the new car. Some companies do offer introductory discounts, but if that still works out more expensive, you might be better off using the no-claims bonus on the kitcar and starting anew with the family bus.

Another factor for the insurance broker to take into account is where you live. Statistics again: if you live in London you are around 75 per cent more likely to have an accident than if you live in Cornwall. Different companies use different statistics, but larger towns and cities carry a loading to even up the odds with your country cousins. Statistics do turn-up the occasional anomaly, though, with some parts of the country proving a better risk than others, for no obvious reason.

The final part of this identikit picture being put together by the company is your occupation. Even though the car probably won't be used for business – and if it is, you'll need business and private, or purely business cover – it does provide some indication of the sort of person you are. Horribly stereotyped, of course, but if you've chosen to become an actor, journalist, or something else wild

and reckless, you'll just have to accept that it will be reflected in your insurance premiums. 'Safest' are clerical and management jobs, but if your job does not live up to its jaunty title, make the point to the broker, and back it up with something in writing from your employer if necessary.

Alternatives

This section covers those schemes and devices that can be used to tailor insurance cover to your particular requirements. There are now a number of schemes aimed specifically at the kitcar builder and owner.

The potential risk really starts immediately the builder begins to collect parts. There could be several thousands of pounds worth of parts in the garage long before the kit itself is delivered, so theft, and even fire damage, are very real threats. This is recognized by some insurance brokers who operate special parts coverage to run from day one through to the completion of the kit. There is a choice of just fire and theft, or accidental damage, fire and theft, and premiums are likely to be moderate when you take this very useful precaution.

Once the car is complete, all that time and effort invested can continue to work in your favour when you shop around for insurance. The reasoning runs like this: a large part of the money paid out in the event of a fully comprehensive accident damage claim is to cover the labour charge involved in putting the vehicle back together. The chances are, however, that the kitcar builder, having built his car, will want to rebuild it himself. So why not offer cheaper insurance, to cover the cost of parts but not labour?

Some companies have already introduced 'parts only' schemes offering considerable savings. Other companies point to the disadvantages. The most obvious of these is the very thing that is saving you the money: the limitations of the cover. It is very important that you fully realize that any money paid out will only cover the cost of the parts, and that you consider the full implications of this. Saying you would be prepared to do the work at the

time of signing on the dotted line is a very different matter to actually getting down to it, to rekindling your enthusiasm, when the crumpled remains of your pride and joy are dumped in your drive. What is more, the 'anti' lobby argues, the ability to build a car from detailed instructions is also very different from repairing damaged body panels and twisted chassis rails. The chassis is in fact a good example of where the system might fall down. Assume a car is involved in an accident which damages the chassis, but not substantially enough for it to be written off. The owner is then left with the expense of buying a new chassis (it's not written off, so it isn't covered by the insurance pay-out), having it repaired, or trying to repair the damaged one himself – perhaps without the necessary skills and equipment.

Having said that, the chassis is often a relatively small part of the overall cost of the finished car, and so is often written off. However, there is still the grey area in the middle that could cause problems. And just to play devil's advocate one more time, what if the company has gone out of business?

Add to this the fact that such a policy offers no cover for the labour costs of fitting a new windscreen, and that personal accident and the loss of personal effects are also excluded, and it might seem that the odds are piled against parts-only cover. However, for the kind of practical person who would feel fully able and willing to rebuild his car in the event of the worst happening, this type of policy can be a big saver.

The other restricted cover scheme, about which there are no such arguments, is limited mileage. These policies first came about when the classic car movement really took off. Owners began to argue that it seemed unreasonable to pay the same premiums for cars that were being used to cover only a few thousand miles a year – or only used in the summer months – as for cars which were covering tens of thousands of miles.

The specialist brokers therefore introduced schemes that offered reduced premiums in return for an undertaking that the car wouldn't cover more than a specified number of miles. The idea has now spread to the kitcar market and policies are available with a variety of mileage restrictions on them: 3000, 5000 and 7500 a year seem the most popular. They are also available over six months with mileage limits of 1500, 2500 and 3750 – the premiums rated accordingly.

The cost

The 'safer' end of the market, small-engined sports and utility-style cars from long-established manufacturers, obviously represent the better risk for the insurance companies, and rates are often close to those of their counterparts in the mainstream motor industry. However, when you start to stir in some of those kitcar variables, such as bigger engines, part-built kits and unusual body styles, matters become a little vaguer.

Ultimately, as in mainstream motoring, it comes down to deciding what sort of insurance cover you want and shopping around for it. The kitcar market being what it is, it offers more variety, with parts-only and limited mileage cover, so there are savings to be made. However, you must always consider very carefully the full implications of the arrangement.

As for shopping around, the specialist kitcar insurance brokers are almost certainly going to give you the best deal. But that 'almost certainly' makes it worth trying a few of the others: at least if they are all more expensive you'll know what you're saving.

The huge number of variables involved make it impossible for us to quote any 'typical' prices, but do remember that the motor insurance business is fiercely competitive. So if a company betters a quote, go back to the first company and point this out – it might just be that something even better is offered.

A little help from your friends

Ideally, this section should include a list of all the kitcar manufacturers and their models. Unfortunately, with well over 100 small companies in the industry (plus new ones arriving all the time), all of which regularly revise their model ranges, and some of which either stop trading or simply move premises, it often proves difficult even for the monthly magazines to keep such information up to date. Out of date information being worse than useless, we have decided not to include that list of makers.

In discussing the choosing and buying of kitcars in earlier chapters, we suggested the specialist magazines and shows as the best source of information on the current models. We wouldn't attach too much value to their quality, however, because this is difficult to assess where kitcars are concerned (the company demonstrator seldom represents a particularly high standard of build), and some magazines obviously find it harder than others. They are, however, a good source of product information, and providing you follow our suggested routine for checking out the manufacturer and the car, you can more accurately assess the quality yourself.

The process of choosing and selecting suggested in those earlier chapters might seem a laborious programme for simply buying a kitcar. However the choice and individuality that makes the kitcar industry so rich and satisfying also makes it a potential minefield for the unwary buyer. But if the opportunity exists for you to find the ideal car exists, what's a little careful shopping?